Library of
Davidson College

War and Peace
in Israeli Politics

Studies in International Politics

*The Leonard Davis Institute
for International Relations,
The Hebrew University of Jerusalem*

War and Peace in Israeli Politics

◆

Labor Party Positions on National Security

Efraim Inbar

Lynne Rienner Publishers ◆ Boulder and London

*To my comrades,
the paratroopers of
Company B, Battalion 50,
who fell in the defense of Israel*

Published in the United States of America in 1991 by
Lynne Rienner Publishers, Inc.
1800 30th Street, Boulder, Colorado 80301

and in the United Kingdom by
Lynne Rienner Publishers, Inc.
3 Henrietta Street, Covent Garden, London WC2E 8LU

© 1991 by Lynne Rienner Publishers, Inc. All rights reserved

Library of Congress Cataloging-in-Publication Data
Inbar, Efraim, 1947-
  War and peace in Israeli politics / by Efraim Inbar.
    p. cm.
  Includes bibliographical references and index.
  ISBN 1-55587-236-0
  1. Mifleget ha-avodah ha-Yisra'elit. 2. Israel—National security. 3. Israel—Politics and government. 4. Israel—Boundaries. 5. Jewish-Arab relations—1973- I. Title.
JQ1825.P373A952 1991
327.5694017'4927—dc20   90-43019
                                                              CIP

British Cataloguing in Publication Data
A Cataloguing in Publication record for this book
is available from the British Library.

Printed and bound in the United States of America

The paper used in this publication meets the requirements
of the American National Standard for Permanence of
Paper for Printed Library Materials Z39.48-1984.

Contents

Acknowledgments vii

Chapter 1 Introduction 1

Chapter 2 Hawks and Doves in the Party 11

Chapter 3 Threat Perception and the Chances for Peace 33

Chapter 4 The Partner in the Envisioned Agreement 57

Chapter 5 The Content of the Future Agreements 85

Chapter 6 The Use of Military Force 121

Chapter 7 The Move to the Left: An Evaluation 149

Appendix A A Plan for Peace and Security 159
Appendix B The Labour Party Platform on Foreign Affairs and Security for the 12th Knesset 161

Bibliography 171
Index 179
About the Book and the Author 184

Acknowledgments

I am obliged to Gad Barzilai, Shai Feldman, Giora Goldberg, Emmanuel Gutman, Yoram Peri, and Yael Yishai for their valuable comments on an earlier draft of this work. The Jerusalem branch of the Labor Party was very helpful during the research period. I am grateful to the Leonard Davis Institute for International Relations of The Hebrew University of Jerusalem for the support lent to this project. Its director, Gabriel Sheffer, who initiated this research and encouraged my work with a critical eye, deserves special thanks. The institute's staff, particularly David Hornik, was of great help in finalizing and improving this product.

E. I.

CHAPTER 1
Introduction

All political parties endeavor to influence governmental policy,[1] on the domestic level as well as in the spheres of foreign affairs and national security.[2] The extent of their actual power varies from nation to nation, but few countries are as affected, both socially and economically, by their political parties as is Israel.[3] In contrast to political systems with weak parties, such as in the United States, parties in Israeli politics are at the crossroads of political decisions. Most have distinct ideological colors, are well organized on a national basis, and impose party discipline on their representatives in the Knesset. And in the area of national security, the main Israeli parties and especially their leadership play a major role.

However, the decisions made by parties, especially when in power, are also shaped by factors beyond party control. Indeed, a complex linkage of constantly changing, externally caused events and internal political forces affects the evolution of national security policies.

Disagreements concerning national security—especially those occurring between Likud and Labor, the two major political forces in Israel since the 1970s—have gradually become the central issue of dispute in the nation's politics. In a poll taken before the November 1988 elections, 71 percent of respondents indicated that the most important criterion in choosing a party was its platform on national security.[4] The context defining the cleavage between left and right in Israeli politics increasingly concerns national security decisions more than any other political domain.[5] When referring here to the rift between left and right, or doves and hawks, I am strictly concerned with how these divisions come to bear upon the area of national security.

Since 1967, the main debate on national security in Israel has revolved around the fate of the territories acquired in the Six Day War, although, as shown later in this work, the hawkish–dovish dispute has also involved other issues, such as the level of threat perception, positions on the Palestinian problem, and attitudes toward the use of force. The dominant divisive issue, however, has been the territorial one, particularly as it pertains to Judea, Samaria, and the Gaza Strip, all part of the historical land of Israel. The eastern part of Jerusalem was annexed immediately after the 1967 war, and since that time a united Jerusalem under Israeli sovereignty has been an article of faith for almost all Israelis. Similarly, the Golan, which was annexed in 1981, does not constitute a bone of contention among Israelis, particularly because of the perceived unabated Syrian enmity toward the Zionist state. Clearly, the future of the Israeli-ruled territories has not only been a question of strategic significance, but one connected to the identity and nature of the future Israeli polity.[6] Its Jewish and democratic character—at least according to one side in the debate—are at stake.

In answer to the question of Israel's eastern border and the fate of Gaza (since the 1978 Camp David Accords, Gaza's future has been connected to the destiny of the West Bank), four basic territorial policies have been proposed in the Israeli body politic. The four options for the final disposition of Judea, Samaria, and Gaza are total withdrawal, partition, autonomy, or annexation. The extreme doves in Israel have advocated a total withdrawal to the 1967 borders (the "Green Line"), and such a position has usually been accompanied by a demand that all Jewish settlements be dismantled and that a Palestinian state be established. For this camp, the return of all Sinai to Egypt and the evacuation of all Jewish settlers from that area serve as precedent and model for a future solution for the eastern border.[7]

The idea of partitioning the territories—in Israeli political parlance a "territorial compromise"—is based on the Allon Plan (named after the Labor leader Yigal Allon). Only in 1977 was this plan explicitly incorporated into Labor's party platform. According to the plan, which is elaborated in Chapter 5, Israel should keep under its sovereignty areas of strategic importance to the secure control of the territory west of the Jordan River, but should not burden itself demographically with the annexation of areas densely populated by Arabs in the mountains south and north of Jerusalem. The Allon Plan proposes that these areas should be demilitarized. Such an approach advocates that a policy of selective settlement in the areas be retained, and that the rest of the territory be handed over to the Arabs, preferably to Jordan.

In contrast to the partition principle embodied in the Allon Plan, the autonomy concept represents the "functional compromise" approach. This approach—originally formulated in the late 1960s by Moshe Dayan, then a Laborite, who later served as Menachem Begin's foreign minister at Camp David—proposes the division of governmental functions, rather than of land, in the territories conquered in 1967. Defense, in particular, must remain in Israeli hands according to this view. Emphasis on the great strategic importance of the West Bank central mountains forms the underlying rationale of this approach, in contrast to the importance ascribed to the Jordan Valley Rift in the Allon Plan. However, since full sovereignty over the mountain area would entail Israeli rule over areas densely populated by Arabs, those who formulated the autonomy plan have proposed instead a functional division of governmental responsibilities. This shared-rule approach was incorporated into the Camp David Accords, which suggested an unspecified type of autonomy in the Israeli-ruled territories as an interim arrangement, leaving a final settlement to future negotiations. Many in Israel regard the functional compromise as a good one for the indefinite future. The Likud has gradually become identified with this prescription.

Finally, the extreme hawks in Israel demand annexation of all territories presently under Israeli military rule, and favor settlement in all of the land of Israel. Some of the extreme hawks propose a transfer of the Palestinian population, while others are willing to grant Israeli citizenship to those Arabs willing to live under Israeli sovereignty.

Thus, the extreme positions of the hawkish–dovish continuum in Israel are annexation at one pole, and total withdrawal at the other. In between these extreme positions can be found the functional approach, which is closer to extreme hawkishness, and the territorial compromise position, closer to extreme dovishness.

This book investigates the Israeli Labor Party positions on national security issues in the 1980s. In order to ascertain the party's direction along the hawkish–dovish continuum, and to distinguish between basic and conjectural positions, the account often makes reference to the period immediately following the 1973 Yom Kippur War, a turning point not only in the history of the party, but for Israel itself. For many, this war shattered long-held beliefs concerning security. More broadly, it precipitated a painful process of self-examination within Israeli society. The changes in the Israeli political system following the war were linked to the political decline of the Labor movement and the Labor Party, for the party gradually lost its hegemony in Israeli politics.[8] The war also brought about a changing of the guard at the leadership level, since several party leaders, including Golda Meir and Moshe Dayan, were discredited for failing to cope with it adequately. Many of the politicians at Labor's helm, however, and many of those who occupied major government positions following the changes in the wake of the war, still remained active throughout the 1970s, 1980s, and the beginning of the 1990s. Of these, Shimon Peres and Yitzhak Rabin are the best-known figures.

I will argue that it was the 1973 crisis that constituted the threshold for a more dovish orientation in the party.[9] Indeed, hawkishness, particularly on the territorial issue, carried the day in the period from 1967 to 1973.[10] Immediately after the 1973 war, a widespread and high level of threat perception persisted. It was believed that the initial Arab military successes of 1973, coupled with growing Arab political leverage in an oil-thirsty world, encouraged further aggression against Israel, and an imminent war was feared by Labor-led Israel.[11] At that time, many in the party still questioned the very existence of a separate Arab Palestinian people; Jordan remained the designated preferred partner in any settlement regarding Israel's eastern border. Thus, until 1977 the party was torn between the functional approach, advocated by Dayan, and the territorial compromise approach, advocated by Allon. At that point, even annexationists were still to be found in the Labor Party.

In contrast, by 1990 the party was positioned further to the left on the national hawkish–dovish continuum. This shift is documented here. At the end of the 1980s the party was formally committed to the Allon Plan, and those who supported annexation and/or the functional approach were no longer Labor members. Informally, the territorial compromise formula was given a very minimalist interpretation in many party circles, an interpretation often quite close to the total withdrawal option. Greater recognition for an independent Palestinian role was incorporated in official party documents by the end of the decade of the 1980s. The peace treaty signed with Egypt in 1979, the prolonged Iran–Iraq war (1980–1988), which neutralized the eastern front, and the PLO's conciliatory statements issued at the end of 1988 were the main contributing factors to a significant lowering of the level of threat perception. Furthermore, as this study shows, the dovish wing in the party increased its strength relative to the hawks in the parliament and at the cabinet level.

The terms *doves* and *hawks*, used here to describe the continuum within the Labor Party, obviously do not correspond to the same terms when used to describe various positions along the national hawkish–dovish continuum. A Laborite hawk, as well as a Laborite dove, both subscribe to the territorial compromise formula. This terminology is maintained because it is part and parcel of the Labor Party's internal intercourse and deliberations. Throughout this book, unless stated otherwise, the terms hawks and doves refer to party positions only. As mentioned previously, Labor's hawkish positions have moved over time in the direction of the extreme dovish position on the *national* continuum.

These changes in the Labor positions were connected not only to internal developments in the party and in Israel, but also to the much more intensive U.S. involvement since 1973 in mediation efforts in the Arab–Israeli conflict. Also influential were developments in the attitudes and policies of Israel's Arab rivals. These factors continued to have an impact on Israel's and Labor's positions in the 1980s. The dovish tendency of Labor gradually became more pronounced, a development that has had significant ramifications, since from 1984 until early 1990 the party found itself once again in a position to influence Israeli policies as part of the National Unity governments.

Labor, a socialist mass party, played the role of the dominant party in the Israeli political system until 1977.[12] After being the major political force in Israeli politics since the establishment of the state and for most of the prestate period, the Labor Party lost the May 1977 elections and was ousted from power. In 1977 the Labor Party was weaker than at any time since 1948, as it was deeply split by a bitter leadership struggle between Rabin and Peres, by intergenerational conflict, and by disputes over foreign and security issues.[13] The 1977 change in government was not directly related to national security issues. But Labor's responsibility for the strategic surprise in the

Yom Kippur War, for the lack of adequate military preparations, and for the subsequent heavy casualties was one factor in its electoral decline.

Six months after the great upheaval in Israeli domestic politics, an even greater change occurred in Israel's foreign relations. Anwar Sadat, Egypt's president, came to Jerusalem, an unexpected move that precipitated a dramatic change in the Arab–Israeli conflict, leading to the 1978 Camp David Accords and the 1979 peace treaty between Israel and Egypt. The Likud-led government, in spite of often being depicted as uncompromising and sometimes even war-mongering, was the first Israeli government to sign a peace treaty with a neighboring Arab country, and the first to open an Israeli embassy in Cairo. This was unquestionably a tremendous achievement, a fulfillment of a dream for most Israelis.

The Labor Party, in disarray following the May 1977 debacle, was taken by surprise—as was everyone else—by the developing peace process.[14] Furthermore, what was happening ran counter to its basic underlying belief and to the argument that it often propounded—namely, that only its platform could be a vehicle toward peace, whereas Likud's positions concerning the Land of Israel and national security issues precluded such a possibility. This was a difficult period of soul-searching for the party, as its leader, Peres, admitted at the time. Labor "had to find its place, to define its role in order not to be erased from the political map."[15] He claimed, furthermore, that the party had never before faced such difficulties nor such despair.[16] Not only was it cast in the unfamiliar and awkward role of a rather impotent opposition, but the peace process and particularly the planned withdrawal from all of Sinai put the party in a difficult dilemma on the key issue of national security.

The Knesset vote on the 1978 Camp David Accords forced Laborites to make a difficult choice: whether to support the peace proposed by the Likud government, or to oppose it because of its stipulation that the Rafiah salient settlements be removed. For most Laborites, it was an article of faith that the retention of this area was important to assure secure borders. At issue on one hand was the precedent of voluntarily dismantling Israeli settlements in the territories taken in 1967. Furthermore, in spite of the fact that Gaza was left under Israeli rule, full withdrawal to the international border constituted in fact a return to the 1967 border with Egypt. Support of the agreement implied relinquishing the principle of secure borders to which the party had adhered. In the past, Labor had rejected any suggestion that Israel should return to the 1967 borders. Nevertheless, most Labor MKs (nineteen), despite some misgivings, decided to vote with the Likud government, helping it to gain the necessary support for its policy. Yet security concerns did prompt four Labor MKs to vote against, while three others abstained—in other words, a quarter of the Labor parliamentary contingent refused to lend support to these agreements.

Thus the Camp David Accords and their territorial and political implications were pivotal and generated considerable debate within the Labor Party, just as they did for the rest of the Israeli body politic. The 1981 elections, furthermore, forced all the various parties to elucidate their thinking, as party platforms had to be offered to the voters. The Israeli air attack on the Iraqi nuclear reactor in June 1981, the Lebanon War and its long aftermath (1982–1985), numerous instances of employing a limited use of force, and the 1984 and 1988 elections also evoked party responses to security issues. The outbreak of the Palestinian uprising, known as the *intifada*, the PLO's moderate statements in October–December 1988, and the subsequent opening of the United States–PLO dialogue aroused still another debate in Israel and within the party. Similarly, the extent to which a partnership with the Likud in the National Unity government could advance the peace process was the subject of intraparty debate. The attitudes and positions of Labor leaders, as well as the party platforms, are the subject of this inquiry.

This book investigates the positions adopted by the Labor Party on national security issues in the 1980s, both while it served in opposition (until 1984) and while it participated in the National Unity governments with the Likud (following the 1984 and 1988 elections). This partnership ended in March 1990, partly because of the difference in perspective between the two parties on how to realize the government peace initiative of May 1989, and in particular because of their differences on how to respond to U.S. involvement in the process. It is difficult, however, to refer to a "party position" on each national security issue. As the vote on the Camp David Accords and other Knesset votes indicate, Labor was not a monolithic bloc. The notion that political parties are cohesive, homogeneous, and centralized organizations is not substantiated by the facts, either in the Israeli political system or in many others.[17]

Yet the party's platform represented Labor's official position, and this document reflected a resolution of the different viewpoints within the party and was, to a great extent, binding on all party members. Labor has always approached the drafting of the party platform, as have other political parties in Israel, with a legalistic-Talmudic frame of mind; every possible shade of meaning is surveyed and evaluated. In the Israeli political culture, in spite of the decline of ideology, the wording of a platform is still deemed to be crucial; it usually generates much interest among party activists and is carefully scrutinized by outsiders as well. Of course, the membership formally has the right to change the platform by democratic means, and the attempts to change the platform during the period investigated here were indicative of the disputes within the party. Disagreements were also present in the highest party echelons—including the ministerial level when the party was in power. Since policy was in the hands of the party leadership, the views of those in the top positions (MKs and particularly cabinet members) had a greater influence on the party's behavior than those of other party members. Therefore, this book focuses on the views of this political stratum.[18] The group researched includes the Laborite contingent in the Knesset and a few other party personalities who, throughout the period researched, did not at all times hold an official party position. Abba Eban—after 1988 no longer an MK but still an articulate voice of the party's doves—is one such person. The research material also includes official party documents that deal with issues pertinent to this study.

As a matter of fact, the struggle between hawks and doves was admittedly not the dominant characteristic of the party in the period we will look at. The divergence between doves and hawks in the party, as well as the use of these terms, began in the mid-1970s.[19] Disputes over foreign policy and security matters were not, however, new to the party. Even during the time that Mapai, Labor's predecessor, was led by the towering figure of David Ben-Gurion, there was no consensus on national security policies.[20] But after 1973, party formulations, primarily as expressed in the party platform, tended to favor one or the other of the camps within the party, or sometimes obfuscation was used in order to allow a kind of "avian coexistence." Identifying the areas of discord and agreement is one of the goals of this book.

Chapter 2 offers some criteria for distinguishing between Labor doves and hawks. I argue that dovish–hawkish disagreements actually constitute a multidimensional continuum. The party organizational divisions relevant to the dovish–hawkish dispute are reviewed in that chapter, and the growing strength of the dovish wing at the parliamentary and ministerial levels is assessed. The third chapter focuses on threat perceptions and differing evaluations among the party leadership of the chances for peace. The level of threat perception in the Arab–Israeli conflict has constituted, to a large extent, the basis for formulating positions on national security issues. Chapter 4 covers the party debate over who should be the partner in talks or negotiations, and also documents the increasing willingness among Laborites to accept Palestinians as a party to an agreement. The details of the envisioned permanent settlement with Israel's neighbors are investigated in Chapter 5. Particular attention is given to the Allon Plan and its minimalist versions, to the character of the various interim agreements considered, and to the suggestions for unilateral measures. Chapter 6 focuses on the attitudes of Laborites toward the use of force. I analyze their perspectives on waging war and on the more limited use of military force, and discuss their attitudes toward the side effects of perennial violence. In the final chapter I attempt to explain the shift of the party toward the dovish pole. This trend seems to contradict conventional wisdom that the Israeli electorate has shifted toward the right, and indeed seems to defy rational political behavior. Parties are supposed to position themselves in a place where they can attract the most voters.[21] Such political behavior—the move leftward—is particularly intriguing in that the dispute over national security issues along the hawkish–dovish continuum has become the most important one in Israeli politics. The explanation, it seems, is to be found in intraparty changes, internal Israeli developments, and the impact of the international environment.

Sources for this work are party documents and the public pronouncements of party leaders. The latter were collected from the written media, Knesset Minutes (KM), and party documents and organs. In addition, intensive interviews were conducted with a number of party leaders, most of the party MKs, and numerous activists. In some cases the positions of the leaders changed over time, so that what was said or written several years ago is not necessarily indicative of later views. Contacts with party activists helped in correctly ascertaining the views that were held at the time of the events in question.

The Labor Party in the 1980s was undoubtedly in decline. Following the breakdown of the National Unity government, it failed in April 1990 to form a government under its own aegis. This political setback has intensified the intraparty struggle for leadership, which could further weaken the party. A detailed look at the changes taking place in the Israeli political system as a whole is beyond the scope of this study; yet it seems too early to eulogize Labor as a political force of the past. Its rival, the Likud, also lost some of its strength during the 1980s, and its leadership is similarly contested, although it did succeed during that period in establishing itself as a ruling party. Nevertheless, Labor was a member of the ruling coalition for most of the decade and still has a role to play, even if in opposition, particularly on the issues of war and peace, an area that requires a great measure of political consensus in Israel. Therefore, through the study of one party, Labor—including its leaders and power contenders—this study also sheds light on Israeli politics in general and on the formulation of national security policies in particular. Indeed, in focusing on the multidimensional hawkish–dovish continuum, this book provides a framework for understanding the main rift in Israeli politics.

NOTES

1. Joseph La Palombara and Myron Weiner, "The Origin and the Development of Political Parties," in *Political Parties and Political Development*, eds. Joseph La Palombara and Myron Weiner (Princeton: Princeton University Press, 1966), p. 3.

2. See Michael Brecher, Blema Steinberg, and Janice Stein, "A Framework for Research on Foreign Policy Behavior," *Journal of Conflict Resolution* 13 (March 1969), pp. 75-101; William Coplin, "Domestic Politics and the Making of Foreign Policy," *Introduction to International Politics* (Chicago: Markham, 1974), chap. 3.

3. Benyamin Akzin, "The Role of Parties in Israeli Democracy," *Journal of Politics* 17 (November 1955), pp. 507–545.

4. For the results of the Modi'in Ezrachi poll, see *Maariv*, 30 August, 1988.

5. Michal Shamir, "Realignment in the Israeli Party System," in *The Elections in Israel—1984*, eds. Asher Arian and Michal Shamir (Tel Aviv: Ramot, 1986), pp. 276–277.

6. For the nonsecurity dimension, see, inter alia, Aaron David Miller, "The Arab–Israeli Conflict, 1967–1987: A Retrospective," *Middle East Journal* 41 (Summer 1987), p. 353; Ian Lustick, "Israeli State-Building in the West Bank and the Gaza Strip: Theory and Practice—A Review Article," *International Organization* 41 (January 1987), pp. 151–171.

7. Few extreme doves believe that the Jewish settlements in the territories have created an irreversible situation leading to a binational state. See Meron Benvenisti, *The West Bank Data Project: A Survey of Israel's Policies* (Washington, D.C.: American Enterprise Institute, 1984). No Israeli political party has adopted such a position, which can be found in marginal extreme dovish circles only.

8. On changes in the party following the 1973 war and on its decline, see Myron J. Aronoff, *Power and Ritual in the Israel Labor Party* (Assen/Amsterdam: Van Gorcum, 1977), pp. 145–165; Yonatan Shapira, "The End of a Dominant Party System," in *The Elections in Israel—1977*, ed. Asher Arian (Jerusalem: Jerusalem Academic Press, 1980); Amos Perlmutter, *Israel: The Partitioned State* (New York: Charles Scribner's Sons, 1985), pp. 229–238; and Asher Arian, "The Passing of Dominance," *Jerusalem Quarterly* 5 (Fall 1977), pp. 20–32. See also Giora Goldberg, "The Parliamentary Opposition in Israel: 1965–1977" (Hebrew) (Ph.D. diss., The Hebrew University of Jerusalem, 1980).

9. For the softening of Labor positions in foreign affairs in its platform for the 1973 Knesset elections immediately following the Yom Kippur War, see Yael Yishai, *Land or Peace: Whither Israel?* (Stanford: Hoover Institution Press, 1987), pp. 92–93; Gershon R. Kieval, *Party Politics in Israel and the Occupied Territories* (Westport: Greenwood Press, 1983), pp. 95–100; and Yossi Beilin, *The Price of Unity* (Hebrew) (Tel Aviv: Revivim, 1985), pp. 141–142.

10. See Avner Yaniv, *Deterrence Without the Bomb: The Politics of Israeli Strategy* (Lexington: Lexington Books, 1987), pp. 177–186.

11. See Efraim Inbar, "Israeli Strategic Thinking After 1973," *Journal of Strategic Studies* 6 (March 1983), pp. 36–41.

12. For the distinction between a mass and a cadre party and for a discussion of the dominant party concept, see Maurice Duverger, *Political Parties* (New York: John Wiley & Sons, Science Editions, 1965), pp. 63–70; 307–309.

13. Perlmutter, *Israel: The Partitioned State*, pp. 253–254.

14. It is true that the origins of the peace process can be related to the 1974 and 1975 Egyptian–Israeli agreements reached during Labor's tenure in office. Yet the main goal of Israeli foreign policy in the 1974–1977 period was the preservation of U.S. support for Israel, whereas relations with the Arabs were of a secondary nature and were subordinated to Israel's U.S. orientation. See Efraim Inbar, "Problems of Pariah States: The National Security Policy of the Rabin Government 1974–1977" (Ph.D. diss., University of Chicago, 1981).

15. Shimon Peres,"Renewal Instead of Power Struggles," *Migvan* 37 (June 1979), p. 4. *Migvan* was Labor's official monthly magazine.

16. Ibid.

17. Giovanni Sartori, *Parties and Party Systems* (Cambridge: Cambridge University Press, 1961), pp. 71–115; for intraparty pluralism in the area of foreign affairs, see, inter alia, Yael Yishai, "Party Factionalism and Foreign

Policy: Demands and Responses," *Jerusalem Journal of International Relations* 3 (Fall 1977), p. 53.

18. For an analysis of the power structure and internal organization of Labor in previous periods, see Peter Medding, *Mapai in Israel* (Cambridge: Harvard University Press, 1972); and Aronoff, *Power and Ritual in the Israel Labor Party.*

19. Aronoff, *Power and Ritual in the Israel Labor Party*, pp. 161, 166–167.

20. On the Ben-Gurion–Sharett dispute, see Michael Brecher, *The Foreign Policy System of Israel* (London: Oxford University Press, 1972), pp. 251–290; see also Gabriel Sheffer, "Resolution vs. Management of the Middle East Conflict," Jerusalem Papers on Peace Problems, no. 32 (Jerusalem: Magnes Press, The Hebrew University, 1980).

21. Anthony Downs, *An Economic Theory of Democracy* (New York: Harper & Row, 1957). On the move of the political system toward hawkishness, see Asher Arian, "Conclusion," in *Israel at the Polls*, ed. Howard R. Penniman (Washington, D.C.: American Enterprise Institute, 1979), p. 301; and Asher Arian and Michal Shamir, "The Primarily Political Functions of the Left-Right Continuum," in *The Elections in Israel—1981*, ed. Asher Arian (Tel Aviv: Ramot, 1983), p. 267.

CHAPTER 2
Hawks and Doves in the Party

ORNITHOLOGICAL DISTINCTIONS

The hawkish/dovish distinction—actually a continuum whose multidimensional character will be delineated later in this chapter—has become the most important issue in national politics in Israel, but it has not been central in intraparty struggles. Labor is composed of many organized party subunits, all of which compete to fill party positions with their own candidates. Power and spoils are their main goals. They can generally be characterized as factions of interest rather than of principle.[1] Immediate and tangible rewards primarily motivate most of these groups, less so the promotion of certain policies. The political power of the various factions during the period investigated here was determined according to numbered ballots taken in the official party forums. Some of the groups were clearly identifiable on the hawkish–dovish party continuum; most were less so. Indeed, the struggle to be elected to certain positions created alliances between various groups in the party that cut across hawkish/dovish distinctions.

Furthermore, since candidates were also considered, to some extent, on the basis of personal merit, their positions on national security issues did not necessarily constitute the most important factors in intraparty balloting. Only a few in the party, primarily those with very strong dovish or hawkish convictions, displayed inhibitions in voting for someone with different views from their own on national security issues. For example, in spite of his ultradovish positions, which eventually led him to leave the party, Yossi Sarid had little difficulty in 1981 and 1984 in mustering the 60 percent of the party Central Council (Merkaz) vote necessary for inclusion on the party list for the Knesset. The Rabin–Peres struggle for leadership, which dominated party politics in the 1974–1984 period, was also not directly related to disagreements over policy on the Arab–Israeli conflict, or on any other issue. Both men received support from doves and hawks alike. Similarly, in the aftermath of the disappointing election results in 1988, demands for a change of leadership were aired by party members with differing political outlooks. The failure of Peres to form a Labor-led government, following the fall of the National Unity government in March 1990, evoked similar responses in the party. Then the old Peres–Rabin feud opened up again, and the second-echelon leadership maneuvered to score points in the party. When it came to advancing their political careers, doves and hawks showed their claws equally.

Yet the party's failure to regain the dominant role in Israel's political system throughout the 1980s, and in particular its lack of success in the October 1988 national elections and in the February 1989 municipal elections, were conducive not only to a demand for a change in leadership, but also to a debate over the party's national security policies. The string of failures was attributed by the hawks to the more dovish image projected by the party. They believed that the party should battle the Likud over the political center, whereas the doves claimed that only a clearer dovish message could arrest the party's decline. The changes in the PLO—and in the U.S. position toward it, which occurred at the end of 1988—created a new situation that further exacerbated tensions within the party. The partnership with Likud in the National Unity government was particularly difficult for the dovish wing under these circumstances. The Likud's more cautious approach to the government peace initiative of May 1989 was viewed in Labor's dovish circles as obstructing the initiative and as a cynical use of Labor to mask Likud's reluctance to proceed toward an agreement.

Nevertheless, since daily party life did not revolve around substantive issues, the attitudes of party activists toward national security issues were often of secondary importance. Group interest, intergenerational conflict, and personal ambitions were powerful factors in blurring the disputes over policy advocacy. Therefore, it is important to stress that the power struggle in the Labor Party was for most of the 1980s only slightly influenced by the debate over national security issues. As mentioned, however, external developments—specifically the outbreak of the intifada, shifts in the PLO position and in U.S. policy—did influence the nature of the power struggle in the latter part of the decade.

Tensions between hawks and doves in the party were also mitigated by the fact that the diversity along the *national* hawkish–dovish continuum was not fully reflected in the party. As noted, the extremes at both right and left had no representation in party forums. For example, no support could be found for a complete withdrawal from all of Judea and Samaria, including East Jerusalem, nor for the annexation of all the land in these regions. A position considered hawkish within the party would have been labeled differently in the context of the entire Israeli political spectrum. A hawkish Laborite would probably have been regarded as to the right, but close to the center, on the national hawkish–dovish continuum.

Furthermore, in spite of a plethora of positions presented by party leaders and activists, there were several basic points that commanded a nearly total party consensus. All agreed on the principle according to which any future agreement with the Arabs was to be reached—namely, territorial compromise. This meant exchanging territories for peace, although the magnitude of withdrawal was not agreed upon. Rule over 1.5 million unwilling Palestinians was regarded by all as a temporary condition, not a permanent one. Party members also agreed that all territories relinquished were to be demilitarized. By the end of the decade, Jordan was still the preferred partner for any negotiations on the final disposition of Judea, Samaria, and the Gaza Strip. Although, as will be shown in Chapter 4, the Palestinians were gradually allowed a greater voice in a future agreement, Jordan was nevertheless regarded as indispensable for reaching a stable political arrangement, in spite of King Hussein's steps during the summer of 1988 toward administrative disengagement from the West Bank.

Formally, the party did not regard the PLO as an acceptable partner. A gradually increasing number of party activists, however, particularly doves, began to demand that this official position be changed. Changes introduced by the PLO in December 1988—at least at the declarative level—implying recognition of Israel and renunciation of terror, and particularly the subsequent U.S. decision to open a dialogue with this organization, strengthened those demanding that the PLO be permitted to take part in negotiations on the future of Judea, Samaria, and Gaza.

In spite of the greater responsiveness to Palestinian political demands, the party has been united in its opposition to an independent Palestinian state, though the intensity of such opposition has varied and over time has weakened. Another area of common understanding, which has always existed, was the awareness that the Arab–Israeli conflict has no military solution. At the same time, however, occasional use of force was viewed as legitimate, though the contingencies that warrant military action were not universally agreed upon. There was also no disagreement over the importance of the peace treaty with Egypt: it was regarded as a historic turning point in the long Arab–Israeli conflict, an achievement that Israel should make efforts to preserve.

As mentioned in Chapter 1, the party has never been monolithic regarding national security issues. Similarly, the consensus that was reached over several principles in the 1980s did not preclude disagreement about the form of their implementation, or about appropriate responses to conjectural developments. How much of the territories is to be bartered away? What is the role of the Palestinians in a future agreement? How are the developments on the Arab side to be evaluated? What are the prospects for a comprehensive peace agreement? What kind of security arrangements are to be incorporated in an agreement and for how long? What is the appropriate level of force to be used in the conflict? On all these questions there was no unanimous opinion within the party. To each question there were several possible answers, a situation that actually created a multidimensional hawkish–dovish continuum. The proposal for an international conference as a forum to overcome procedural obstacles in attempting to resolve some problems in the Arab–Israeli conflict—an idea that gained prominence in the latter part of the 1980s—was one example of a conjectural development, responses to which did not necessarily reflect the hawkish/dovish distinction but, rather, tactical considerations. Another example was the question of how to respond to the U.S. suggestions for realizing the May 1989 Israeli peace initiative. Hawks, however, tended to be more cautious even on tactical matters.

The ideal type (in a Weberian sense) of a 1980s Laborite hawk—as was true of hawks in other Israeli parties or elsewhere in the world—had a high level of threat perception. They were also skeptical about the possibility of achieving peace with the Arabs in the near future, and therefore preferred long-term interim agreements to attempts to reach comprehensive solutions. In accordance with the Allon Plan, they tended to favor the retention of approximately 30 percent of Judea and Samaria, most of it lightly populated by Arabs, and insisted on holding onto most of the Golan Heights. Their solution for the territories was primarily motivated by strategic considerations, but they were not impervious to the historical Jewish links to the land of Israel. The Laborite hawk's motto, as with hawks in other parties, was that peace can be attained only through strength.[2] The Palestinian role was minimized and subordinated to a Jordanian outlook. Hawkishness was also reflected in support for a greater coercive dimension in policies involving national security.

In contrast, Laborite doves tended to have a lower level of threat perception and to believe that peace was within reach following a major Israel withdrawal. Their view of the time factor was in fact drastically different from the hawks'. Paradoxically, in spite of the low threat perception, a great sense of urgency was displayed in the doves' search for a solution to the Arab-Israeli conflict, stemming from the belief that without such a solution war was imminent and inevitable. Doves by and large regarded the status quo as dangerous, since international developments did not necessarily favor Israel. Therefore, delaying negotiations would, from the dovish point of view, only lead to a less satisfactory outcome of the peace process.[3] Indeed, this theme of urgency was new in Laborite thinking. In contrast, hawks tended to feel less threatened by the status quo and were willing to wait until the Arabs reconciled themselves to accept the types of agreements they favored. The ideal dove was skeptical about this possibility and willing to suggest that the Palestinians could enjoy a greater role in a future agreement, at the expense of, but not necessarily to the exclusion of, Jordan. Under certain circumstances, even the PLO could constitute one side to an Israeli–Jordanian–Palestinian accord. Dovishness was also directly related to a reluctance to use force in the conflict. Doves believed that excessive use of force by Israel was counterproductive, since it raised the Arab level of threat perception. Furthermore, toward the end of the 1980s some doves put forward arguments minimizing the importance of military power in international politics, thus downplaying the significance of Arab arsenals.

In general, both hawks and doves professed to adhere to the principles of realpolitik.[4] Neither the hawks nor the doves were concerned with what might happen to the local Palestinian population following a retreat—for example, a ruthless suppression of political liberties. Labor dovishness was primarily instrumental, rather than normative. Yet the doves were slightly more inclined to use and accept moral arguments, such as right of self-determination. As I have stated, all Laborites valued the peace treaty with Egypt. Yet a dove tended to believe that this treaty was extremely fragile and was worried that the peace process might come to an end. In contrast, the hawk had a different evaluation of the constraints that bound Egypt to its treaty obligations and pointed out the Egyptian interests, at least in the short term, in preserving the status quo. The multidimensional nature of the Labor hawkish–dovish continuum suggests that clear distinctions were in many cases very difficult to make:[5]

	Dovishness and Hawkishness in the Israeli Labor Party		
Dovishness	Low	Threat Perception	High
	High	Probability of Peace	Low
	High	Sense of Urgency	Low
	Palestinian	Partner	Jordan
	Almost total	Extent of Withdrawal	Major
	Low	Predilection to Use Force	High

Was there any litmus test for belonging to one of the camps? There were indications that the attitude toward the PLO could possibly serve as a dividing line. Willingness to accept the PLO as a negotiating partner (even when it was qualified by several preconditions), the implication of which was the possibility of the establishment of a Palestinian state, seemed to serve as a necessary, but not sufficient, condition for a dovish orientation.[6] Support for a PLO role has often been expressed off the record, particularly before December 1988. The realization that negotiating with the PLO implied the possibility of establishing a Palestinian state was the main reason for the reluctance of many Laborites, and others as well, to deal with them. Yet since 1989, reluctant acceptance of a PLO role has been increasing among non-doves also. This is further evidence of the leftward move of the party during this period and of the typological difficulties as well.

WHO IS WHO?

Classification of the Labor party leadership on the multidimensional hawkish–dovish continuum is indeed not an easy task. Public statements systematically covering all the issues are often lacking. Furthermore, in contrast to a small proportion of party activists who clearly professed during the 1980s to be either doves or hawks, there were many in the party who held positions somewhere in between. In addition, political actors are typically inconsistent on national security issues.[7] There were also some who preferred not to clearly position themselves on the continuum, for fear of estranging potential voters in party forums when running for office.[8] Moshe Shahal, a minister in the National Unity governments and an aspirant for the premiership, seemed to have adopted such a strategy of cultivating an unclear image, although he was closer to the left. In fact, this phenomenon helped to minimize tensions in the party between doves and hawks. Some even presented themselves as belonging to a separate, in-between category called "*yonetz*" (a Hebrew coinage meaning "dove-hawk"), without really clarifying the differences among the three categories. This obviously allowed for some flexibility. Some of the yonetz-type Laborites displayed a combination of firm positions on territory and security arrangements on one hand, stemming from a fairly high threat perception, and moderation on the Palestinian or the PLO issue on the other. Even the yonetz group, however, was far from homogeneous. Mordechai Gur, a former chief of staff, a cabinet member in the National Unity governments, and another aspirant for the premiership, was one example of this "slippery" category. In politics, clarifying one's views is not necessarily expedient.

There were occasions, however, when party members were forced to make decisions, and their true political leanings would come to the fore. Differences of opinion on security and foreign affairs were significant when the party platform had to be written, or when the party, as such, had to react to events of national security significance. There was an obvious tendency to come up with formulations satisfactory to all members or at least to a majority. Yet not all issues lent themselves to such linguistic artistry. For example, the question of whether to insist on sovereignty in certain areas defined as security zones was, by nature, dichotomizing, and the vote would clearly indicate hawkish or dovish tendencies. Such clear-cut choices were rare, however, and the difficulties in classifying the party leaders are still substantial. Another difficulty lies in the changing views of the politicians: many adopted gradually more dovish positions as time went on, although there are examples of Laborites moving in the opposite direction as well. Nevertheless, the following is a preliminary mapping of the dovish–hawkish tendencies in the party.

Shimon Peres, the party chairperson and leader since 1977, served in various cabinet positions in the 1980s: prime minister (1984–1986), foreign minister (1986–1988), and finance minister (1988–1990). Once a hawk, he gradually moved leftward; his views on many issues in the 1980s reflected a dovish outlook. Further evidence for placing Peres on the left comes from the composition of his staff. His close advisors in recent years have been, with almost no exception, professed doves such as Yossi Beilin and Avraham Burg. (Both succeeded, thanks largely to the efforts of their boss, in entering the Labor list for the 12th Knesset and in becoming MKs in 1988.) Nevertheless, Peres refrained from participating in any dovish party forums; as the leader of the party, he preferred to occupy a more central position.

Left of Peres, we find Abba Eban, formerly a foreign minister, and a Knesset member until 1988. Unbound by governmental responsibility since 1974, he was freer to express his own convictions and often served as the spokesperson for the dovish camp. Yitzhak Navon, formerly a popular president (1978–1983), and the minister of education from 1984 until 1990, was also to the left of Peres. Ezer Weizman, a Likud leader in the 1970s who joined Labor in 1984 and who then served as a minister in the National Unity governments, also projected a more dovish image than Peres; indeed the doves welcomed him to their camp.

To the right of Peres we find Yitzhak Rabin, the defense minister from 1984 to 1990 and the second-ranking leader in the party power hierarchy. Considered to be a hawk, many of his positions on national security issues have even commanded the respect of the rival party, Likud. Aryeh Nehamkin and Shoshana Arbeli-Almozlino, both in ministerial positions in the first National Unity government (1984–1988), were self-identified hawks and can be positioned to the right of Rabin. Nehamkin was the representative of the *moshav* (agricultural cooperative) movement, which has traditionally displayed hawkish tendencies.[9] Arbeli-Almozlino, who voted in 1978 against the Camp David Accords, had a background in Achdut Haavoda, an activist-socialist and hawkish faction of the party which no longer exists.

The other first-rank Laborites who have held ministerial positions since 1984, such as Chaim Bar-Lev, Gad Yaakobi, Mordechai Gur, Yaakov Tzur, and Moshe Shahal, can all be placed somewhere between Rabin and Peres. Bar-Lev, who had served as the party's secretary-general (1977–1984) before becoming a cabinet minister, had a dovish image that, when running for a place for the party Knesset list in 1988, he explicitly made efforts to dispel. His positions at that time were closer to the hawkish side, and he occasionally participated in the party's hawkish forums, which he explicitly joined in the fall of 1989. Yaakobi maintained a mixture of hawkish and dovish positions. As mentioned, Gur classified himself as a yonetz. Shahal usually displayed dovish positions, but refrained from identifying himself as a dove. Tzur had a dovish image, but on the issue of territory he was far from dovish: he voted in the Knesset for the annexation of the Golan (1981), and, after southern Gaza was excluded as a security zone from the party platform in 1986, he demanded that it be included.

The other Laborites who acquired the prestigious status of cabinet member in 1988 were Avraham Katz-Oz and Rafi Edri. Katz-Oz, although he displayed some hawkishness, such as voting in favor of the Golan annexation in 1981, was suspected by the hawks of not really being one of their species because of his close relations with Peres. Edri was left of Peres on the hawkish–dovish continuum. He and Weizman were the only two Labor ministers to deny support to the Israeli government's peace initiative of May 1989—which included an offer for elections in the territories—because they believed it was necessary to negotiate with the PLO. Another party leader with some influence, who was offered a cabinet post in 1988 but declined the honor, was MK Uzi Baram, who since 1984 had served as the party's secretary-general (replacing Bar-Lev). Baram is a pronounced dove who refused to serve in the government together with the Likud. In February 1989 he resigned as Labor secretary-general so as not to be associated with the Likud–Labor government policies and to prepare himself for the political battle for the party leadership. His replacement as secretary-general was MK Micha Harish, a yonetz with a dovish past.

Cabinet membership is the highest level in the party hierarchy. Ministers have at their disposal budgets and jobs, which can compensate their supporters and entrench their power. There are, of course, differences of rank among ministers. The premiership is allotted to the party leader; other powerful and prestigious ministries are defense, finance, foreign affairs, and education. An additional measure of ministerial status is participation in the inner cabinet, which, in the National Unity governments, had an equal number of representatives from Labor and Likud and dealt with sensitive national security issues and the peace process. It was the prerogative of Peres, as party leader, to choose Labor's ministers, their posting, and who was to be included in the inner cabinet. This discretionary power was somewhat limited, however, by the priority he placed on not estranging parts of the party from each other and particularly by his desire not to renew his political feud with Rabin. Such considerations were also relevant, but less so, to the faction's allotments of seats in prestigious Knesset committees and particularly to the position of committee chairperson.

The distribution along the hawkish–dovish continuum not only was the result of various personal responses, but also reflected different traditions in the party. The Labor Party was established in 1968 as the result of the merger of three independent parties: Mapai, Achdut Haavodah, and Rafi. The three groups continued to function as recognized factions within the Labor Party until 1975, when the factional regime disappeared.[10] The demise of these organizational structures did not, however, erase the differences in outlook among the various factions' members. Yet as time passed, the significance of the past traditions diminished. Younger members were socialized into a united party, in a general atmosphere of less ideological fervor.

Usually, former Achdut Haavoda and Rafi activists showed a greater tendency toward hawkish positions. The Achdut Haavoda Party and its kibbutz movement (Hakibbutz Hameuchad) have favored a "tough" policy toward the Arabs, and until more recently, a strong settlement program in all of the land of Israel. Hakibbutz Hameuchad also exerted pressures on Labor, when the latter was in the opposition, to support the 1981 annexation of the

Labor Cabinet (1984–1990) Members' Identification		
Doves	*Yonetz*	*Hawks*
Peres[a]	Bar-Lev[a]	Rabin[a]
Weizman[a]	Shahal[b]	Arbeli-Almozlino[f]
Navon[a]	Yaakobi[c]	Nehamkin[f]
Edri[d]	Tzur	
	Gur[e]	
	Katz-Oz[d]	

[a]Inner cabinet member, 1984–1990.
[b]Inner cabinet member, 1989–1990.
[c]Inner cabinet member for part of 1990 (Yaakobi replaced Weizman, who was dismissed for his alleged contacts with the PLO).
[d]Cabinet member, 1988–1990.
[e]Gur resigned from the cabinet in 1986 and was replaced by Arbeli-Almozlino. He reaccepted ministerial responsibility in 1987.
[f]Cabinet member until 1988.

Golan.[11] Actually, only in June 1976 (after the death of its leader Yitzhak Tabenkin) did Hakibbutz Hameuchad accept a resolution in favor of a territorial compromise as advocated by Yigal Allon, one of its younger leaders. Allon was Rabin's mentor from the days of the prestate Palmach military organization, and although Rabin was not an Achdut Haavodah member he was considered close to its leaders and its political line.

Rafi was a group led by David Ben-Gurion, Moshe Dayan, and Shimon Peres that split off from Mapai in 1965. Its membership consisted of the more "activist" circles within the party, all of which were security oriented. It too was generally more inclined to support hawkish policies.

Many former members of these two groups who were still active in Labor in the 1980s were part of the Central Stream group. To what extent this group was actually situated at the center of the party continuum, as it claimed and as its name suggested, was debatable. Although it professed strict adherence to the party platform, it was viewed by many both inside and outside the party as being the backbone of the hawkish camp. It met occasionally, had a semipermanent secretariat, and its leaders included MK Shlomo Hillel, a former minister and speaker of the 11th Knesset (1984–1988); Immanuel Zisman, the boss of the party organization in Jerusalem who became an MK in 1988; and Simcha Dinitz, former ambassador to the United States, former MK, and presently chairperson of the Jewish Agency.[12] Nehamkin and Arbeli-Almozlino also identified themselves as members of this group. Bar-Lev, though not clearly within the Central Stream until late in 1989, occasionally showed up at its functions. The group was founded in 1984 to counteract the dovish tendencies of the party, but its roots can be traced back to 1978, when some of its future members disapproved of the Camp David Accords.[13] The Central Stream, in contrast to other party groups, was not power oriented, and as such it refrained from the public struggle for party positions.[14] It preferred to project a friendly image to other power groups in the party, instead of competing with them.

Rabin was, conspicuously, not a member of this group. He had his own power organization, known as the Rabin camp. In addition, because of his leadership aspirations and position, he preferred, like Peres, to maintain a more central position and not to be clearly identified with any group more definitely placed on the party's hawkish–dovish continuum.

Past affiliation with the activist factions of the Labor Party, Rafi, and Achdut Haavodah could be misleading, as the rather dovish positions of Peres and Navon, both once Rafi members, indicated. MK Aharon Harel, for example, was a lesser known dove with a Rafi past. Similarly, Tzur, who often expressed dovish attitudes at the ministerial level in the grand coalition, was the representative of Hakibbutz Hameuchad, once associated with Achdut Haavodah.

Interestingly, some of the Central Stream hawks claimed Peres as a member of their own camp.[15] Others in this group, such as MKs Nachman Raz and Edna Solodar, while not claiming him as a fellow member, did not classify him as a dove.[16] This, too, underlines the difficulties faced by anyone seeking to clearly position the leaders somewhere along the hawkish–dovish continuum. Possibly, this attitude toward Peres among some hawks was a sign of political wisdom. Blurring the fact that the party's leader had become a dove may have served their interest, diverting attention from leftward movement within the party. This could have been useful in intraparty struggles, as well as in electoral politics.

At the hawkish extreme of the party we may identify a group named after Ben-Gurion; among its better known leaders were Asher Ben-Natan and MK Amnon Lin, both of whom had a Rafi past.[17] The Dor Hemshech ("continuing generation") group, composed of members in the forty to fifty age bracket, displayed some hawkish tendencies, although it was primarily power oriented. Some of its leaders, for example MKs Micha Goldman and Raanan Cohen—new Knesset members in 1988—were also active members of the Central Stream. Similarly power driven, the Young Guard group displayed a pronounced dovish orientation.[18] Among its leaders, the best known were MK Chaim Ramon and the new (1988) MK Amir Peretz. Most other groups in the party, such as the well established Leshiluv, include in their ranks hawks as well as doves and cannot be neatly classified.[19] The leader of the Leshiluv group has been MK Micha Harish, the new secretary-general, who is himself a yonetz. Similarly, the Rabin camp, the emerging Gur camp, and the regional party organizations were purely power oriented and included members of differing convictions. Shahal and Yaakobi also had informal groups of followers.

There were, however, a few more homogeneous dovish groups. For example, the Mashov group, headed by MK Yossi Beilin, a confidant of Peres whom he chose to serve as director general of the Foreign Ministry as well as deputy minister of finance, and by MK Avraham Burg, were clearly oriented to the left.[20] Similarly, manifestly dovish views were undisputed within the Kfar Hayarok group, led by MK Chaim Ramon and Nissim Zvili. Following the November 1988 elections a new dovish group was formed, the Forum for the Promotion of Peace, which included most doves in the party. This seems to be the dovish version of the Central Stream—ideological fervor with no power orientation. Another dovish bastion, though not officially Labor affiliated, was the International Center for Peace in the Middle East, whose members included doves such as Abba Eban, party veteran and former justice minister Chaim Tzadok, popular MK Ora Namir, MK Shevach Weiss, and MKs Yaakov Gil and Aharon Harel. In this framework, they can lend support to formulations that deviate from the Labor Party platform. This center also hosts doves from parties and circles left of Labor.

In January 1989, a new body was formed in the party, the Political Center. This marked the first time that a yonetz forum was organized. Its organizers, among them the veteran MK David Libai and Knesset newcomers Avraham Shochat, Hagai Merom, and Eli Ben-Menachem, claimed that this group's purpose was to continue the historic pragmatic approach of Mapai. They belonged to various power groups in the party. The establishment of this body could have been significant, as it suggested the possible crystallization of three separate camps with distinctly different outlooks on war and peace: doves, hawks, and yonetz. This development also seemed to indicate an increased importance of national security issues in party life. Nevertheless, this group did not gain prominence and in 1990 the yonetz disposition was not yet clearly institutionalized, primarily because of the lack of a single leader with stature in the party.

THE STRENGTH OF EACH CAMP AND CONFLICT RESOLUTION

As pointed out at the beginning of this chapter, the Labor Party was not preoccupied during the 1980s with national security issues; it rarely debated topics of defense and foreign policy, and its institutions were hardly involved at all in policy formulation when the party was in the government. This pattern was typical also of Mapai, Labor's predecessor.[21] When partner to the ruling coalition, the locus of decisionmaking was at the cabinet level; while in opposition, there was a somewhat wider participation in molding the party positions.

When not in power (1977–1984, 1990–   ), Labor could only give advice or criticize the government; for the most part it played a reactive role. The party position, as expressed in its platform and approved by the party's Central Council (a body convened every few months), could serve only as a general guideline that was not always relevant to government decisions on particular cases, which demanded ad hoc reactions. The response to the June 1981 air raid on the Iraqi reactor, for example, or to the June 1982 outbreak of the Lebanon War, or to cuts in the defense budget, could not be derived from the party platform or from the Central Council (Merkaz) resolutions. The mere fact of being in opposition allowed Labor MKs greater latitude in voicing their personal views; they had no obligation to support a particular policy. This is true, of course, in other parliaments as well.[22] Yet when it came to national security affairs, Laborites were somewhat restrained by the fear of being accused of irresponsible criticism (see Chapter 6), although Israelis have tolerated increasingly higher levels of criticism since 1973.

Apart from sporadic personal reactions, the party did attempt to issue formal responses in various forums. The largest was the Executive Bureau (Lishkah). This forum of approximately one hundred members, elected by the Central Council, meets on an almost weekly basis. For example, in January 1982 the Executive Bureau discussed the possibility of engaging in hostilities along the Lebanese border, and voiced approval for a limited military operation in the event of a Palestinian attempt to wage a war of attrition. Another example was its July 30, 1982 call to refrain from bombing civilian targets in Beirut during the Israeli siege of that city. The parliamentary faction was regularly convened to discuss national security issues as well, and this is where parliamentary responses were often decided upon. A more limited, informal forum dealing with national security issues in the early 1980s was Havereinu, which included only those Labor MKs who were members of the prestigious parliamentary Foreign Affairs and Defense Committee and several additional Labor MKs. Peres, Rabin, Bar-Lev, Gur, Eban, Hillel, Harish, Sarid, and Dani Rosolio represented the party in this committee when the Lebanon War broke out. This body was active in coordinating the party's policy toward the government's military involvement in Lebanon.

The party also established a small "Reactions Committee," which included a few MKs and several other party activists. This forum was actually quite open and those most interested, even if not formally members of the committee, could participate in the wording of the party's responses. Hawks and doves alike participated in these forums. The final wording of the resolutions was usually assigned to a small group, which attempted to issue communications acceptable to all; these "experts" on drafting resolutions were usually able to resolve the disagreements between hawks and doves. As in earlier periods, voting as a mechanism for conflict resolution was seldom used in the Labor Party during the 1980s.

In 1984, when Labor formed the National Unity government together with the Likud, party participation in national security issues became more limited. As the party's representatives took charge of national security affairs—Rabin as defense minister and Peres as prime minister (1984–1986) and later foreign minister (1986–1988)—the locus of decisionmaking moved to the cabinet level and of necessity now involved the Likud, primarily Shamir. An inner cabinet dealing with national security issues, consisting of ten ministers equally divided between Labor and Likud, was created in 1984. In spite of the desire of all ministers to join this forum, the body that coordinated high policy in the 1984–1988 period was the "prime ministers' club," the name given to the informal meetings of Peres, Rabin, and Shamir (who had all been prime minister at least once). The higher echelons of the bureaucracy that served those three ministers, only some of whom were politically nominated, played an important role in minimizing party inputs. When in government, Labor leaders could expect the support of the Knesset faction and the party institutions for their policies, although some criticism was tolerated. In contrast to Labor parties in other countries, the Israeli Labor Party was rather disciplined.[23]

In the aftermath of the November 1988 elections, another National Unity government was formed, this time headed by Shamir but preserving the status of Peres and Rabin as the leading Laborite decisionmakers in the cabinet. The forum of the inner cabinet was also preserved, but was increased to twelve. Peres, though he was appointed finance minister and vice-premier and was no longer formally responsible for foreign affairs, and Rabin, who remained as defense minister, continued to be members of the inner group formulating high policy. The "prime ministers' club" was enlarged to include also the new foreign minister, Moshe Arens of the Likud, who was for the time being only an aspirant to the premiership. Among the Laborites, Rabin was the chief political beneficiary of the formation of the new National Unity government in 1988; he was among those who worked hard to forge the grand coalition. After 1984 his position as defense minister was not seriously challenged either in Labor or Likud, which increased his authority on national security affairs. This was one of the reasons he was most reluctant to break up the coalition in March 1990.

Since 1984, a party forum called Sareinu ("our ministers") has held regular weekly meetings to discuss, among other topics, defense and foreign affairs issues on the government's agenda. Sareinu included all Laborites in ministerial positions; and Rabin and Peres occasionally met or discussed over the telephone issues to be raised in this forum, to make sure there would be coordination between the two of them. Sareinu allowed little involvement on the part of other party institutions, however, evoking some criticism. The party secretary, MK Uzi Baram, even threatened to resign (January 1988) unless greater participation in decisionmaking was assured him. He clearly wanted to be included in the Sareinu forum; he also advocated greater involvement of the formal party forums in the decision-making process. The

Executive Bureau and the Central Council, which were regularly convened, served mostly to legitimize decisions made elsewhere.

In the final analysis, the ones who made the decisions on the main issues in the 1980s were Peres and Rabin. They were careful not to challenge each other on topics to which either of them assigned great importance. Peres, for example, agreed to follow Rabin in the 1987 decision to scrap the Lavi airplane, a national project he had initially supported. Similarly, Rabin decided to overcome his skepticism about Peres's plan for an international conference that would open the way for negotiations with Jordan. Both men were instrumental in securing Labor's support for the May 1989 peace initiative of the National Unity government. And only their cooperation put an end to this government in March 1990.

One of the main arenas of conflict between doves and hawks was the writing of the party platform. As mentioned previously, party planks generate much interest in Israel, and party activists assign great importance to their precise wording. As a matter of fact, any party document on national security issues evokes a certain predictable struggle. This intraparty factional struggle has always served, to some extent, as a mechanism for providing alternative policy choices to the party.[24]

When, at the April 1986 party congress (*veida*)—a 3,000-member body that generally convenes every four years—the doves proposed an amendment to substitute for the term *sovereignty* (which previous platforms had used for describing the future status of Israeli security zones in the territories) other terms less unacceptable to the Arabs, the vote became a test of the power of the doves versus the hawks. This dovish amendment attracted only about 40 percent of the delegates. On the other hand, the hawkish amendment at the same *veida* to restore Southern Gaza to the party list of security zones, following its deletion by the preparatory committee, was also backed only by approximately 40 percent of the convention.

Both votes demanded clear-cut choices, and their outcome is indicative of the difficulties involved in assessing the distribution of Laborites along the party hawkish–dovish continuum. The second vote also manifested, however, the delegates' tendency to accept the consensus reached in the preparatory committee (establishing a preparatory committee to smooth tensions before a vote is taken in a party forum is a common practice).[25] Another example of the preparatory committee's work took place in the summer of 1988, before the elections and following Hussein's measures toward disengaging Jordan from the Israeli-ruled territories. In this case, certain party leaders demanded that the platform be adjusted to the new reality. As is typical, a committee was appointed to reach consensual formulations, which were subsequently approved by the party Central Council (Merkaz). Only on rare occasions was the committee's suggested draft rejected by the party forums. Such committees are carefully selected in order to give representation to all the main orientations in the party. Furthermore, Rabin and Peres have made sure that they are well represented in such bodies. What struggle occurs is therefore generally within the committee, and the party's formal institutions are usually spared the trouble of making a choice.[26] Since 1984 the party has undergone a process of democratization, particularly in the area of nominations; but many votes, as observed in the literature on parties in general, still served a ritualistic rather than a decision-making purpose.

Election propaganda in the 1980s was less subject than the platform to intraparty quarreling, because all wanted the appeal to be as broad as possible. In the 1984 elections, the party made a conscious effort to come up with formulations that obfuscated the differences between its hawks and doves.[27] During the 1988 elections campaign, however, the party presented a rather dovish profile that was far from pleasing to the hawks.[28] But they preferred not to dispute the party message vocally, so as to avoid focusing attention on its dovish character or presenting Labor as a divided party. Nevertheless, in the late 1980s the hawks displayed increasing concern about the party's dovish emphasis, both for electoral and substantive reasons.

Since advancement within the party hierarchy was not strongly connected during the 1980s to one's position on the Arab–Israeli conflict, the personal inclinations of party members were not overly influenced or constrained by the party consensus. Because of the scant involvement of the party institutions in national security issues, those in the leadership positions at the ministerial and parliamentary level had the greatest input. Indeed, the hawks' greatest concern was over the party's representation in the Knesset, where the doves were gradually increasing their strength. This increase was intriguing, since the party institutions seemed to be less dovish than the MKs who were elected. But since dovish members were already in the Knesset, they were able to develop power bases in the party that were not directly connected to national security issues. The relations between the party leaders and the party activists are based on mutual dependence, and the two groups need each other to govern effectively.[29] This was a further indication of the secondary importance attached to the candidates' positions on national security issues. The parliamentary faction also supplied the cadres for the top ministerial positions. Indeed, one of the functions of parties in every political system is the selection of leaders.[30]

At the cabinet level, the doves' strength was more or less equal to the hawks' in the 1984–1988 period. But with Nehamkin and Arbeli-Almozlino outside the cabinet after a new National Unity government was formed in December 1988, the doves gained the upper hand, as can be seen clearly in the table on page 19. The only hawks left in the cabinet were Rabin and Bar-Lev, who, as mentioned, joined the ranks of the hawks late in 1989. Among the new candidates considered for a cabinet post during the ultimately unsuccessful attempt to form a Labor-led government in the spring of 1990, only one, MK Michael Bar-Zohar, was a hawk. MKs Libai and Shochat were yonetz, while Baram, Namir, and Ramon were doves. Masha Lubelski, the head of the party-ruled women's organization, Naamat, who also was considered a ministerial prospect, was an unmistakable dove. At that time, the hawks feared that Peres might pack the new government with doves and Hillel even threatened to refrain from supporting it unless it had a respectable hawkish representation.[31] Interestingly, already at the beginning of the decade, in 1980, in expectation of a Labor victory in the 1981 elections, the hawks in the party feared that Peres would elevate the status of many party doves to ministerial rank.[32]

A close look at the turnover in the party Knesset representation since 1977 also indicates a dovish increase. In 1981, the new list did not include any net loss to the hawks at the expense of the doves. Yet in the 11th Knesset (1984–1988) the Labor dovish contingent in the Knesset increased by three; it increased by two more in 1988. The total addition of five dovish MKs was quite significant, taking into consideration the fact that the size of the Labor Knesset faction as a whole (not to be confused with the strength of the erstwhile Labor–Mapam Alignment) remained stable in the 1980s. The electoral appeal of Labor, in contrast to its parliamentary strength, was clearly in decline throughout that decade; its electoral alliance with leftist Mapam (in 1981 and 1984) and with the Independent Liberals (in 1984) received progressively less support in each election in the 1980s—a loss of 7 percent between 1981 and 1988.[33]

The composition of the party's 12th Knesset (elected in 1988) faction allows us to gauge the strength of the hawks and doves and also to project the balance of power into the early 1990s. As we have seen, the changes in the composition of the Knesset membership in 1988 strengthened the dovish camp within the parliamentary faction. Among the thirty-nine Laborites sitting in the 12th Knesset, only eleven were clearly hawks: Rabin and Bar-Lev—the only hawks serving at the ministerial level; the veteran MKs Arbeli-Almozlino, Hillel, and Solodar; the new MKs Bar-Zohar, Cohen, Gal, Goldman, and Zisman; and Shitrit, who identified himself as a yonetz but substantively took hawkish positions, was active in the Central Stream, and was counted by the hawks as one of them.

Fourteen MKs constituted the dovish contingent: Peres, Navon, Weizman, and Edri at the ministerial level; veteran MKs Arad, Baram, Namir, Ramon, and Weiss; and new MKs Beilin, Burg, Dayan, Eliav, and Peretz. The Arab MK on the 1988 party list, Massalha, further increased the doves' strength to fifteen. This camp, moreover, included nationally prominent doves such as Eliav (a former secretary-general of the party who left Labor in 1975 in protest against what he felt were its hawkish positions but returned in 1986) and Burg, both of whom were active in the Peace Now movement. Indeed, it was the first time that Labor had sent representatives to the Knesset who were clearly associated with Peace Now.[34] Another extreme dove was Ramon, who even stated that at the cabinet level there was not even one Laborite with indubitably dovish views.[35] The great support that Namir

Labor Parliamentary Turnover in Terms of Hawks and Doves Since 1977

	Hawks	Doves	Yonetz	Hawks	Doves	Yonetz	Dovish net addition
	who were not reelected			new on the Knesset list			
1981	3	3	2[a]	6	9	4[b]	0
1984	5	3	1[c]	2	1	2[d]	3
1988	7	4	3[e]	6	5	3[f]	2

Note: This table takes into consideration only those MKs who sought election on Labor's list in the Labor Party. It does not include the MKs of leftist Mapam, which was in alignment with Labor until 1984. It includes, however, the joining of MKs Amnon Lin and Yitzhak Peretz in 1980, and the MKs of Ezer Weizman's Yahad Party in 1984, because they were absorbed into the party.
"Dovish net addition" shows the number of new doves minus new hawks added to numbers of ex-doves minus ex-hawks. Mid-term Knesset changes were also considered.
[a]Moshe Dayan, Yigal Allon, and Amos Hadar were the hawks; the doves were Chaim Tzadok, Yitzhak Navon, and Yehoshua Rabinovich. Aharon Yadlin and Eliyahu Moyal were yonetz. Navon was elected as president and was replaced by Avraham Katz-Oz, a yonetz (April 1978). In place of the deceased Allon entered Yehuda Hashai, a hawk. In 1980, MKs Amnon Lin and Yitzhak Peretz, both hawks, left the Likud and joined Labor.
[b]Michael Bar-Zohar, Aryeh Nehamkin, Raanan Naim, Aharon Nachmias, Dani Rosolio, and Chaim Herzog were hawks. The doves were Nava Arad, Rafi Edri, Aharon Harel, Uri Sabag, Shevach Weiss, Naftali Blumenthal, Yaakov Gil, and Musa Harif. Herzog, who became president, was replaced in 1983 by Nachman Raz, another hawk. Harif was replaced by Edna Solodar, a hawk; Rosolio's replacement was Chaim Ramon, a dove. This left the ratio of hawks to doves the same as it was in 1981. Dov Ben-Meir, Mordechai Gur, Rafi Swissa, and Yaakov Tzur were yonetz.
[c]The hawks were Tamar Eshel, Michael Bar-Zohar, Raanan Naim, Yehezkel Zakai, and Yehuda Hashai. The doves included Yerucham Meshel, Uri Sabag, and Naftali Blumenthal. Rafi Swissa was a yonetz.
[d]The hawks were Simcha Dinitz and Efraim Shalom; the dove was Yitzhak Navon; Yisrael Keisar and David Libai were yonetz. Dinitz, the hawk, and Harel, the dove, left the Knesset in 1987 and were replaced by Yaakov Gil, a dove, and Avraham Shochat, a yonetz. In 1984, Yahad, Weizman's party, joined Labor. It included Weizman, a dove, and Binyamin Ben-Eliezer and Moshe Amar, both yonetz.
[e]The hawks were Aryeh Nehamkin, Nachman Raz, Amnon Lin, Efraim Shalom, Jacques Amir, Aaron Nachmias, and Yitzhak Peretz. The doves were Menachem Hacohen, Yaakov Gil, Adi Amorai, and Yossi Sarid. Moshe Amar, Eliyahu Speiser, and Dov Ben-Meir were yonetz.
[f]The doves were Lova Eliav, Yossi Beilin, Avraham Burg, Eli Dayan, and Amir Peretz. The hawks included Michael Bar-Zohar, Raanan Cohen, Gedalia Gal, Micha Goldman, Shimon Shitrit, and Immanuel Zisman. Hagai Merom, Eli Ben-Menachem, and Efraim Gur were in the yonetz camp.

and Eliav received from the party Central Council (Merkaz) during elections to the party list was noteworthy. To what extent the dovish views of such backbenchers—views which are not in accordance with the party platform—will be adopted by the party leadership remains to be seen. As for the rest of the parliamentary faction, thirteen MKs could not be clearly identified either as hawks or doves. But the dovish camp in the parliamentary faction of the 12th Knesset was larger than the hawkish one, and larger than the emerging yonetz camp as well. The elected faction chairperson was also a dove, Ramon.

The continuing deadlock in Israeli politics between Labor and Likud, as well as changes in the international environment, exacerbated the conflict over which political road should be taken. Most doves opposed partnership with the Likud in a grand coalition. Developments in the Likud—specifically, during the summer of 1989, the consolidation of the internal opposition to Prime Minister Shamir and to the May 1989 peace initiative—led the Labor doves to demand again to leave the government. This exacerbated the tensions between the dovish and hawkish wings in the party. In a move indicative of the growing tension, MK Zisman proposed in September 1989 to expel from the party those dovish members who worked against the party platform. In this debate, MK Baram called the party hawks a "dogmatic and outdated group," and called himself and his dovish colleagues "the realistic group" in the Labor Party.[36] Their analysis led them to prefer the status of parliamentary opposition to continued cooperation with the Likud in the government. They failed, however, to put an end to the Likud–Labor government until Rabin too went along with such a step in March 1990.

These tensions were not divorced from the power struggle within the Labor Party. Peres and Rabin were both in their late sixties, yet judging from the history of Israeli politics they were young enough to run the party for several years to come. The potential for a renewed political battle between the two for the top spot in the party arose again in 1989, as a result of the contrast between Labor's electoral failures and Rabin's general popularity and pivotal role in Israeli coalition politics. At that time Rabin displayed reluctance to renew the struggle once again, seeming to be satisfied with a power constellation assuring him the defense portfolio. Yet, following the fiasco of Peres's attempt to form a Labor-led government, Rabin opened up the old feud. Many in the party, including professed doves Weizman, Tzadok, and even the Kfar Hayarok group, had considered, since the summer of 1989, lending strong support to Rabin for the leadership position in the next elections, to be held in November 1992. Initially, Rabin's chances to replace Peres looked good. Yet in July 1990 he failed in his attempt to elicit the support of the majority of the Central Committee (Merkaz) for his demand for an early confrontation over the leadership position. Peres, an artful politician, once again showed his talent at intraparty politics and defeated Rabin.

Of course, this fact had little influence on the younger Laborites attempting to take the reins. Gur, Yaakobi, Shahal, and Baram, each in his fifties, were all competing for the first spot, and hoped to retire Peres and Rabin at the earliest opportunity. Of the four, Shahal had probably built the largest power base in the party and also had an advantage in having been promoted to membership in the inner cabinet in 1989. Yaakobi reached the rank of inner cabinet member a year later, though he had a longer ministerial career and was widely regarded as Labor's most authoritative speaker on economic affairs. It is significant that the hawks had no representation among the new contenders for the party's leadership. Hillel, who is in his sixties, entertained such aspirations, but in the 12th Knesset he was relegated to the status of an ordinary MK. Indeed, as we have seen, the hawks were rather poor in candidates for cabinet positions. In the not too distant future, the absence of any hawk in a leading position could be of great significance. It is not yet clear at what point the party will have to decide on its leader. May 1991 is the date for the next party congress; but the competition for the leadership position could end earlier, particularly if there will be national elections before the scheduled November 1992 elections.

NOTES

1. For this distinction, see Giovanni Sartori, *Parties and Party Systems*, pp. 76–77. Sartori actually prefers the term *fraction* to describe such party subunits (see his discussion on pp. 71–82).

2. For a similar distinction on the U.S. scene, see Graham T. Allison, Albert Carnesale, and Joseph S. Nye, Jr., *Hawks, Doves and Owls* (New York: W.W. Norton, 1985). The debate here is primarily over the type and amounts of nuclear weapons.

3. This thinking is similar to E. H. Carr's theme that change is inevitable and that the weaker side should display flexibility to prevent war. See his *The Twenty Years Crisis, 1919–1939* (London: Macmillan, 1946). On such thinking in the extreme Israeli dovish circles, see Rael Jean Isaac, *Israel Divided: Ideological Politics in the Jewish State* (Baltimore: Johns Hopkins University Press, 1976), pp. 94–95.

4. For the principles of the school of political realism in international relations, see Hans Morgenthau, *Politics Among Nations*, 4th ed. (New York: A.A. Knopf, 1967), pp. 3–14.

5. The hawkish–dovish tendencies described here are not necessarily characteristic of other parties. The striking difference between Labor's hawks and Likud's, for example, is the choice of the Arab partner. Laborites clung to the Hashemite option, whereas Likud's hawks opted for a non-PLO Palestinian partnership. Another example is the common evaluation of some extreme doves, as well as Likud hawks, that partition is no longer a realistic option because of the intensive settling in Judea and Samaria. A more elaborate discussion of the characteristics of hawks and doves in Israeli politics generally, a fascinating topic, is beyond the scope of this work.

6. Many interviewees pointed out that the position on the PLO was a basic difference between doves and hawks.

7. This is true even of communist political systems where ideological rigor and consistency are highly valued. See Alexander Dallin, "The Domestic Sources of Soviet Foreign Policy," in *The Domestic Context of Soviet Foreign Policy*, ed. Seweryn Bialer (Boulder: Westview Press, 1981), p. 345.

8. Many party leaders interviewed for this work have pointed out this fact. The classification here will be based on the self-image and on the image projected, taking into consideration the positions on the multidimensional continuum, as well as the party peers' judgment. The discussions the author held with many party activists served as a basis for evaluation.

9. His predecessor as the moshav movement's representative, Yehezkel Zakai, was one of the Labor MKs to vote against the Camp David Accords. The moshav movement representative who replaced Nehamkin in the 12th Knesset, Gedalia Gal, was also known to be a hawk. The present secretary-general of the movement, Nissim Zvili, is an arch-dove, however. This is also indicative of the changes taking place in the party.

10. For the positions of those parties on security and foreign affairs until 1968, see Michael Brecher, *The Foreign Policy System of Israel*, pp. 169–167, 180–182, 318–371; for their positions following their merger into the Labor Party in 1968 until 1973, see Yossi Beilin, *The Price of Unity*.

11. See Yael Yishai, *Land or Peace: Whither Israel?*, p. 84; Eyal Kafkafy, "From Wisdom to Sagacity," *State, Government and International Relations* 27 (Hebrew) (Winter 1987), pp. 56–57.

12. For the views of the Central Stream group, primarily on the territorial issue, see Shlomo Hillel, "The Allon Plan Has Come of Age," *Spectrum* 1 (March 1983), pp. 13–15 (*Spectrum* is an English-language magazine published by the Labor Party); Immanuel Zisman, "At Maale Efraim Peres Was Strengthened," *Davar*, November 15, 1987; Simcha Dinitz, "The Road to Change Goes Via the PLO," *Baavoda*, no. 10 (October 1986).

13. Interview with Dr. Amos Carmel, one of its main activists, on November 25, 1987. The Central Stream's predecessor was the Manof group, founded in 1981.

14. Evidence suggests that Simcha Dinitz was elected to his post as chairman of the Jewish Agency, in 1987, with the organized help of the Central Stream, which wished to block the path of Nissim Zvili, an arch-dove.

15. Interview with Immanuel Zisman, December 30, 1987.

16. Interviews with MK Nachman Raz, December 12, 1987; and MK Edna Solodar, December 12, 1987. Both represented the kibbutz movement. Raz was not reelected to the Labor Knesset list in 1988.

17. Asher Ben-Natan has had a rich government career in the security and foreign affairs area. In the 1970s he served as an advisor to Peres, then a hawk. Lin returned to the party in 1980 after several years' flirtation with Likud. He has been considered an expert on relations with Israeli Arabs. For this group, see Yishai, *Land or Peace: Whither Israel?*, p. 85.

18. For its positions, see Grisha Arloser, "Wasted on the Young!?" *Spectrum* 2 (March 1984), p. 23.

19. For the Leshiluv group's views on national security, see Shmuel Bahat and Israel Gat, eds., *A Selection of Decisions and Conclusions on "Leshiluv": A Zionist-Socialist Circle in the Labor Party* (Hebrew) (Tel Aviv: Labor Party, 1986).

20. For its views, see Yair Hirschfeld, "Labor Initiative," *Spectrum* 2 (June–July 1984). The author, an expert on Arab affairs, is one of its leaders.

21. See Peter Medding, *Mapai in Israel*, p. 218; for criticism of Ben-Gurion's unwillingness to allow party involvement in national security issues,

see Yossi Beilin, *Sons in the Shade of Their Fathers* (Hebrew) (Ramat Gan: Revivim, 1984), pp. 41–42, 78.

22. On the latitude of backbenchers in the British parliament, see, inter alia, Neville Thompson, *The Anti Appeasers* (Oxford: Oxford University Press, 1971), p. 7.

23. For British Labor Party forums adopting resolutions against the recommendations of the Labor-led government, see John Roper, "The Labor Party and British Foreign Policy," in *The Foreign Policies of West European Socialist Parties*, ed. Werner J. Feld (New York: Praeger, 1978), pp. 10–12.

24. Gershon R. Kieval, *Party Politics in Israel and the Occupied Territories* (Westport: Greenwood Press, 1983), p. xi.

25. For the importance of consensus in party life, see Medding, *Mapai in Israel*; and Myron J. Aronoff, *Power and Ritual in the Israel Labor Party*, pp. 83–90.

26. For the functions of committees in the Labor Party, see Aronoff, *Power and Ritual in the Israel Labor Party*, pp. 79–97.

27. See Jonathan Mendilow, "Israel's Labor Alignment in the 1984 Elections: Catch-All Tactics in a Divided Society," *Comparative Politics* 20 (July 1988), pp. 443–460.

28. Efraim Inbar, "War and Peace, Hopes and Fears in the 1988 Elections," in *Israel at the Polls: The Elections of 1988–89*, eds. Daniel J. Elazar and Shmuel Sandler (Detroit: Wayne State University Press, in press).

29. Samuel J. Eldersveld, *Political Parties: A Behavioral Analysis* (Chicago: Rand McNally, 1964), p. 10.

30. For political parties' functions, see Sigmund Neumann, *Modern Political Parties* (Chicago: University of Chicago Press, 1956), pp. 395–400.

31. *Haaretz*, March 23, 1990.

32. See *Yediot Ahronot*, October 30, 1980.

33. The number of seats reserved for those two parties aligned with Labor on the Knesset list was out of proportion to the two parties' real electoral strength.

34. For Lova Eliav's views on the Arab-Israeli conflict, see his *Eretz Hatzvi* (Hebrew) (Tel Aviv: Am Oved, 1972). For the Peace Now movement, see Mordechai Bar-On, *Peace Now* (Hebrew) (Tel Aviv: Hakibbutz Hameuchad, 1985).

35. *Davar*, September 8, 1989.

36. *Jerusalem Post*, September 1, 1989.

CHAPTER 3
Threat Perception and the Chances for Peace

The perceived threats, along with the evaluation of developments in the Arab–Israeli conflict, are the two main factors molding the positions of Laborites on national security issues. This is the predominant dimension of the multidimensional hawkish–dovish continuum. Attitudes toward the chances for peaceful coexistence with Israel's Arab neighbors and toward the possibility of acceptance of the Jewish state by the Arab world affect all other dimensions of the continuum. Such attitudes are rooted in various personal experiences and dispositions, and their formation is beyond the scope of this work. Generally, Laborites' judgments tend to be presented in pragmatic rather than ideological terms. All Laborites, doves and hawks alike, profess to be realists, but their interpretations of what reality is and what is achievable, given all the regional constraints, differ.

The acute Israeli threat perception in the recent past stemmed from the common belief that the Arabs' goal was the destruction of Israel as a political entity—i.e., *politicide*.[1] Nowadays, politicide as an all-Arab policy goal is no longer an unquestioned assumption within the party. Some do believe that changes have taken place in the Arab countries toward acceptance of Israel. The implications of the differences in threat perception are clear: the more acute the feeling of insecurity, the more stringent is the insistence on various security arrangements, including a larger scope of border rectifications.

Threat perception also influences the attitude toward time. The time factor, i.e., how long Israel should delay a political agreement until the best results are achievable, is another intraparty issue of dispute. Hawks believe that time is needed to allow changes in Arab positions toward Israel to take place. They argue that Israel must have patience until a solution it regards as desirable is accepted in the Arab world. Furthermore, time is considered an important element in testing Arab claims of moderation. Conversely, among doves, perceived signs of moderation—the basis for their lower level of threat perception—are to be capitalized on in order to achieve an agreement. The realization that the Arab transition to more moderate positions is not necessarily a one-way process, coupled with the feeling that time plays a negative role as far as Israel is concerned, leads to a sense of urgency, which is translated into a greater willingness to reach an agreement with Arab actors even if the terms are not ideal. As mentioned, doves tend to have lower levels of threat perception, yet paradoxically press harder to reach an agreement quickly.

Most in the party, however, regardless of ornithological affiliation, agree that in the aftermath of the 1978 Camp David Accords and the 1979 peace treaty with Egypt, Israel has faced considerably fewer threats to its security. Egypt, Israel's most powerful Arab rival, seemed to have chosen to abjure force, at least in the short range, in its dealings with the Zionist state. This marked a break in the violent pattern of the Arab–Israeli conflict, and did not fail to impress most Israeli leaders. As a matter of fact, the peace treaty has withstood several strains, such as the 1981 Israeli air raid on the Iraqi nuclear reactor and the 1982 Israeli invasion of Lebanon. Furthermore, Egypt's gradual return to the Arab world in the 1980s, after it had been ostracized for its peace treaty with Israel, did not result in any of the changes in its relations with Israel that the other Arab states had demanded. At the end of 1989 even Syria and Lybia normalized their relations with an unreformed Egypt. The unflinching Egyptian commitment to the peace treaty was duly noted by the Israeli political elite, including Labor's leadership.

Similarly, Jordan, in terms of intent or capability, is regarded as only a minor threat. Years of intricate relations with Jordan have taught Israeli leaders that King Hussein is a moderate, pragmatic leader, who can be expected to engage in warlike activities against Israel only in extreme circumstances where the benefits of such actions very clearly outweigh the risks. The PLO, regardless of its perceived intentions of destroying Israel—a perception that became increasingly questionable after its statements of December 1988—possesses little military capability to do so. Syria, however, remained throughout the 1980s a powerful and committed enemy. Nevertheless, its rivalry with Iraq and Jordan, as well as the prolonged Iran–Iraq war (1980–1988), which has continued to simmer at a low level, reduced the probability of a coordinated military effort against Israel on its eastern front by Syria, Jordan, Saudi Arabia, and Iraq. The Iraqi invasion of Kuwait, which evoked the opposition of Syria, Saudi Arabia, and Egypt, further increased tensions in the Arab world and further reduced the chances of a united front forming against Israel.

A countering factor in the direction of increased threat perception toward the end of the decade was the presence of long-range missiles and chemical warheads in the Arab arsenals. Indeed, the Iraqi threats in spring 1990 to use chemical warheads indiscriminately against Israel, made all the more ominous by Iraq's conquest of Kuwait in August—an obvious act of politicide—clearly increased the threat perception among Laborites, as well as most other Israelis. The weakening of the Hashemite regime in Jordan, beginning in the late 1980s, was similarly regarded as worrisome. Yet the assessment that there has been some overall mellowing in the Arab enmity toward Israel has not basically changed among Laborites, and they continue to differentiate in their apprehensions of various Arab actors.

THE DOVES

In a typically dovish manner, Abba Eban argued in 1987 that after the Six Day War the destruction of Israel was no longer entertained as a possibility by clear-headed people.[2] In an earlier and more balanced statement, he distinguished three Arab approaches toward Israel. Formally, he maintained, only Egypt and Lebanon (as a result of the May 1983 agreement) had ended the state of war, but Jordan, Morocco, Tunisia, and possibly Saudi Arabia had relinquished the dream of Israel's destruction. He asserted, however, that politicide remains the goal of some Middle East international actors such as Syria.[3] Indeed, under its pressure, Lebanon abrogated its agreement with Israel in April 1984.

Similarly, Ezer Weizman had little fear of a politicide campaign. Once considered a superhawk, he changed his views following Sadat's visit to Jerusalem. Serving then as defense minister in the Likud-led government, he played a leading role in the successful conclusion of the Camp David Accords and the 1979 peace treaty. In 1984, following the elections in which he ran on a separate list, Weizman joined Labor and even became an outspoken leader of its dovish wing. He believed that there was a possibility of moving into a new interim period, characterized by an Israeli attempt to integrate into the Middle East, which might put an end to the Arab–Israeli conflict.[4]

The historic precedent that led Weizman to such a belief was the Franco-German relationship, once an ongoing bloody conflict that has turned into an amicable partnership in the European Community.[5] Weizman distinguished between a stable peace and a peaceful situation with a potential for war. The transition from intense antagonism to a stable peace, he maintained, has to include an interim stage in which the possibility of warlike acts accompanies the peaceful relationship. Egyptian–Israeli relations in the 1980s were, according to Weizman, undergoing a delicate interim stage of this sort.[6] His analysis implied that a transition to a situation such as the Franco–German rapprochement, free from hostilities, could also occur between the Arabs and Israel. Although Weizman displayed a historical perspective, he is no historical determinist. His views implied that stable peace is a historical possibility, but that the historical process is open-ended, leaving the future to be defined by actions taken by people. This explains some of his desire for Israeli activism and initiatives. Interestingly enough, while rejecting the dove and hawk labels, he nonetheless felt more attracted to the symbol of the hawk, because "the hawk represents speed, power, activity—what is known in political jargon as 'activism'; the hawk represents the people who are willing to take the static situation of the status quo and change it from the foundations."[7] This linguistic preference did not change the dovish substance of his views.

In spite of the fact that Weizman conceded that Egyptian–Israeli relations were in a fairly unstable interim stage, his threat perception was quite low.

He dismissed the summer 1988 news of Arab missiles and gas warheads, and declared he would need a gas mask only to protect himself during the coming elections.[8] He claimed, in fact, that destructive technology can have positive effects of leading to cooperation rather than conflict.[9] Furthermore, his appraisal as of 1988 was: "We have the strongest armoured and air force we have ever had and an excellent command. We have a peace settlement with Egypt with a huge potential; the United States is on our side; and the Soviet Union is much less against us than it used to be."[10] Weizman's assessment that Israel had become an entrenched reality in the Middle East, a fact to which most Arabs have learned to reconcile themselves, was a typical dovish position.[11]

Weizman similarly dismissed any Palestinian plans to eliminate Israel. He even minimized the importance of the Palestinian National Covenant, which explicitly advocates such an aim, as well as violent actions perpetrated by the PLO in Israel: "I am always reminded that the Palestine Covenant calls for the destruction of Israel. Let them try. From my experience, when someone seriously intends to destroy you, he fights with tanks, aeroplanes, a marching army. If someone puts a bomb into a rubbish bin somewhere, he is demonstrating weakness and frustration."[12]

Labor doves have gradually come to perceive less threat from the Palestinians and even the PLO. For example, in 1987 Yossi Beilin, then second in command to Peres at the Foreign Ministry, ordered that the distribution of the Palestinian National Covenant as propaganda material be discontinued. This document was probably no longer seen as reflecting current Palestinian positions. Similarly, MK Ora Namir reported to her dovish colleagues in the party, early in 1988, that she had heard moderate voices among Palestinians, some of them associated with the PLO.[13] She even concluded that "the conflict between us and the Palestinians is mostly emotional."[14] In minimizing the importance of the dispute over land, Namir seemed to suggest that emotional problems are more easily dealt with than a territorial conflict of interest. Her opinion also echoed Sadat's insistence that the Arab–Israeli conflict was essentially psychological, a position that belittled Israeli concerns about security arrangements. Weizman shared the emphasis on psychological factors, claiming that the burden of a ghetto mentality, in which everyone on the outside is perceived as an enemy, hindered the peace process. He suggested that the Jewish "prism" in Israeli foreign policy had to be discarded. To this distorting effect he attributed the failure to recognize that changes in the latter part of the 1980s in Europe—leading toward a decrease in international tensions and an increase in interstate cooperation—are bound also to affect the Middle East.[15]

Weizman and other doves had little fear about the capability of the Arab countries and the Palestinians to challenge Israel's actual existence, and questioned the reality of such an intention on their part. Nevertheless, in a dovish manner Weizman also warned that a failure to reach an agreement soon with the Arabs would lead to another war. The inevitable political tensions could bring about an uncontrollable escalation. Like other doves, he feared that Egypt might join such a war. He regarded the political efforts of Labor to reach an understanding with Jordan and the Palestinians in the 1987–1988 period as the last chance before a terrible "bloody war" would befall Israel that, in his opinion, would cost it tens of thousands of lives.[16] Such a "terrible war" was likely to break out, in Weizman's evaluation, before the year 2000.[17]

Indeed, the Labor doves, although stressing in their analysis and their political prescriptions the perceived process of moderation among the Arabs, did not rule out the possibility of future wars. Ironically enough, they were much more worried about imminent war than the hawks. It was argued that the moderation process taking place in the Arab world was not irreversible, and that therefore it had to be actively encouraged by Israel. For example, MK Chaim Ramon, one of the leading young doves, lamented the lack of Israeli flexibility in reaching an agreement with the Arabs. The insistence on too many conditions by Israel, as well as by some Arabs, was, he asserted, an unrealistic stance that might lead to further rounds of violence. Although this evaluation was a response specifically to the policies of the National Unity government in the 1986–1987 period, it was also meant as a criticism of his party's hawks.[18] With the approach of the November 1988 elections, Ramon believed that Israel was at a crossroads. One road, he felt, led to war.[19] Therefore he supported the May 1989 peace initiative, although he advocated a faster pace. Like other doves, he expressed his willingness to take chances in the peace process.[20] The dovish analysis emphasized Israeli responsibility for preventing a political impasse and avoiding future military confrontations. In contrast, the hawks saw Arab enmity as the main cause of the Arab–Israeli wars. This fear of war has been the underlying assumption behind the doves' sense of urgency. Preventing war and avoiding unnecessary, futile loss of Israeli lives was their top priority in the period we are examining. Some singled out Israeli recalcitrance in dealing with the Palestinian issue as the primary cause for the dangerous Middle East impasse.

In the Labor Party, the most eloquent, comprehensive argument stressing the urgency of bringing political efforts to fruition was made by Shimon Peres. By the early 1980s he was already considered to be closer to the dovish wing of the party. He explained to his colleagues in a party forum in 1985 that "peace can come when rare constellations occur in the history of the two sides of the conflict. Such constellations are rare indeed. At times they happen and sometimes they can be created."[21] In 1987 he stressed to his Executive Bureau colleagues that "since the Six Day War, and perhaps since the War for Independence, no better occasion was created to open negotiations to settle the conflict between us and Jordan and to solve the Palestinian problem. Moreover, if this opportunity is lost, it is possible that in the coming years, in the next decade and in the next twenty years, no such chance

will recur. There are things that happen just once and they pass away."²²
Peres believed that during the tenure of the first National Unity government
(1984–1988), an agreement with Jordan and a solution to the Palestinian
problem was a real possibility, particularly following the understanding he
reached with King Hussein in April 1987 (the London Agreement, which
dealt with the modalities involved in convening an international conference to
formally open Israeli–Jordanian peace talks).²³ He needed, however, to
overcome the hawks' apprehensions about an international conference. In
July 1989, after the second National Unity government presented its peace
initiative, he again emphasized that Israelis, as well as Palestinians, do not
have much time to reach an agreement.²⁴

If this unique opportunity were to be missed, Peres foresaw a bleak
future. The Arab world would return to waging war against Israel.²⁵ He
believed that such warlike tendencies were reinforced by the severely
deteriorating economic conditions in Arab countries such as Egypt and
Jordan. Any catastrophic development could encourage only the most
negative and extreme forces on the Arab side.²⁶

A critical factor leading to Peres's acute sense of urgency was his grave
concern about the possibility of the introduction of nuclear technology into
the Arab countries. The possibility of such a scenario meant for Peres that
Israel had to make great efforts to reach political arrangements before the
nuclearization of the Middle East.²⁷ Furthermore, in contrast to the situation
during the 1970s, he expressed apprehension about Israel's economic ability
to withstand successfully a prolonged arms race with the Arabs.²⁸ Difficulties
in mobilizing the necessary economic resources for building a strong enough
conventional force could, he believed, increase the pressure for Israel to adopt
an open nuclear posture.²⁹ The introduction of long-range missiles and
chemical weapons in the Arab world thus evoked a sense of urgency in regard
to the need to make peace. Interestingly, the developments that contributed to
an increase in threat perception constituted for Peres and other doves catalysts
for moderation and urgency, rather than enhancing suspicion of Arab attitudes
toward Israel.

Some of the pessimistic expressions of Peres were obviously colored by
the failure to implement the April 1987 London Agreement and by
difficulties encountered in 1988 by U.S. Secretary of State Shultz in his
attempt to resolve the Arab–Israeli conflict. As the Likud partner in the
government coalition blocked both the London Agreement and the U.S.
initiative, Peres and other doves in the party lamented what was perceived to
be a passing opportunity to make peace. They were much more disappointed
than Labor's skeptical hawks by the failure to convene an international
conference. For Peres, the international conference was not just a procedural
matter; he seemed genuinely convinced that Israel of the 1980s was living on
borrowed time. Similar reactions were expressed concerning Likud's
reluctance to go along with U.S. attempts to promote the May 1989 peace

initiative. This time, in March 1990, the hawks reluctantly joined Peres's efforts to bring down the government.

Peres's admonitions about the tragic consequences of Israeli inability to capitalize on a unique historic opportunity echoed the arguments made by the Peace Now movement. Indeed, Peres had already declared in 1978 that "the principles of Peace Now are identical" with those of the party.[30] Then, this statement evoked severe criticism in the party, most of whose members regarded that movement as being far to its left. Typically for the left wing in Israeli politics generally and in the party itself, the sense that time was running out and that war was imminent was accompanied in Peres's outlook by the conclusion that politicide was no longer a real possibility.

Holding up a rather pessimistic picture as the only alternative to "peace now" marked a new departure in Peres's thinking. A past member of the Rafi faction in the Labor Party, Peres was once clearly a hawk.[31] Nevertheless, in the 1970s he showed greater optimism, since he viewed the Middle East as deterministically moving into a transitional stage between a war period and a postwar period in a world divided into prewar, war, and postwar regions. He believed "that the main problem in the Middle East is how to pass through the corridor that leads from a period of suffering the burdens of war to one which, acccording to proven dialectics, is a 'postwar' era. The problem is how to pass through this corridor while avoiding additional wars."[32] In his view, this interim period was characterized in the 1980s by greater war dangers, and its transformation into a postwar condition seemed less certain in the near future.

Events in Eastern Europe a decade later renewed and confirmed his optimism. Peres took the view that similar change is, sooner or later, inevitable in the Arab world. Democratization, in his opinion, would have to lead to lower military expenditures and to economic and scientific cooperation in the Middle East, with the inclusion of Israel.[33] Such an assessment was an elaboration on his earlier attempts to lower the level of threat perception of his party colleagues and of the general public. For example, during the election campaign in the summer of 1988, he made a point of being unimpressed by arguments about existential threats: "We will not push the Arabs into the desert and they will not throw us into the sea."[34] This optimism about reconciliation with the Arabs coexisted with the fear of an imminent outbreak of hostilities—a symbiosis typical of the Israeli left.

Not only did Peres's threat perception change, as well as his attitude toward the time factor, but his style toward the Arabs also became more conciliatory, stressing the urgent need for efforts to end the conflict. I shall analyze his positions in greater depth later; for now, suffice it to say that he was obviously driven by the desire to prevent a war, and particularly by the awareness that the younger Israeli generation, the one that carries the security burden, deserved to be convinced, if a war did break out after all, that no effort had been spared to foster better relations with the Arabs. Peres seemed to recognize that social cohesiveness is an important element of national strategy.[35] Following the war in Lebanon, the Israeli political elite in general was alerted to the fact that in the absence of national consensus, large-scale military operations, which also involve reserve units, are politically problematic and could be socially destructive as well.

Another reason often used to stress the need for reaching an understanding with the Arabs soon was the fear of an imposed superpower solution. Israelis usually accord great value to Israel's contribution to the Western alliance, but also understand that the United States has a clear interest of its own in reducing the tensions in the Arab–Israeli arena. Since 1973 U.S. involvement in the peace process has grown drastically, leading to several agreements between the parties, including a peace treaty. The United States has also exerted pressure on Israel from time to time in order to increase its sensitivity to U.S. desires. Doves have occasionally welcomed U.S. pressure to change Israeli positions that they regard as intransigent. For example, MK Ora Namir related the Israeli government's May 1989 offer to hold elections in the territories to U.S. pressure.[36] Not pleased with the progress made toward implementing the elections, MK Burg called in the summer of 1989 for U.S. pressure to speed up the peace process.[37] A few doves even subscribed to the thesis that only U.S. intervention could force Israel to make the necessary concessions to reach an Arab–Israeli rapprochement.[38] U.S. prodding was considered reasonable and not overwhelming, but coordinated U.S.–Soviet pressure was seen as less responsive to Israeli concerns. Thus the improving U.S.–Soviet relations in the late 1980s were viewed as particularly conducive to a scenario in which the superpowers would pressure their respective Middle Eastern clients to end the dispute. The U.S.-coordinated international effort, under UN auspices, to boycott Iraq in the summer and fall of 1990 made such international intervention in the Arab–Israeli conflict even more credible in the eyes of many doves.

Weizman, Ramon, and Yossi Sarid regarded the outcome of the negotiations with the Arabs, difficult as they might be, as preferable to an agreement imposed by the two superpowers.[39] In 1987 Peres warned his Labor colleagues about such an unfavorable scenario in the absence of progress in the peace process.[40] As a matter of fact, it was assumed that in case of collusion by the superpowers, Israel would be forced to return to the 1967 borders;[41] most party doves, in spite of their territorial minimalism, did not regard such a prospect favorably. Therefore, the doves called on Israel to be both energetic and flexible so as to ensure a negotiated settlement. The fear of an imposed solution also spread to other quarters in the party. For example, Yaakov Tzur, a yonetz cabinet member, seemed to have been convinced as early as 1984 that such a scenario was quite possible. Another yonetz, Gad Yaakobi, expressed similar apprehensions at the end of 1988, following the opening of the dialogue between the PLO and the United States.[42]

In general, as we have seen, the doves regarded the passage of time negatively. One pressing reason for this was their fear that the Israeli settlements in the Arab-populated areas of Judea and Samaria might become a fait accompli. It seemed clear to them that the burgeoning Israeli presence in those regions might lead to an irreversible, tragic situation in which the separation of the two communities fighting over the land of Israel would no longer be possible. It is noteworthy that in contrast to the pessimistic evaluation of marginal dovish circles outside the party, both doves and hawks within Labor still regarded partition as a practical solution.

Indeed, all factions of the party played an important role in placing the "demographic problem" on the Israeli political agenda. This was part of Labor's campaign to point out the problems connected with annexation, which some of its political rivals on the right were advocating. Essentially, the demographic problem meant that the Jews would not be able to maintain a majority in western Palestine. Therefore, Labor argued cogently, annexation could only result in the establishment of a binational state. The expectation that massive Jewish immigration could change the demographic picture was not realized, and by the end of the 1980s only a great measure of ideological fervor could still sustain such a vision.[43] Even the growing numbers of Soviet immigrants in 1990 and the expected continuation of this wave of immigration could not drastically change the demographic picture in Palestine (despite Arab apprehensions). Yet Labor's success during this decade in sensitizing Israel to the demographic reality simultaneously weakened the argument put forth by Labor's hawks that parts of the homeland could be colonized successfully, as in the Zionist past, though primarily for security reasons. But this did not bother the doves, who regarded the hawkish plans for territorial adjustment as totally unrealistic in any case.

Arguments focusing on the demographic problem tended to dovetail with warnings about the difficulties posed by occupation. As an arrangement based on the Allon Plan—to dispense with the areas densely populated by Arabs—failed to materialize, and as Israel's stay in the territories began to look permanent, the reality of ruling over one and one-half million unwilling Arabs gradually became a moral and political dilemma. Indeed, since 1981 the Labor party platform has carried a clause pointing out the moral erosion in Israel caused by the occupation. Yet in contrast to the hawks, who preferred to pay greater attention to the strategic importance of parts of the territories, the doves' attention was captured mainly by the territories' inhabitants. Ramon, for example, regarded the continuation of the status quo as leading to "a non-democratic state, which will lose its Jewish character and moral image."[44] With the exception of the issue of occupation, however, moral arguments were rarely used even by doves in the debate over national security.

The Palestinian uprising, or intifada, which started in December 1987, galvanized the doves into stiffer opposition to the continuation of the status quo. Even before the Palestinian civil unrest broke out, the role of the IDF as occupier of the territories had been considered as having a corrupting effect on Israeli society. Yet the period of "benign occupation" was replaced in 1988 by a harsher military rule and by greater friction between the IDF and the Arab population. The increasing instances of excessive use of force by the army were considered an indication of the grave potential for brutalization of Israeli society, and for undermining the rule of law by obfuscating the borderline between lawful and criminal behavior. Namir, for example, regarded the Palestinian uprising as the cruelest war Israel had fought. She maintained that it corrupted Israeli values, that "the adjustment to occupation causes changes in our worldview."[45] Furthermore, the IDF's difficulties in suppressing the uprising were, in the eyes of the doves, a clear signal that the status quo had to be changed as quickly as possible. Peres, in his role of finance minister, pointed out on several occasions that the intifada had a most negative impact on Israeli economic performance. The costs of the Israeli military presence were perceived to outweigh any security benefits it might have. The continuation of the unsatisfactory status quo in the West Bank was also seen as endangering relations with Egypt. MK Eliav's 1989 evaluation that the only alternative to a resolution of the Israeli–Palestinian conflict "is a continuing nightmare"[46] reflected the dovish sentiment.

The fact that Rabin, a Laborite, was in charge of the territories as defense minister muted some of the dovish criticism in the party, particularly in the period preceding the October 1988 elections. Usually, backbenchers have less freedom of action when their own party is in power. Yet after the elections some Laborite doves, as shall be noted in Chapter 6, were less restrained in their statements about Rabin's policy.

In general, the party doves argued that the more time that passed, and the more opportunities Israel missed, the less satisfactory would be the final agreement. Like the doves outside the party, the party doves believed that a settlement of the Arab–Israeli conflict was within reach, particularly after the Egyptian–Israeli peace treaty. Little emphasis was placed on interim stages for reaching a comprehensive agreement. Once negotiated, its stability could be assured. This belief was based on a perceived moderation in the Arab camp. Such an analysis did not lead necessarily to a reduced threat perception, however. It was argued that the lack of progress in settling the conflict would weaken the moderate elements on the other side and fuel a process of conflict escalation. Although in the doves' view an all-out war to destroy Israel was not the most likely scenario, were the deadlock to continue, "limited" wars—which might still be horrendous in scope—to rock the status quo or to gain some political or territorial advantages were a foregone conclusion. Therefore, peace warranted even taking risks in the present to prevent bloodshed in the future.

THE HAWKS

On the hawkish side we have a quite different set of views. Yitzhak Rabin, an authoritative speaker on security affairs, was the voice for the hawkish persuasion in the 1980s. As mentioned, no other hawk in the party enjoyed a commensurate political stature. Rabin recognized the significance of the Sadat initiative and in 1978 pointed out what he saw as its implications: (a) for the first time an Arab leader declared that Israel was an established political fact, one to be recognized and to coexist with peacefully; (b) the Israeli interpretation of peace was accepted; and (c) an Arab state had proved willing to negotiate with Israel directly, rather than through intermediaries.[47] Later on, in 1986, he still placed a high value on the new relationship with Egypt. In his opinion, the preservation of this peaceful relationship should be of the highest priority for Israel's foreign policy.[48] In his capacity as defense minister of the National Unity government, he emphasized that only because of the peace treaty had a $600 million cut in the defense budget been possible, allowing the rehabilitation of Israel's deteriorating economy.[49] Rabin recognized the strategic fact that Egypt was, at least for a substantial period of time, unlikely to reopen hostilities with Israel. The changes in relations with Egypt obviously contributed to lowering his level of threat perception, as it did for other Israelis. He regarded the agreement with Egypt as an important, though not permanent, element of Israel's national security.

In the mid-1980s, Rabin expressed his opinion that Israel's military superiority until the mid-1990s was assured, although its margins of security had been dangerously eroded by Israeli budgetary cuts and by Arab weapons procurement plans.[50] In 1986 Rabin explained that the unfavorable general military balance between the IDF and the Arab armies was mitigated by political factors, such as the peace treaty with Egypt, Jordanian moderation, and the diversion of Iraqi forces to the Iranian front.[51] Similarly, the thaw in the superpowers' relations seemed to weaken the Soviet backing of Syria. Yet, he argued, the cease-fire reached in the Persian Gulf war in the summer of 1988 could bring about a new, less favorable strategic reality in the near future.[52] Furthermore, Rabin realized that the post-1973 period had been characterized by Israel's inability to sustain by itself the economic effort needed to counterbalance qualitative and quantitative improvements in the Arab military forces.[53] As the Knesset discussed the significance of the 1988 Anglo–Saudi arms deal, which had surprised Israel, Rabin expressed his concern that Knesset members were insufficiently aware of the huge amounts of high-quality military hardware being supplied to the Arabs, while Israel was having economic difficulty in preserving required force levels.[54] In 1989, Rabin expressed great apprehension about advances made in several Arab countries in developing ground-to-ground missiles, and in their production of chemical weapons. This development threatened to blur the boundary between the battlefield and the home front, thus constituting a clear escalatory potential.[55]

Despite the negative trends observed, Rabin was satisfied with Israel's strategic situation. In March 1990, at a memorial to Yigal Allon, Rabin stated that during the previous decade Israel had reached an unprecedentedly comfortable strategic position. He explained this to be the result of the peace treaty with Egypt, the Iran–Iraq war, and the erosion in Soviet support for Syria.[56] He concluded that toward the end of the 1980s Israel's main Arab rivals were in no position to challenge it militarily.

In respect to the future, however, Rabin was less sanguine. He, like other hawks in the party, did not dismiss continuing existential threats to the state of Israel created by Arab enmity.[57] Occasionally, he voiced concern that Israel faced the predicament of "to be or not to be."[58] In a remark similar to the views of extreme hawkish circles in Israel, Rabin suggested that "Israel's War of Independence has not yet ended"; for him, the Arab quest for politicide was not a thing of the past.[59] Such fears were reinforced by voices in the Arab world calling for action to prevent the growing numbers of Jews emigrating from the Soviet Union from reaching Israel. This was a trigger for many Israelis, particularly hawks in Labor and outside it, to be reminded of the "evoked set" of past uncompromising enmity by the Arabs to Jewish immigration.[60] Such opposition amounted to the denial of the Zionist state, whose raison d'être was ingathering of the Jews in the land of Israel. Indeed, Dinitz criticized Palestinians' activities against Jewish immigration and added: "Opposition to immigration amounts to opposition to the continued existence of the state of Israel."[61] Rabin, too, was concerned; in an appearance before the Knesset Foreign Affairs and Defense Committee in February 1990, he warned that there was a danger that the Arabs could achieve unity against Israel based on a consensus against Jewish immigration.[62]

Despite his vote in favor of the Camp David Accords, and a lowered threat perception, Rabin was haunted by memories of 1967, when Arab armies had stood along the Green Line (the 1967 borders). His traumatic experience as chief of staff at that time had a formative effect on his outlook. He was never reconciled to the full withdrawal in Sinai to the 1967 international border, which, in his opinion, does not constitute a secure border; actually, he would have preferred delaying the peace several years until such borders could be negotiated. In light of the difficulties involved in negotiating the peace treaty with Egypt, Rabin said: "There is no way of finding a middle ground, even with the best intentions in the world. Our most sensible policy is to stall."[63] In a typically frank manner, he expressed his opinion that the peace treaty, though important, was essentially just an interim agreement.[64] Rabin has always displayed willingness to make some concessions in order to help reduce regional tensions, or to please the United States, whose support he considers critical to Israel's security. But he also did not hesitate to play for time while passing through difficult diplomatic periods as prime minister, and had no qualms about fighting a long diplomatic rearguard battle in the hope of inducing favorable changes in rivals' positions.[65] In contrast to the doves, Rabin was essentially in no hurry to attempt negotiations with the Arabs, so long as the differences were seen by him as unbridgeable.

In general, Rabin was skeptical about the possibility of a direct transition from war to peace. He rejected the "Peace Now" slogan and indicated that a slow and gradual process was necessary in order to reach peaceful relations in the region.[66] He considered the peace process a very long one, requiring much patience: "Any attempt . . . to solve the problem by a single act," he declared, "will lead nowhere."[67] Rabin still feared existential threats and saw no reason not to prolong the political process of tension reduction so long as there was some chance of achieving a better deal. When confronted in 1988 with the argument that his prescription for a settlement on the eastern border, the Allon Plan, was a nonstarter in Arab quarters, Rabin's answer was: "Then we will wait until they will accept it."[68] Commenting on the extended period of the Palestinian uprising, he stressed: "In every protracted conflict there is a component of 'who gets exhausted first.' I believe that we will not be the first to break down."[69] Wearing down the opponent to accept Israeli conditions was part of the strategic game Rabin was playing. He also recognized the importance of national determination in Israel's strategy versus its Arab rivals. Faith, patience, and perseverance were preconditions for reaching an acceptable peace agreement. Israeli weariness of the protracted conflict was seen as having a negative effect on Israel's bargaining position.

Interestingly, in spite of the fact that Rabin had a higher level of threat perception than the doves in his party, he was less concerned than Peres about the introduction of nuclear weapons in the Middle East. Although admitting that his proposal for a Nuclear Weapons Free Zone had been rejected by the Arabs, he nevertheless expressed his belief at a party forum in 1987 that "in the next ten years, at least, the Middle East will not go nuclear."[70]

The Palestinian uprising, which strengthened the doves' determination to find a solution, had a mixed effect on Rabin. At the beginning, he declared that the intifada did not constitute a challenge to Israel's basic security, and regarded it only as a "current security" problem.[71] Rabin recognized that only a political settlement could put an end to the uprising and that it could not be eliminated by military means alone; as a "current security" problem, however, he felt it was manageable. He advocated a patient approach, consisting of the use of limited force together with economic and administrative pressures to lower the level of Palestinian resistance. Yet Rabin gradually became aware of the political ramifications of the events taking place in the territories, an aspect he found far more threatening. He claimed that the Palestinians have "far-reaching political goals that are a threat to the state of Israel and its future,"[72] and recognized in the Palestinian uprising the "evoked set" of unabating Arab enmity and the desire to destroy Israel. In Rabin's eyes, the IDF's duties in the administered territories became a struggle for Israel's very existence.[73] In his analysis, the uprising was also the result of Israel's unhappy adventure in Lebanon; the phased withdrawal influenced Palestinian perceptions of Israel's diminished capacity to engage in a low-level conflict over a long period. This, Rabin believed, strengthened the extremists in the Palestinian camp.[74]

The PLO's diplomatic successes in the winter of 1988–1989, following the changes in their formulations toward Israel, which were in part a result of the developments in the territories, made the demands for a Palestinian state seem more realistic. Rabin, however, dismissed the PLO's new language as linguistic acrobatics, and a Palestinian state still constituted for him, as well as for many others in the Israeli political elite, a mortal danger. Therefore, the intifada, although regarded as a "current security" problem not much different from the terrorist attacks originating in Lebanon, increased Rabin's threat perception. This did lead Rabin, as with the doves, to adopt more flexible positions concerning Palestinian representation (though Rabin was not as forthcoming as the doves) and to seek political ways to end the uprising. But in contrast to the party doves, Rabin was also sensitive to the Likud positions: in his opinion, no progress on a political solution could be made without broad support, including the Likud's, and the range of practical solutions was therefore more limited.[75] The May 1989 National Unity government peace initiative, which included an offer to hold political elections in the Israeli-ruled territories, was the product of his close relations with Yitzhak Shamir, the Likud prime minister. Rabin also used arguments from the internal political arena, primarily the necessity to maintain a working relationship with Likud, and to moderate dovish inclinations in his party toward a faster pace of negotiations and more "flexible" positions.

Rabin's views were characteristic of what was termed, in the 1980s, the hawkish camp. Once a mainstream Laborite whose positions remained stable for long periods, in the 1980s Rabin came to be regarded as representing the party's hawkish positions, although organizationally he did not belong to hawkish forums in the party such as the Central Stream.

Labor hawks seemed to consider politicide a plausible Arab goal if Israel were to lose its general deterrence capability.[76] An Israel perceived as weak could conceivably become the target of an Arab attack to dismantle the Jewish state. For example, at the end of 1987, Aryeh Nehamkin (a hawk with little influence in the party beyond the moshav movement) did not exclude the possibility of a joint Syrian–Jordanian military undertaking against Israel. Similarly, Nehamkin said in regard to Egypt that "we gave everything back and still no one knows what the future has in store."[77] And the aggressive Iraqi behavior of 1990, of course, also appeared to hawks in the party and outside it as corroboration of their existential fears. Because of their high threat perception, the hawks advocated a gradual process of reducing tensions in the region. For example, Dinitz said in 1989: "I do not believe that peace is achieved through a single dramatic act in which we go from belligerency to peace and the exchange of ambassadors. There are interim stages, as there were with Egypt . . . it is a process."[78]

Interestingly, in spite of their greater apprehensions about Arab intentions, in the absence of a settlement the hawks did not see war as the only logical alternative remaining to the Arabs. Arab perceptions of Israeli intransigence, they believed, could indeed place a strain on Israel's relations with Egypt, but so long as Egypt upheld its obligation to refrain from military activities, the Arab option for a large-scale war was drastically limited. Relations with Egypt had already been tested on several occasions, and furthermore, the hawks viewed them as less fragile than did the doves. If the Arabs entertained thoughts of changing the situation by force, they also had to take into consideration Israel's strength and alertness, as well as various international developments. Therefore, it was argued that the calculus of going to war was more complicated than the doves suggested. Moreover, with their more pronounced realpolitik outlook, the hawks considered war as part and parcel of the Middle Eastern reality for some time to come.[79] War could and should be delayed, but could not be eliminated.

Differences between the two orientations in the party were also manifested at the tactical level. The peace conference that Peres advocated has never had a great appeal among the party's hawks. It took Peres some time to secure lukewarm support from Rabin. In 1987 Nehamkin, then a minister in the National Unity government, said of the conference: "I believe on balance the risks outweigh the chances for a positive outcome."[80] Another hawk, MK Raanan Cohen, even demanded that the issue be dropped from Labor's 1988 elections propaganda. The Israeli instinct toward realpolitik, embodied in the party's hawks, encouraged suspicion toward international forums. Furthermore, the chances of reaching peace on the eastern front in the near future were not regarded by Labor's right as very good. Peace was desirable if within reach, but since it was not regarded as something that would necessarily last, hawks were less willing to pay a high price for it. Similarly, they showed much greater patience with the evolving diplomatic process following the May 1989 peace initiative, whereas the doves continuously demanded leaving the Likud–Labor government in protest of the perceived procrastination by Likud.

BIRDS OF ANOTHER FEATHER

Those party leaders not clearly identifiable on the hawkish–dovish continuum, or those in the yonetz category, held varying views on these matters. For example, Mordechai Gur showed hawkish inclinations that were not incompatible with his self-description as a yonetz. He pointed out with satisfaction that among Israel's enemies only a few still believed that Israel could be militarily wiped out. Therefore, future wars would have limited goals. Yet he warned in 1987 that an Israeli military defeat could revive previous Arab plans to eliminate Israel.[81] Furthermore, in 1981 he expressed his regret that the party voted in favor of the withdrawal from Sinai to the 1967 borders, which he felt constituted a dangerous precedent.[82] Indeed, he believed a tougher bargaining posture could have yielded a better result.[83] Furthermore, because of the realities of human nature and also of the Middle East, it was plausible that the fragile peace with Egypt could revert to a state of war, according to Gur's realpolitik outlook.[84] He could hardly envision the Middle East becoming a stable and peaceful region in the near future.[85] For these and other reasons, Gur, a former chief of staff, has consistently supported an increase in the defense budget. In the summer of 1989, he advocated allocating additional funds to the IDF for its campaign to suppress the intifada. That campaign was seen by Gur, as it was by some of his colleagues, as "a struggle for the existence of the state."[86]

Nevertheless, tension reduction was possible by reaching various understandings with Arab states. Gur was known to advocate a tacit agreement with the Syrians in Lebanon. Securing interim agreements, whose purpose was to test Arab intentions and minimize security risks, could eventually lead to a peaceful relationship with Israel's neighbors. In his opinion, this was the basis for a more realistic national policy.[87] He rejected the theme of urgency. In spite of the fact that he regarded the PLO as a possible negotiating partner and viewed its new stance as a drastic change he believed that this organization still had a long way to go. Time also was needed, according to Gur, to allow changes in the Likud[88]—a view similar to Rabin's. Indeed, in terms of threat perception and attitude toward time, Gur could not be distinguished from the party's hawks.

In contrast to Gur, Chaim Bar-Lev, a past secretary-general of the party (1977–1984) and a former chief of staff, was more optimistic, and regarded the signing of the treaty with Egypt as the end of one period and the beginning of a new era in Arab–Israeli relations. He believed that the general tendency in the region would be an expansion of the peace process. In his opinion, Israel's security was greatly improved in the 1980s by the change in its relations with Egypt, as well as by the fragmentation of the eastern front.[89] His rather low threat perception placed him for most of the 1980s in the yonetz category.

Moshe Shahal was clearly identified with neither of the party camps. He was rather optimistic about the possibility of reaching peace with the Arabs, and put forward an interesting argument: Islamic fundamentalism, primarily after the Islamic revolution in Iran, had come to be perceived by the moderate Arab countries as a greater threat than Israel. Shahal believed, therefore, that since the Arab moderates regarded the Arab–Israeli conflict as fueling the strength of the radical Muslims, there was a clear incentive for the moderates to try to end the dispute with the Israelis.[90] The reacceptance of Egypt in the Arab world on its own terms also lowered his level of threat perception. The renewal of diplomatic relations in December 1989 between Egypt and Syria was for him an additional proof of the Arab world's willingness to adopt the Egyptian approach to the Arab–Israeli conflict.[91] Like other doves in the 1980s, he perceived Iraq as having considerably mellowed its enmity toward Israel. In his view it had joined the moderate, pragmatic Arab camp, which was interested in reducing tension in the Arab–Israeli core area of the Middle East so as to better concentrate its forces against the dangers of Islamic extremism. According to Shahal, a tacit alliance had been forged among Israel, Egypt, Jordan, Iraq, Saudi Arabia, Kuwait, and the Gulf Emirates.[92]

Many doves, Weizman in particular, preferred to side with Iraq rather than Iran in the Gulf war. MK Uzi Baram, then Labor's secretary-general, in 1987 expressed the view that Muslim fundamentalism constituted a greater danger than Iraq. Whereas the latter could eventually change its outlook, the Muslim perspective would in all probability remain constant.[93] In contrast to the traditional, realpolitik, pro-Iranian orientation of the hawks, which emphasized geopolitics, some doves preferred to emphasize the Egyptian–Iraqi alliance, which seemed to soften the Iraqi opposition to the Egyptian–Israeli peace treaty. This, in turn, was in accordance with the doves' belief in the increased acceptance of Israel by the Arab world. Therefore, all in all they saw the Gulf war as less threatening for Israel. Like Weizman, Shahal hoped Israel would capitalize on the changes in Iraq to strengthen the peace process with Egypt.[94] The attitudes toward the Iran–Iraq war were another instance (in addition to the international conference) of the left-right distribution as manifested by a passing regional development. As noted, a sobering change of attitude toward Iraq took place in 1990.

By the end of the decade, Shahal had adopted the dovish "urgency thesis." He commented on his ministerial colleagues: "The ministers who believe that we have time and there is no reason to hurry to find a political solution do not live in the real world."[95] He even envisioned the possibility of U.S. sanctions on Israel, like those imposed on Red China following the Tiananmen Square events.[96]

Gad Yaakobi, a minister in the National Unity government with a Rafi past, who gradually moved from hawkishness to more moderate positions, also subscribed to the urgency thesis. The idea that "time is on our side" was, he maintained, a delusion.[97] The civil unrest in the administered territories that began in the winter of 1987 constituted, for him, an additional refutation of such an illusion.[98] The continuation of the status quo in Judea, Samaria, and the Gaza Strip seemed to strengthen annexationist tendencies, and in the absence of a political solution, Yaakobi feared the emergence of a situation similar to that in South Africa or Lebanon.[99] He also pointed out that a great economic price was being paid for the intifada, as it prevented economic growth.[100] Yaakobi had a feeling of urgency and believed that peace was within reach. He was impatient with the slow pace with which the May 1989 peace initiative was being pursued and expressed concern about the possibility of wasting such a good opportunity to make progress in the peace process.[101] Peace was, for him, a precondition for Israel's "continuous human, economic, and technological development," and for the maintenance of its democratic institutions.[102] He was even one of the few Laborites at the ministerial level to call for unilateral measures in the territories, including a partial withdrawal (see Chapter 5). This was in contrast to the gradualist approach, which insisted on interim agreements, and which was generally supported by all quarters of the party. Though this view was usually emphasized by hawks, few in the left wing of the party believed that peace could descend upon the region in one fell swoop.

Among party leaders in the yonetz category, Gur stands out for his skeptical, realpolitik outlook. The others—Bar-Lev, Shahal, and Yaakobi—have lower levels of threat perception and for most of the 1980s were closer to Peres and to the dovish wing. In the party struggles, more often than not, they cooperated with Peres rather than Rabin.

CONCLUSION

Shimon Peres and Yitzhak Rabin both had long records of dealing with national security affairs. Each had served as both prime minister and defense minister; Peres had also been foreign minister. Because of their leadership positions in the party, both refrained from identifying organizationally with either the dovish or hawkish organizations. Rabin was, however, more closely identified with the hawkish wing of the party than was Peres with the dovish wing. Their differences of opinion on the matters covered in this chapter were, to a large extent, characteristic of the dovish–hawkish debate within the party. Peres belittled the possibility of existential threats and regarded peace as within reach. In his estimation, failure to reach an accommodation with the Arabs was certain to exact a terrible price: namely, an imminent war. Rabin, on the other hand, was more concerned with carefully evaluating specific threats posed by Arab military establishments, and at the same time felt less urgency to reach an agreement. He considered peace a possibility, but only as the end result of a lengthy historical process marked by interim agreements. Both leaders shared an awareness of the demographic problem, and the realization that only political avenues could put an end to the occupation and to the Palestinian uprising. Rabin, however, seemed less perturbed by the continuation of the status quo. Most other party leaders shared dovish evaluations of the level of threat and the chances for peace.

It is difficult to measure exactly the overall level of threat perception and whether it moved toward the lower end of the continuum. Labor party platforms during the 1980s displayed a rather high level of threat perception. For example, in 1988 the platform was formulated not very differently from those of earlier elections, and stated: "The growing military power of the Arab states and their hostility requires Israel to maintain a quantitative military force with a qualitative edge over the Arab armies."[103] It also noted the massive delivery of high-quality weapons to the Arab states and in particular the strategic significance of their surface-to-surface missiles and chemical weapons.[104] It is significant, however, that the article of the 1981 platform on the need to preserve and develop a deterrent force even after peace agreements were reached was deleted in subsequent party platforms.[105]

NOTES

1. The term politicide was coined by Yehoshafat Harkabi. See his *Fedayeen Action and Arab Strategy*, Adelphi Papers, no. 53 (London: IISS, 1969), p. 1. Harkabi believes Jordan and even the PLO no longer hold politicide as an operative goal, as distinct from a grand design for the future. See his "Main Features of the Arab–Israeli Conflict" (Hebrew), Policy Papers, no. 22, The Leonard Davis Institute for International Relations, The Hebrew University, January 1988, p. 1; for a similar distinction, see Martin Seliger, "Fundamental and Operative Ideology: The Two Principal Dimensions of Political Argumentation," *Policy Sciences* 1 (Fall 1970), pp. 325–338.

2. Abba Eban, "The Six Day War: A Chance, But No Solution," *Skirah Chodshit* 34, nos. 3–4 (1987), p. 18.

3. Abba Eban, *The New Diplomacy* (London: Weidenfeld & Nicolson, 1983), p. 198.

4. Ezer Weizman, *The Battle for Peace* (Hebrew) (Jerusalem: Edanim Publishers, 1982), p. 163.

5. Weizman, *The Battle for Peace*, p. 43.

6. Weizman, *The Battle for Peace*, p. 279.

7. "Ezer Weizman on 'Doves' and 'Hawks,'" *Spectrum* 5 (April 1987), p. 12.

8. *Haaretz*, June 29, 1988.

9. "Interview with Weizman," *Spectrum* 6 (June 1988), p. 10.

10. *Jerusalem Post*, July 15, 1988.

11. See also MK Aharon Harel, "Messianism and Realism," in *The State of Israel and the Land of Israel*, ed. Adam Doron (Hebrew) (Beit Berl: Beit Berl College, 1988), pp. 393–394; and interviews with MK Ramon, MK Yossi Beilin, and MK Yossi Sarid. Sarid, once the arch-dove of the Labor Party, decided to leave it in 1984, in protest against Labor's decision to join with the Likud in the National Unity government.

12. "The Dovecot," *Spectrum* 5 (April 1987), p. 12.

13. *Spectrum* 6 (February 1988), p. 13.

14. *Davar Magazine*, December 23, 1988.

15. "Interview with Weizman," *Spectrum* 6 (June 1988), p. 10; Gideon Samet, "If Weizman Is Right, We Are in Trouble," *Haaretz*, September 15, 1989. For the Jewish attitudinal prism in Israeli foreign policy, see Michael Brecher, *The Foreign Policy System of Israel*, pp. 229–244.

16. Ezer Weizman, "Before War," *Yediot Achronot*, January 1, 1988; Samet, "If Weizman Is Right."
17. *Maariv*, May 3, 1988.
18. Interview with MK Chaim Ramon, January 31, 1988.
19. "Interview with Chaim Ramon," *Spectrum* 6 (September 1988), p. 32.
20. See *Haaretz*, January 18, 1990.
21. Shimon Peres, "The Struggle for Continuing the Peace Process" (Hebrew), *The Israeli Labor Party*, February 1986. The periodical is an occasional publication of the Labor Party; the article is a transcript of a speech by Peres in a party forum on November 25, 1985.
22. Shimon Peres, "The Struggle Over the Continuation of the Peace Initiative" (Hebrew), *The Israeli Labor Party*, June 1987. This was a speech delivered in the Executive Bureau (Lishka) on May 7, 1987.
23. For the text of the agreement, see the *Jerusalem Post*, January 1, 1988.
24. *Haaretz*, July 18, 1989.
25. English transcript of Shimon Peres's speech before the Knesset, October 10, 1983, made available by the Israeli Labor Party.
26. *The Israeli Labor Party*, no. 10, December 1986, p. 8. This was part of a speech delivered by Peres to the party center on August 7, 1986, following his visit to Morocco.
27. Shimon Peres, "Futurology and Foresight," in *Towards the 21st Century: Targets for Israel*, ed. Alouph Hareven (Hebrew) (Jerusalem: The Jerusalem Van Leer Foundation, 1984), pp. 93–94.
28. *Haaretz*, February 19, 1988. In the 1970s, when serving as defense minister, he denied the claim that Israel lacked the resources to match the Arabs' investments in their military establishments. See "Interview with Shimon Peres," *Davar*, April 30, 1976.
29. For the difference between an ambiguous and an open nuclear policy, see Shai Feldman, *Israeli Nuclear Deterrence* (New York: Columbia University Press, 1982). This is a dovish argument for going nuclear. It has not yet gained any support among Labor's leadership.
30. *Haaretz*, May 26, 1978, quoted in Yael Yishai, *Land or Peace: Whither Israel?* p. 162. See also Mordechai Bar-On, *Peace Now*.
31. For Rafi and Peres before 1973, see Yossi Beilin, *The Price of Unity*; for Peres in the 1974–1977 period, see Shlomo Aronson, *Conflict and Bargaining in the Middle East* (Baltimore: Johns Hopkins University Press, 1978), pp. 256–330.
32. Shimon Peres, "Strategy for a Transition Period," *International Security* 2 (Winter 1978), p. 11. This article was translated from a section of his book *Tomorrow Is Now* (Hebrew) (Jerusalem: Mabat, 1978).
33. Shimon Peres, "The Middle East in a Brave New World," *Jerusalem Post*, December 8, 1989; see also "Interview With Shimon Peres," *Spectrum* 8 (January 1990), p. 8.
34. *Maariv*, July 21, 1988.
35. See Michael Howard, "The Forgotten Dimension of Strategy," in *The Defense Policies of Nations*, eds. Douglas J. Murray and Paul R. Viotti (Baltimore: Johns Hopkins University Press, 1982).
36. See Dan Shilon, "Interview with Ora Namir," *Haaretz*, May 19, 1989.
37. See Avraham Burg, "The Main Thing Is to Push On," *Haaretz*, August 28, 1989.
38. For the best-known statement of this thesis, see George W. Ball, "How to Save Israel in Spite of Herself," *Foreign Affairs* 55 (April 1977), pp. 453–471.

39. See Weizman's statement in *Maariv*, February 18, 1988; interviews with MK Sarid and MK Ramon.

40. *Maariv*, August 7, 1987.

41. Harel, "Messianism and Realism," pp. 382, 395.

42. For the views of Tzur, see Israel Peleg, "The Left on Rights," *Spectrum* 2 (January–February 1984), p. 7; for the views of Yaakobi, see *Maariv*, January 1, 1989.

43. Even political circles right of Labor had to pay greater attention to the demographic reality. Indeed, the renewal of the "transfer" idea in certain extreme hawkish circles, mostly outside the Likud, was a reaction to the realization that the Zionist dream of the Ingathering has practical limitations.

44. "Interview with Chaim Ramon," *Spectrum* 6 (September 1988), p. 32.

45. Israel Landers, "Interview with Ora Namir," *Davar Magazine*, December 12, 1988. See the discussion in Chapter 6 on the side effects of the use of force.

46. Arie Lova Eliav, "Back to the Future," *Spectrum* 7 (May–June 1989), p. 11.

47. Yitzhak Rabin, "A Peace Plan," *Migvan* 28 (July 1978), p. 3. In this article Rabin deplored the fact that no party forum discussed the Sadat initiative until then.

48. See his "The Israeli–Egyptian Relationship: Whereto?—An Israeli Perspective," *Dapei Elazar* 9 (1986), p. 106; and *The Israeli Labor Party* (Hebrew), no. 10, December 1986, p. 11. This was part of a speech given to the party Central Council (Merkaz) on June 7, 1986.

49. *The Israeli Labor Party*, December 1986, p. 11.

50. See his "War, Terror and Peace," *Bama*, February 1, 1986. This is the organ of the Jerusalem Labor organization.

51. Ibid.

52. Yitzhak Rabin, "Goals for the IDF," *Yediot Achronot*, September 25, 1988.

53. See Asher Maniv, "A Conversation with Yitzhak Rabin," *Migvan* 46 (April 1980), p. 4.

54. *Maariv*, July 14, 1988.

55. *Jerusalem Post*, May 5, 1989.

56. *Haaretz*, March 8, 1990.

57. Rabin, "War, Terror and Peace."

58. See, inter alia, his speech at the Memorial Day of the Engineering Corps in *Hatzofe*, August 18, 1988.

59. *Jerusalem Post*, May 5, 1989; see also *Davar*, June 2 and September 1, 1989.

60. For the "evoked set," see Robert Jervis, *Perception and Misperception in International Politics* (Princeton: Princeton University Press, 1976), pp. 213–216.

61. *Haaretz*, April 20, 1990.

62. *Yediot Achronot*, February 21, 1990.

63. *Newsweek*, January 1, 1979.

64. Chaim Izak, "Interview with Yitzhak Rabin," *Davar*, October 27, 1978.

65. See Efraim Inbar, "Problems of Pariah States: The National Security Policy of the Rabin Government," parts 2 and 3.

66. Bezalel Amikam, "An Evaluation with No Illusions—In the Aftermath of a Meeting with Yitzhak Rabin," *Al Hamishmar*, February 22, 1980.

67. Yitzhak Rabin, "Middle East Chess: King's Move," *Spectrum* 1 (April–May 1983), p. 7; see also his statement to *Maariv*, August 3, 1986.

68. Yoseph Harif, "Rabin Suggests Waiting Period," *Maariv*, October 19, 1988.
69. *Maariv*, January 20, 1989; see also *Davar*, September 1, 1989.
70. *Spectrum* 5 (September 1987), p. 8; for his views against nuclearization, see Efraim Inbar, "Israel and Nuclear Weapons Since October 1973," in *Security or Armageddon*, ed. Louis Rene Beres (Lexington: Lexington Books, 1986), pp. 64–73.
71. Israeli strategic thinking distinguishes between challenges to "basic security," i.e. threats to Israel's very existence, and "current security" problems that include limited threats to its territorial integrity and the well-being of its citizens.
72. *Maariv*, January 11, 1989.
73. *Maariv*, December 27, 1988; *Davar*, June 2, 1989.
74. Yitzhak Rabin, "IDF's Objectives," *Yediot Achronot*, September 25, 1988.
75. Amnon Abramovitch, "Interview with Rabin," *Maariv*, February 2, 1989.
76. For a discussion of general and specific deterrence, see Patrick M. Morgan, *Deterrence* (Beverly Hills: Sage Publications, 1977).
77. "Interview with Nehamkin," *Spectrum* 5 (October 1987), p. 9.
78. "Interview with Dinitz," *Spectrum* 7 (May-June 1989), p. 13.
79. For the realistic school in international relations, see Hans Morgenthau, *Politics Among Nations*, pp. 3–14.
80. *Spectrum*, 5 (October 1987), p. 9.
81. Mordechai Gur, "The Lavi and the Preparations for the Next War," *Maariv*, July 27, 1987.
82. "Emda Medinit," *The Israeli Labor Party*, no. 1, December 1981, p. 13. This was part of a speech delivered at the party Central Council (Merkaz) on October 22, 1981.
83. Interview with Mordechai Gur, December 28, 1987.
84. Mordechai Gur, "Military Might and Freedom of Choice," *Davar*, March 27, 1981.
85. Interview with Mordechai Gur, December 13, 1987.
86. *Maariv*, July 18, 1989.
87. Asher Maniv, "A Conversation with Motta Gur," *Migvan* 41 (October 1979), p. 41.
88. Gideon Levi, "Interview with Gur," *Haaretz Magazine*, February 10, 1989.
89. See Zeev Schiff, "Bar-Lev in a Waiting Position," *Haaretz*, April 24, 1981, and Knesset Minutes (KM), May 3, 1981, p. 2159.
90. *Maariv*, January 20, 1988.
91. *Haaretz*, December 28, 1989.
92. See *Haaretz*, August 10, 1988.
93. "Who's the Greater Threat?" *Spectrum* 5 (February-March 1987), pp. 20–21.
94. Ibid.
95. *Maariv*, February 20, 1989.
96. *Maariv*, June 14, 1989.
97. See his "The Three Delusions," *Jerusalem Post*, February 26, 1988.
98. *Maariv*, June 6, 1988.
99. *Maariv*, April 28, 1987; *Haaretz*, March 12, 1989.
100. *Haaretz*, March 12, 1989.
101. *Haaretz*, October 18, 1989.

102. *Maariv*, June 6, 1988.
103. See 1988 Party Platform, Appendix B, article 1.6.5; see also 1.6.4 and 1.6.16.
104. Appendix B, article 1.6.16.
105. *The Platform for the 10th Knesset* (The Alignment: Israeli Labor Party–Mapam, June 1981), article 3, p. 7.

CHAPTER 4

The Partner in the Envisioned Agreement

Divisions between hawks and doves played a significant role in the question of who was to be the partner in a future agreement. Discussions in the party revolved primarily around the desired formal agreements, which had to include a political quid pro quo for Israeli concessions, the nature of which will be discussed in the next chapter. Informal agreements with Arab leaders were of less concern in the party's debates, since they reflected various configurations of national interests of an ephemeral quality. Informal understandings were also viewed as less binding. In addition, the traditional Israeli quest for international recognition made formal agreements appear particularly attractive. It was clear that on the issue of the Golan, the negotiating partner would have to be Syria. Just as clear was the fact that Assad of Syria showed little interest in reaching a formal agreement with Jerusalem. Less obvious was the choice of partner in an agreement with Lebanon. Since the Lebanese central government, never very strong, had gradually disintegrated, particularly after the outbreak of the civil war in 1975, its ability to fulfill any pledges it might make appeared dubious. In contrast to Likud, Labor has always had few illusions about the value of an official document signed by the representatives of a government unable to govern. For these reasons, as long as Lebanon continued in a state of crisis, Laborites, without exception, preferred informal agreements that seemed to suit better Israel's security interests. They showed little enthusiasm for the Likud-led government's efforts to reach a peace treaty with Lebanon in 1983. Indeed, after a short period of euphoria at the beginning of the Lebanon War, Labor supported a phased withdrawal by Israeli troops and strengthening of the security zone north of the border with Lebanon. As a result of Labor's efforts, this program was implemented by the first National Unity government (1984–1988) in 1985. Yet the choice of partner in the negotiations over the future of Judea, Samaria, and Gaza remained a highly charged issue, both politically and emotionally.

THE JORDANIAN VERSUS
THE PALESTINIAN OPTION

The stance adopted by most of the Labor party leadership throughout the 1980s viewed Jordan as the best partner in negotiations. Another option, rejected by the party platform as well as by the majority of its leadership, was to negotiate with the PLO, which claimed to represent Palestinian national aspirations. Various political organizations in the country to the left of Labor had, for some time, advocated mutual recognition and subsequent bilateral negotiations with the PLO. These circles, in Israel and outside, served to a great extent as a reference group for Labor's doves on the Palestinian issue. Other alternatives were to meet with a Jordanian–Palestinian delegation, or solely with Palestinian (non-PLO-affiliated) representatives. These last two alternatives gradually gained acceptance and became incorporated into the party platform. As mentioned in Chapter 2, dovishness in the Labor Party was manifested by an inclination to allow the Palestinians a greater role in a future settlement.

Labor's orientation toward Jordan was not without its historic roots. As the Zionist movement in the prestate period became more aware of the Arab opposition to its colonization efforts and its political goals, it accelerated its attempts to reach some level of agreement with the Arab nationalist movement. In regard to the Arab inhabitants of western Palestine, the Zionists have still scored little success. However, the rulers of Jordan, the Hashemites, have always displayed a greater readiness to enter into a dialogue with the Zionists than have those Arabs residing west of the Jordan River.[1] In 1948, Israel and Jordan were the main beneficiaries of the partition of Palestine. Despite the fact that Jordan was formally committed to the anti-Israel consensus among the Arab states, a complex relationship characterized by both conflict and cooperation developed between the neighboring states. After the 1967 Six Day War, which resulted in Jordan's loss of the West Bank, Labor-led Israel demonstrated interest in negotiating with Jordan's King Hussein about the return of some of the territories captured in that war. On many occasions Hussein met unofficially with Labor leaders to discuss possible means of settling the conflict. These efforts did not succeed in producing a formal settlement, but the two countries did arrive at numerous informal understandings. In part, the failure was due to Israeli reluctance to make major concessions in return for the minor practical improvement in bilateral relations that Jordan could offer.

As of 1967, when Israel initiated the policy of "open bridges" over the Jordan River (the border between Israel and Jordan), a two-way free passage of resources and people (with the exception of Israeli Jews, who are not allowed by Jordan to cross the border) has existed. Indeed, in 1973 Hussein refrained from initiating a new front against Israel and the "open bridges" policy remained undisturbed. Instead, rather than opening a new front along the

Jordan, one of his brigades was sent to Syria to fight Israel on the Golan as a token of support for the Arab cause. In 1978, after a short "wait and see" period, typical of Jordanian foreign policy, Jordan refused to join the Camp David peace process, in which it was offered a role involving the future of the territories. Yet, in September 1984, it was the first Arab country to restore full diplomatic relations with Egypt, which had been to an extent ostracized by the Arab world for its peace treaty with Israel. Thus in the 1980s Israel's relations with Jordan, on a practical level at least if not a formal one, seemed to rank even better than its relations with Egypt.

Hussein appeared to be a moderate leader, who had in the past proved his ability to honor his agreements and maintain his control over an unruly Palestinian population. Jordan was also a known political quantity. Therefore, if parts of the territories acquired in 1967 were to be handed over to an Arab factor, Hussein appeared to be a more promising observer or guarantor of an agreed-upon modus vivendi than did Yasser Arafat. Until the mid-1980s, Hussein's pro-Western orientation was also seen as preferable to an anticipatedly pro-Soviet PLO. In the period from 1984 to 1990, the Labor Party was again able to influence foreign policy. Peres in particular, in his capacity as prime minister (1984–1986) and subsequently foreign minister (1986–1988), made great efforts to entice Hussein into entering a formal process of negotiations. These endeavors culminated in the London Agreement (April 1987) between the two leaders. To Labor's chagrin, however (particularly its dovish wing), their Likud partner blocked the Jordanian option, which was at that period conditional on Israeli participation in an international conference on the Middle East.[2] Likud was opposed to international involvement, and Labor's hawks, despite their emphasis on the Jordanian option, displayed similar lack of enthusiasm for that political avenue. Secretary of State Shultz's initiative in 1987, which attempted to bring about negotiations between Israel and a Jordanian–Palestinian delegation, also failed to bear fruit.

Yet, toward the end of the decade, an increasing number of senior Laborites came to the reluctant realization that Hussein's role in the West Bank might be at an end, a realization that was strengthened by Jordan's gradual loss of influence in the West Bank and the diminishing of its interest in the territories. Furthermore, King Hussein's declaration of July 31, 1988 concerning his disengagement from the West Bank, in tones not entirely new, but backed up this time by administrative steps, put an additional strain on the stance held by most Laborites that Hussein was a necessary partner in a political settlement. Moreover, the civil unrest that had permeated the country since December 1987 (i.e., the intifada) elevated the status of the claim of the Palestinians—Hussein's competitors—to the territories. Finally, Hussein's rival, the PLO, succeeded in changing the official U.S. policy of excluding the PLO from the political process, a policy which had been in effect since 1975. This occurred following the Algiers Palestinian National

Council resolutions (November 1988), in which PLO chairman Yasser Arafat proclaimed the establishment of a Palestinian state and issued several vague statements that could be interpreted as an acceptance of UN Resolutions 242 and 338, renouncing the use of terror and recognizing the state of Israel. Upon U.S. insistence, in December 1988 Arafat went on to clarify some of his earlier statements, thus opening the way for an official dialogue between the United States and the PLO, one constituting an important political milestone that could not easily be ignored.

Nevertheless, the party's official position, accepted by the majority of its leaders—that Jordan was an indispensable partner in reaching a lasting comprehensive agreement (as distinguished from an interim agreement)—was still in effect by 1990. In August 1988 (after Hussein's disengagement speech), Peres underlined the geopolitical fact that Jordan still possessed the longest border with Israel. Therefore, whoever ruled Jordan was a potential partner for peace with Israel. In addition, Peres believed that Hussein was still interested in some link to the West Bank and that the Jordanian role could be revived under certain circumstances.[3] Rabin similarly could not envision at this period any permanent agreement without Jordan, since the two countries shared a common border and both were faced with the Palestinian problem.[4] In the past, Israel and Jordan had been allies against the Palestinian national movement. Rabin assumed that the past would repeat itself, which could well be described as a typical fallacy in strategic and historical analysis.[5] Other Labor ministers, such as Bar-Lev, Tzur, and even Weizman, refused to consider Hussein's disengagement steps in August 1988 as his last word on the matter, but rather as a challenge to the PLO and Israel.[6]

During its campaign before the November 1988 elections, Labor made great efforts to show that the Jordanian option was still alive. It even succeeded in enlisting King Hussein's help in this endeavor, when he agreed at Peres's prodding to appear together with Peres on the U.S. television program *Nightline* a few days before the Israeli elections.[7] An unequivocal relinquishment of the Jordanian option was, thus, not considered wise. In addition, a separate Palestinian delegation for a permanent agreement, it was argued, would in all probability lead only to an independent state, which was still rejected by most party members.

The Jordanian orientation was upheld even after the new developments in the PLO position and the subsequent U.S. decision to hold talks with this organization. Peres, for example, phrased it succinctly in March 1989: "We have to return the Jordanian horse to the stable," but added, "in the meantime we have to begin with the Palestinians."[8] He was referring to holding elections in the territories to establish a Palestinian partner in an interim agreement. Gur, although known for accepting the idea of a dialogue with the PLO, argued that a Jordanian role was necessary to prevent the emergence of a Palestinian state.[9] He envisioned using Jordanian involvement to curb the PLO's political ambitions.

Another reason that Jordan had been the preferred historic partner was that the Palestinian national movement had failed up till the late 1960s to impress the Israeli political elite as a force to be reckoned with,[10] a perception shared by other Middle Eastern elites and even by the Palestinians themselves. Moreover, in the early 1970s, the existence of a separate Palestinian nation was still questioned in the Labor Party, and the Palestinian issue was still referred to as primarily a refugee problem. The assumption that the Arabs of Palestine could express themselves politically in any Arab country, and that the condition of the refugees was a humanitarian question properly the responsibility of their Arab brethren, was rather convenient to the Israelis. They pointed out that, in contrast to the Arabs in Palestine, Zionist political aspirations could only be fulfilled in the land of Israel. A new Palestinian national identity necessitated a political solution much more exacting, territorially and morally, on Israel and its national revival movement, Zionism. Thus, the mere existence of a Palestinian nation was often denied. Golda Meir's remark in 1969 about the nonexistence of a Palestinian nation, then quite accepted in most quarters of the party, later became a famous political gaffe.[11] Only gradually did the party, at the doves' prodding, come to recognize the reality of an emerging Palestinian identity. Yet it was argued that this identity was developing, albeit more slowly, beyond the Jordan River as well, where the Palestinians, in contrast to the Bedouin component of the population, constituted a majority. Hawks and doves alike in the party did not exclude a scenario in which the Hashemite royal regime would collapse, leaving Jordan ruled by Palestinian elements. This, however, only strengthened the opposition to the establishment of a "third" state in the region, notwithstanding the fluctuating fortunes of the Palestinian national movement. Undermining the Hashemite regime in order to allow the emergence of a Palestinian state in Jordan, an idea aired by Likud's Ariel Sharon, was not considered by the party leadership in the 1980s as a practical option; its wisdom was also questioned. Indeed, as noted, the difficulties of the Hashemite regime in the late 1980s and 1990 caused great concern among Laborites.

Practical reasons tended to dictate a Jordanian orientation. As of 1967, the only organized Palestinian leadership in existence was the PLO. Yet the PLO was ideologically and unequivocally committed to the destruction of the state of Israel, as its basic document, the National Covenant, indicated.[12] Israelis took the Covenant just as seriously as they regarded their own parties' platforms. Therefore, the Labor Party, except for a few dissenting opinions, regarded this organization as totally unrealistic and uncompromising, and saw no possibility of its reaching an accommodation with the Jewish state. The dissenting view would later, of course, gain strength in the party.

The convential pro-Jordanian viewpoint began to be challenged by some Labor doves primarily in the mid-1970s. Initially, they argued that Hussein had long refused to be the partner to Labor's envisioned territorial compromise. In addition, the question of whether there was a real Hashemite interest in regaining control over the lost territories and particularly over their inhabitants, who were undergoing a process of "Palestinization," was increasingly raised. The doves in the party, under the influence of the more leftist circles, were the first to recognize the development of a new national identity among the Arabs in Judea, Samaria, and the Gaza Strip, an identity that emerged in part in response to the Israeli occupation. After 1967, new foci of identity appeared and the traditional leadership, oriented toward the Hashemite regime, lost ground to the PLO. With the passing of time, a progressively smaller proportion of West Bank inhabitants had experienced living under the Hashemite regime and sharing a history of political allegiance to Jordan. Gradually, the doves ceased to regard the Jordanian option as acceptable to the Arabs of Judea, Samaria, and Gaza.

As a result of developments among the Arabs in the administered territories, therefore, the doves demanded a revision in the party's policy. Furthermore, it was argued that the PLO had become more pragmatic; that its moderation had to be encouraged; and that the organization reflected the authentic nationalistic desires of the Palestinian national movement, which could not be suppressed.[13] A few Laborites also objected to negotiations with a fragile monarchic regime "doomed by the forces of history," and pointed to the need to deal with the "forces of tomorrow." The general aim of the argument was to undermine the assumption that Jordan's Hussein could become the partner in a future agreement.[14] The doves primarily emphasized the anticipated benefits to Israel of a dialogue with the Palestinians—PLO supporters or others—rather than the normative dimension of Palestinian demands for collective political rights.

In actuality, until the end of 1988, a wide consensus prevailed in the Labor Party against any dialogue with the PLO, which was regarded as Israel's arch-enemy, particularly since such a dialogue would revolve around a questionably viable separate Palestinian state in the administered territories. Even more ominous was its potential for irredentist claims both west (Israel) and east (Jordan), a clear prescription for regional instability.[15] The PLO demand for statehood and "the right of return" (of Palestinian refugees to their homes in Israel) was extremely threatening. It was also pointed out that the PLO's main constituents were the refugees, the most radical part of the Palestinian population. The Laborite argument against dealing with the PLO was aptly summed up in the sentence: "Whom you talk with determines what you talk about." To a large extent, demands by many, in the party and elsewhere, for the PLO to accept UN Security Council Resolutions 242 and 338, to renounce terror, to cancel the Palestinian National Covenant, and to give up the "right of return" were ploys to prevent any PLO participation in the political process occurring in the Arab–Israeli arena. Other members of the party, particularly toward the end of the decade, insisted on various preconditions in order to acquire a better negotiating position vis-à-vis the PLO.

During the period in the 1980s when the PLO was ruled out as a potential partner but the "pure" Jordanian option was becoming less and less feasible, the addition of a Palestinian element in that option became necessary. Through the 1978 Camp David Accords, in which the Palestinians of Judea, Samaria, and Gaza were given a say in the implementation of the autonomy plan, their semi-independent participation in negotiations over the future of those areas was incorporated into an internationally binding document. The inclusion of Palestinian representatives from the Israeli-ruled territories thus accorded with the formal position of the party. While it still met resistance in some hawkish quarters, such participation was gradually accepted as inevitable, though it was understood to be under Jordanian tutelage. The Camp David Accords, although lacking Jordan as a signatory, envisioned a Jordanian role in the implementation of the autonomy plan—an interim solution—and, later on, in the effort to attain a permanent settlement. This aspect of the accords pleased the Labor Party, which only in the summer of 1988 was willing to accept a limited independent role for the Palestinians.

The need for political backing from the Palestinians for any future agreement gradually came to be recognized by all in the party. The main problem was mobilizing Palestinian leaders in the Israeli-ruled territories who were willing to negotiate with Israel and who were sufficiently detached from the PLO. In 1984, when Labor was once again in the government, its representatives there, primarily Peres and Rabin, began their ongoing practice of meeting numerous local leaders in an attempt to start a meaningful dialogue and to find appropriate Palestinians to participate in a Jordanian–Palestinian delegation. Delegation members would have to be disconnected from the PLO, yet close enough to this organization to be identified as true nationalists. The doves in the party were less exacting about the credentials of the potential partners. Abba Eban wryly observed that Israel should not expect its interlocutors to be "members of the Zionist Executive," but rather Palestinians "with a disturbing past."[16] At the beginning of 1988, Yossi Beilin, Peres's confidant, claimed that Israel had made a mistake in refusing to enter into talks with a group of Palestinians who were not pro-Jordanian. He noted their acceptance of PLO leadership, yet called for Israel to accept such a group as plausible partners in a dialogue.[17] Though Beilin was serving at the time as General Director of the Foreign Affairs Ministry, this did not prevent him from making a rather controversial statement. Other doves in the party, for example MK Chaim Ramon, were interested in similar discussions.[18] Peres also showed some flexibility, and was even criticized by Rabin for his meetings with Arabs in the West Bank who were identified as PLO supporters.[19]

Rabin censured any "flirting" with the PLO. Yet, already at the end of

1980, in a party forum discussing the party platform for the coming 1981 elections, Rabin had reconciled himself to a Palestinian role in a Jordanian context: ". . . the key is partly in the hands of the leadership of the territories, maybe more than in Hussein's. Therefore, I name my proposal Jordanian–Palestinian."[20] In the latter part of the 1980s he believed that a moderate Palestinian leadership, with no PLO links, could emerge in Judea, Samaria, and Gaza. The example he gave in 1987 was of the late Rashad A'Shawa of Gaza.[21] Ironically, he was even more optimistic in the winter of 1987–1988, when the full magnitude of the Palestinian uprising came to light. Appearing on television, he told the nation, "The unique feature of what is happening here is that, for the first time, it is the residents of the territories who are leading the Palestinian struggle."[22] Rabin was impressed, and accepted the proposal aired by his party's doves for holding elections in the administered territories. He hoped the elections would allow the emergence of Palestinian representatives not subservient to the PLO.

The argument for a greater Palestinian role was, however, left mainly to the doves; others attached more weight to extracting the acquiescence of the Arab countries to a political arrangement that included a Palestinian component. For example, in 1982, Rabin saw the solution of the Palestinian problem primarily in terms of securing Egypt's, Jordan's, and even Saudi Arabia's tacit approval.[23]

Differences of opinion concerning the role of the Palestinians were in fact connected to the way in which the Arab–Israeli conflict was seen. The doves gradually accepted the view that the Palestinian problem was at the "heart of the conflict." Early proponents of this stance, as far back as the late 1960s, were Navon and Eliav.[24] Weizman, a new dove, also declared in 1987 that the "root of the conflict was the lack of solution of the Palestinian problem."[25] In his opinion, the only way for Israel to integrate into the Middle East was through solving the Palestinian problem.[26]

In contrast, Rabin and other hawks denied this claim. The hawks placed the responsibility for the conflict on the general Arab refusal to accept a Jewish state in the region. The Arab countries and the Palestinian leadership were blamed for the Palestinian tragedy. Despite Rabin's assertion that "we have to offer a reasonable solution to the Palestinian problem," he declared emphatically in 1983 that "the Palestinian problem is not the heart of the Arab-Israeli conflict."[27] In 1988 he deplored "the transfer of the focus of the confrontation between ourselves and the Arabs, from the Arab states to the Palestinians."[28] In this article, written after the outbreak of the intifada, Rabin pointed out the dangerous implication of such a change in perception. "Diverting the focus of a solution . . . to the Israeli–Palestinian level would be a serious mistake for it would mean Israel's facing the PLO."[29] The hawks in the party emphasized the interstate aspect of the Arab–Israeli conflict, whereas the doves paid greater attention to the intercommunal dimension, whose resurgence had resulted from Israel's conquest of Judea, Samaria, and

Gaza in 1967.[30] The Labor Party's gradual recognition of this intercommunal dimension, and of the growing importance of the Palestinians in the conflict, was reflected in revisions that were demanded in the party platform.

Naturally, the changes in Laborite perceptions of the Palestinian issue were connected to Middle East developments and the changing fortunes of the PLO. The 1980s, in fact, may be said to have been characterized by the "Palestinization" of the Arab–Israeli conflict, meaning that the Palestinians became a growing political threat and an issue with a high public profile.[31] Previously, as we have seen, the Camp David Accords and the peace treaty with Egypt had reduced the level of threat perception among Laborites and others. Then, as time went on, attention was diverted from the interstate dimension of the Arab–Israeli conflict to the Palestinian issue. Israel's invasion of Lebanon, which attempted, among other things, to destroy the PLO, was in part the result of the Likud leadership's realization of the greater resonance of the Palestinian issue and of the greater threat—less military than political—posed by the PLO. The hawkish wing of the Labor Party supported this understanding of the Lebanon War (see Chapter 6). Indeed, the expulsion of the PLO from Beirut weakened the organization, and strengthened Jordan for some time after, but did not reduce the necessity of finding a partner to negotiate with Israel on the destiny of the Israeli-ruled Palestinians.

The decline in PLO fortunes increased Labor's reluctance to deal with Arafat and his organization. It also contributed to the emergence of pragmatic politicians in the administered territories with PLO and/or Jordanian loyalties, who displayed a modicum of independence in their positions.[32] Yet such politicians consistently displayed unwillingness or inability to assume leadership in regard to an independent or semi-independent role in the peace process, and this enhanced the positions of the PLO and Jordan. Jordan's influence in the territories, however, dwindled over time, culminating in Hussein's announcement of formal disengagement from the West Bank in the summer of 1988, a development that dovish Laborites pointed to as confirming their reading of the Middle Eastern political map.

The intifada pushed the Palestinian problem to an even higher place on the Israeli and international agendas. The intifada was seen as a major milestone by many senior Laborites. Bar-Lev and Tzur argued that it constituted a break with the past and that Israel faced an entirely new situation.[33] Gur called it "the most dramatic event since the establishment of the state in 1948."[34] Rabin, as we have noted, similarly attached great importance to it. This development was very threatening, but it brought to the fore new forces capable of leading the Palestinians in the territories. Although the Palestinian uprising was not initially led by the PLO, it clearly strengthened its position versus Jordan. It also strengthened the option of a more active role for the Palestinians living under Israeli rule.

Rabin summed up the search for a partner to a peace process in the

1980s as follows: "In 1982–83, Egypt decided to stop leading the political process.... In July 1988, Jordan... decided to stay out.... As a result of the decisions by Egypt and Jordan we have one choice: the Palestinians."[35] As far as Rabin was concerned, the only door open for continuing the peace process had a Palestinian address on it. He hoped the Arab countries would later join the process. The changing circumstances also affected the party's platform and the stances taken by members.

CHANGES IN THE PARTY PLATFORM

In regard to choice of a partner in the process of regional reconciliation, the party clearly moved in a dovish direction in the 1980s, i.e., toward greater responsiveness to the inclusion of Palestinians in the political process. While references to the general perception of threat and to the chances for peace were not clearly incorporated in the party platform, the issue of the desirable partner was regularly defined there. On this issue, therefore, it is easier to refer to a party position and to attempts to change it. The revisionist thrust in the party was prompted by its doves.

The beginning of the shift toward the left occurred in 1973. In that year, the party platform mentioned a Palestinian identity for the first time. Article 9 in the Peace and Security section reads: "The self-identity of the Palestinian and Jordanian Arabs could be expressed in the neighboring Jordanian–Palestinian state."[36] This also marked the first time the term "Jordanian–Palestinian state" was included in the platform.

Considering the reluctance of many Israelis at that period to accept the fact that a Palestinian nation was being formed, the significance of the use of this term should not be underestimated. Indeed, political circles left of Labor regarded these changes in the 1973 elections platform as a radical shift in their direction.[37]

Since the PLO's international stature had increased, and since its demand for partnership in any Middle Eastern settlement had become more accepted in many world capitals, particularly after the 1973 October War, the Labor party platform for the 1977 elections emphasized that negotiations were to be conducted solely with sovereign governments. It also explicitly excluded the PLO from the peace process,[38] regarding it as a terrorist organization set on destroying the Jewish state and as incapable of changing its character as expressed in its own covenant. Furthermore, nobody in Labor at that time was willing to grant the PLO what it wanted—a Palestinian state.

An additional change occurred in 1977, when the party platform for the first time permitted the inclusion of Palestinian representatives from Judea and Samaria in a Jordanian delegation for negotiations with Israel.[39] This constituted a clear alteration in the perception of the Palestinian problem. It was a move that had been long demanded by the left, both in the party and in the Israeli political arena. It also indicated the erosion of Labor's Jordanian orientation. Jordan, it was perceived, could no longer exclusively negotiate the future of the Palestinians in Israeli-ruled territories. This platform change reflected an earlier revision in the leadership positions. Already in 1975 Rabin had promised U.S. Secretary of State Kissinger that Israel would accept the inclusion of Palestinians from the territories in a Jordanian delegation. This promise was a response not only to a U.S. request but also to the decision of the October 1974 Rabat Arab Summit to recognize the PLO as the sole legitimate representative of the Palestinians. Rabin also clarified that his country insisted on interstate negotiations.[40]

The Gaza Strip was not mentioned in the 1977 party platform, because it was regarded as an issue belonging to bilateral relations with Egypt. Only following the 1978 Camp David Accords was the future of Gaza explicitly linked to the solution for Judea and Samaria. Indeed, the 1981 platform added Gaza to the areas to which representatives of a Jordanian delegation would be sent.[41] Begin's insistence on not allowing the restoration of Egyptian rule to the Gaza Strip, which was regarded as part of the land of Israel, contributed to the general tendency to regard all Arabs within the borders of post-1922 mandatory Palestine as sharing a common political problem and future. This heightened the awareness among all Laborites, as well as other politically interested Israelis, of the Palestinian problem.

A further softening of the position toward the Palestinians occurred in 1981, when the election platform expressed readiness to incorporate representatives of the inhabitants of the territories in the autonomy talks. This left room for the inclusion of Palestinians not residing there. In addition, the platform expressed willingness to hold discussions with "Palestinian personalities and bodies who will recognize Israel and denounce terrorism," thus explicitly widening the range of acceptable Palestinian partners.[42]

The change in these positions was not welcomed by all party members. MK Amos Hadar, for example, one of the party's hawks who had voted against the Camp David Accords, claimed at the end of 1981 that the changes in the party platform on the Palestinian issue during that year were a mistake. The sections in the platform that recognized the rights of the Palestinians and expressed readiness to talk with them were, he felt, unnecessary.[43] In 1981, the hawks in fact succeeded in limiting the degree of openness expressed toward Palestinian participation. A new clause in the platform specified, "The PLO, as based on the Palestinian Covenant, and any other organization which rejects Israel's right to exist and the national existence of the Jewish people, or which uses terrorist means, cannot be partners to such negotiations."[44] This new precondition for eligibility as a partner, which added additional obstacles to including the PLO in the peace process, was the result of a hawkish attempt to forestall any pressure to allow a PLO role. At a later stage, the doves consoled themselves that this article could be interpreted as permitting some dealings with the PLO even without a formal renunciation of the Palestinian Covenant. By the end of the 1980s in fact they were satisfied with what they perceived as a de facto change in the PLO.

Despite qualification by the new clause, the article in the 1981 platform that allowed for a less discriminating selection of negotiating partners among the Palestinians—as long as they recognized Israel and denounced terrorism—was quite close to the Yariv–Shemtov formula. Named after Laborite Aharon Yariv, a major general of the reserves, and the leftist Mapam leader Victor Shemtov, this formula stipulated recognition of the PLO in exchange for PLO recognition of Israel and disengagement from terror. The formula, rejected by the Rabin government in 1974 when Yariv and Shemtov were both cabinet members, was backed by dovish elements in the party, who argued that it was vital for Israel to project an image of flexibility, and that playing the Palestinian card could enhance Israel's leverage vis-à-vis Hussein.[45] Some doves, for example Eban, Ramon, and Beilin, claimed at the end of the decade that the Yariv–Shemtov formula was actually included in the platform—referring to the article in the 1981 document. Eban did not use the Yariv–Shemtov terminology, but claimed in 1988 that the platform allowed, under certain conditions, contact with the PLO.[46] Though the platform could be interpreted as such, it did not explicitly mention the PLO by name, as Yariv and Shemtov had advocated.

The hawks disagreed, of course. Rabin and others rejected the formula, because, in their opinion, negotiations with the PLO would inevitably lead to a Palestinian state.[47] They pointed out that the platform emphatically rejected the PLO as a partner. Some also distinguished between "talks" and "negotiations." They maintained that the platform only permitted negotiations with states, and not with Palestinian representatives, except when they were part of a Jordanian delegation.[48] Indeed, in 1986, at the party congress, an attempt was made to substitute the term negotiations for "talks," but it was successfully put down by the hawks. Yariv then suggested dropping the clause explicitly banning the PLO as a negotiating partner. The party congress in 1986 rejected this amendment.[49]

In the aftermath of the 1978 Camp David Accords concluded by Begin's government, which recognized the "legitimate rights" of the Palestinians, it became politically easier for the Labor Party to incorporate in its program a greater consideration of the Palestinian national problem than it had shown previously. Laborites, most of whom were pragmatic, accepted the political facts created by the Likud-led government and included into their platform a greater accommodation of Palestinian interests. During the 1980s, difficulties in arriving at an agreement with Hussein, and the realization that the Hashemites might not be interested in retrieving the West Bank, coupled with increased perception of a Palestinian national identity, led many Laborites to regard the Palestinian option as indispensable in terms of disconnection from the densely Arab populated areas of Judea, Samaria, and Gaza. Jordan seemed no longer capable of reaching an agreement with Israel on its own. Some Palestinian cooperation to grant Hussein the needed legitimacy for such a step was recognized by Labor as necessary. In the doves' view, it was vital. Yet the hawks insisted on the inclusion of Palestinian representatives from the administered territories, to circumvent the possibility of dealing with the PLO.

Some doves in the party even wanted to assent to certain formulations not mentioned in the Camp David Accords. Already in 1977, the Leshiluv group had called for recognition of the Palestinian right to "national self-determination."[50] Yet it explicitly opposed a "third" (Palestinian) state. Sarid and Beilin suggested in October 1980, before the 1981 elections, a substitution of the term "self-determination" for "self-identity."[51] An attempt to alter the party platform to include the term self-determination was made again at the party congress in 1986. By this time, the term was well accepted in circles left of Labor such as Mapam and Ratz (Citizens Rights Movement). Abba Eban, anticipating opposition on the ground that such a term was equivalent to a Palestinian state, explained at the party Central Council (Merkaz) on June 7, 1986 that such a recognition would not necessarily lead to an independent Palestinian entity. He claimed that greater flexibility was needed to attract Palestinian representatives to negotiate with Israel, and hinted at more enticing formulations in order to overcome Palestinian reluctance.[52] In 1987, Edri, Baram, Ramon, Beilin, Namir, Eliav and other doves supported an acknowledgment of Palestinian "self-determination." They signed a declaration of the Center for Peace in the Middle East that called for "mutual recognition, based on territorial compromise and self-determination."[53]

This term was of course opposed by the hawks. MKs Hillel, Arbeli-Almozlino, Hadar, and Rosolio rejected Beilin's suggestion in October 1980.[54] Dinitz voiced similar opposition in 1986.[55] Rabin even called those in favor of self-determination for the Palestinians "a danger to Israel's security."[56] Reluctance to adopt such a formulation was not limited to hawks alone. Moshe Shahal, a yonetz with dovish leanings, joined the hawks on this issue. In a speech to the party's Central Council (June 7, 1986), he responded to Eban's arguments asserting that "the disputed term clearly indicated an independent state and that the proposed change made the chances for negotiations even more remote."[57] Self-determination for the Palestinians was, finally, not included in the party platform.

Yet, in an unprecedented manner, at the 1986 party congress Shimon Peres, then prime minister, declared Israel's recognition of the Palestinians as a nation.[58] Although the Camp David Accords (drafted in English) did include the term Palestinian people, as Peres himself mentioned, the Hebrew word *am* is less ambiguous than the English term "people." Peres did not embrace the term self-determination, but he came close. This was the first time an

Israeli prime minister had ever made such a statement. Interestingly enough, the party congress did not introduce this phraseology into the party platform.

The Labor Party hoped that some Palestinian leadership would emerge in the territories acquired in 1967, and associate itself with an Israeli–Jordanian agreement. However, the extent to which emerging local leaders were able to free themselves from the PLO's directives became increasingly questionable. Israeli attempts, mostly half-hearted, to encourage the development of an independent local leadership or to strengthen the pro-Hashemite elements did not prove successful.[59] As a matter of fact, after 1976 (when Peres was defense minister), Israel refrained from holding municipal elections in the territories. Labor was in a position to do so after 1984, since it held the defense portfolio. But Rabin feared that, as in 1976, such elections would elevate PLO supporters to leadership positions—an unwelcome development, as he saw it. In 1988, however, he came to view general—not municipal—elections in a different light, as shall be discussed later.

These failures, as well as developments in the region related to the intifada, strengthened the dovish claim that greater responsiveness to the Palestinians and the PLO was necessary. In addition, Hussein's policy since the spring of 1988 of signaling disengagement from the West Bank made the party's preference for a Jordanian–Palestinian partner appear less realistic. Thus more members of the party have embraced the dovish position.

Before the November 1988 elections, another important revision took place in party positions concerning Palestinian participation in the peace process. For the first time, the idea of an independent Palestinian delegation was accepted, in connection with negotiations for an interim agreement, though not necessarily for a final settlement. Peres announced this differentiation between the interim and permanent agreements in August 1988.[60] This distinction in regard to the negotiating partner, a new development in the party, was made in response to the events in the territories, to Hussein's new policy, and to internal pressure from the doves. As a result, a Palestinian independent delegation was accepted as a viable partner for negotiating an interim agreement over the immediate future of Judea, Samaria, and Gaza. This new formula was assented to by most party hawks as well, and was incorporated in the 1988 party platform.[61]

As expected, it was the doves who initiated this reversal. Abba Eban led the demand for a change in Labor's stance on the issue of Palestinian representation.[62] He and Shahal were responsible for drafting the new formula. Shahal questioned the viability of a Jordanian option in the wake of Hussein's disengagement speech, as did others in the party.[63] Beilin and Ramon, the more radical doves, proposed that the platform permit the inclusion of a Palestinian independent delegation in a permanent settlement as well.[64] Eban also demanded that the party delete from its platform any clause specifying groups with whom Israel refused to talk, obviously having the PLO in mind.[65] These proposals were rejected, however. The hawks were not prepared to allow too many revisions. Nevertheless, the new political developments, together with the coming elections, provided the doves with an opportunity to make significant alterations in the party platform in the dovish direction.

The party was ripe for the granting of exclusive Palestinian representation in an interim agreement. In actuality, though, in the past the doves had advocated greater responsiveness to the Palestinians than this; some were now eager to adopt a Palestinian instead of a Jordanian orientation in all contexts. The party, however, was not ready to relinquish the Jordanian option altogether.

Rabin's stance on this issue was apparently critical in regard to the party's adoption of the new formula. Already by the spring of 1988 he was willing to consider an independent local Palestinian partner for a limited agreement, even before Hussein's disengagement speech.[66] In reaction to the uprising, he observed that for the first time the Palestinians of the territories were a leading factor in the struggle. This led him to hope that a local leadership might arise that was willing to reach an accommodation by direct negotiations with Israel, although he could not yet detect such a development.[67] Rabin's new evaluation on the possibility of arriving at an interim agreement without Jordanian participation paved the way for the change in the platform introduced by the doves. Without Rabin, the hawkish party leaders had little chance of blocking the adoption of the new formula.

The main problem with the new formula, particularly for the hawks, continued to be the exact nature of the Palestinian partner. As far as Rabin was concerned, the potential partner (a delegation comprising residents of the territories) was not yet in existence. Some in the party suggested the Arab mayors, while others mentioned individuals with a clear PLO affiliation. Since there was a leadership vacuum in the administered territories, in the sense that there were few Palestinian political figures who were recognized beyond their immediate areas, the new formulation seemed to be a blatant invitation for the PLO. This was, indeed, exactly what some doves had in mind.

Aware of the great opposition to including PLO representatives in a delegation to negotiate with Israel, some doves like Yossi Beilin, Avraham Burg, and the veteran party leader Chaim Tzadok began early in 1988 to suggest elections in Judea, Samaria, and Gaza to foster the development of an elected leadership.[68] Many claimed that Israeli attempts at nursing a moderate leadership had in the past ended in fiasco, and that only the Palestinians could choose their own leaders. These would probably be oriented toward the PLO, but if elected in a democratic process, they could not be easily rejected by the Israelis. Moreover, their status as elected representatives could give them enough legitimacy to develop a modicum of independence from the PLO, which was after all a self-appointed leadership. Such a leadership might, to some extent, be more realistic in its dealings with Israel than would the

PLO, which was removed from the region and more susceptible to the pressures exerted by its extreme factions.

It was not only doves who subscribed to this view. Yaakov Tzur, a yonetz, concurred, as he sided with the doves on the Palestinian issue.[69] Even Rabin accepted the need for elections in the spring of 1988, a clear reversal of his earlier opposition to this step. As noted previously, his assessment was that local forces could take the lead. Rabin did not intend to hold municipal elections, which he considered politically irrelevant. He favored "elections for the body that will run the self-administration" in the territories.[70] Before Israel went to the polls in November 1988, Rabin and Peres, in the name of the party, suggested that elections be held in the territories, hoping that those elected would enter into negotiations with Israel over the form of the interim agreement. Furthermore, they indicated that the "biographies" of the elected negotiators would not be thoroughly checked, in other words, ending the ban on PLO supporters. However, both Rabin and Peres stipulated that such elections could be held only after the civil unrest ceased for a few months, a problematic condition considering that the intifada showed no signs of ending.

In 1989, Rabin, within the National Unity government formed after the November 1988 polls, became the moving force behind the May 1989 peace initiative based on elections in the territories. Rabin and Peres both joined in the effort to convince Labor ministers and the party's Executive Bureau (Lishka) to promote the government's peace program, which the most dovish as well as the most hawkish elements in the party refrained from backing. The ministers Weizman and Edri preferred an outright PLO orientation and did not believe that the elections could circumvent a PLO role; therefore they did not vote in the government in favor of the peace initiative. MK Beilin similarly opted for immediate negotiations with the PLO. In contrast, hawks like MKs Hillel, Zisman, and Raanan Cohen stressed, among other things, the dangers of entering into an indirect dialogue with the PLO through the elected Palestinians.

The party platforms and the policies supported by Labor during the 1980s clearly manifested a dovish tendency. The more extreme hawks, as well as the most dovish elements in the party, were dissatisfied with the changes in policy, for different reasons; but as long as party positions were supported by Peres and Rabin, no serious challenges on the Palestinian issue could be effective.

THE PARTY AND THE PLO

At the meeting of the Palestinian National Council in Algiers (November 1988), the PLO proclaimed its own state and issued vague declarations that could possibly be interpreted as an acceptance of UN National Security

	Evolution of the Party Platform on the Palestinian Issue
1973	"Palestinian identity" and "a Jordanian–Palestinian state" first mentioned; opposition to a Palestinian state
1977	Representatives from Judea and Samaria allowed in a Jordanian–Palestinian delegation; opposition to a Palestinian state; and the PLO explicitly excluded from the peace process
1981	Representatives of the inhabitants of Judea, Samaria, and Gaza permitted into a Jordanian–Palestinian delegation; talks with "Palestinian personalities and bodies that will recognize Israel and denounce terrorism" allowed; opposition to a Palestinian state, the PLO excluded from the peace process; organizations basing themselves on the Palestinian Covenant not acceptable
1984	No significant changes
1988	Willingness to negotiate an interim agreement with authorized representatives of the inhabitants of Judea, Samaria, and Gaza; opposition to a Palestinian state; the PLO excluded from the peace process; organizations basing themselves on the Palestinian Covenant not acceptable

Resolutions 242 and 338, renouncing the use of terror and recognizing the state of Israel. Following U.S. insistence on more explicit statements as well as pressure from Egypt and other international actors, the PLO offered new formulations. The Reagan administration found these added clarifications satisfactory, and in December 1988 decided to hold formal talks with this organization. The flexibility displayed by the PLO and the subsequent reversal in U.S. policy surprised the newly formed Israeli National Unity government, of which Labor was an important part.

Many doves in the Labor Party welcomed these developments, however, as they seemed to substantiate their theories about a moderation process taking place in the Arab world. They no longer regarded the PLO as a mortal enemy and believed that peace was within reach. In fact, prior to the late 1988 developments, the number of Laborites willing to revise the official party position concerning the PLO was on the increase and included first-rank leaders such as Gur, Eban, and Weizman. As early as October 1981 Gur had suggested talking to the PLO if it would cancel its covenant and recognize Israel's right to exist. He was then very much criticized in the party. Eban, even in 1988, was more oblique, which reflected the perceived unpopularity of advocating dealings with the PLO. He expressed his pleasure at Secretary of State Shultz's meeting with two Palestinian–American professors, members of the Palestinian National Council;[71] he also criticized the law banning talks with the PLO. In January 1988, Labor's Young Guard had recommended talks with the PLO upon that organization's acceptance of 242 and 338 but, conspicuously enough, made no mention of canceling the covenant or of recognizing Israel, both of which were cited in the platform as preconditions for such a step.[72] Even before the uprising in the territories, another well-known dove, MK Ora Namir, declared that "there is no way to reach peace without the PLO."[73]

Possibly Peres himself had changed his stance somewhat on this issue. In a speech at Eilat in March 1988, he said, "PLO—yes, Arafat—no."[74] He later claimed that he was misunderstood; he may have meant PLO sympathizers in the territories. There have been indications, however, that Peres and his close advisors were in fact mellowing in their opposition to negotiations with the PLO. For example, during his tenure at the Foreign Ministry, the use of the Palestinian National Covenant as propaganda material was discontinued, an action for which he was severely criticized in the party. In a more veiled manner, when enunciating Labor's principles for the coming elections, Peres spoke of the Jordanian–Palestinian delegation as the "preferred partner for negotiations,"[75] and hinted that there was another possible choice of a negotiating partner. This other option was the PLO.

Yet, in contrast to most doves, Peres was cautious in dealing with the new situation in the aftermath of the developments of October–December 1988. Initially, he belittled the significance of the statements in Algiers; they were too vague to satisfy him.[76] With the exception of Weizman, the other Labor ministers displayed similar skepticism.[77] Furthermore, Peres expressed his sorrow at Jordan's recognition of the state the PLO had proclaimed at Algiers, a step that complicated the situation, but that did not exclude Jordan from future negotiations.[78] He called the U.S. decision to begin talks with the PLO "a sad day."[79] While he still continued to see Jordan as an indispensable partner, he nevertheless did not hesitate to welcome the later changes in the PLO's position in December. But he did recommend waiting some time to find out whether these changes were merely linguistic, or whether they reflected a real reversal in policy.[80] Earlier on, he had realized that "if we talk to the PLO, we cannot talk to Jordan."[81] He was hesitant to play the PLO card, which was to a great extent an irreversible move.

Any other position would have led to a party and governmental crisis. Considering the challenges to Peres's leadership following the November 1988 elections, recognition of the PLO was not the best issue with which to win a political battle in his party. Furthermore, a commitment to a new policy toward the PLO could have brought down the National Unity government. Under the coalition agreement this would have meant new elections, which would have intensified the struggle to replace the existing leadership. This was not a scenario to be encouraged by Peres. The idea of bringing down the government on the issue of dealing with the PLO, and holding national elections with this issue as the central topic, did not (with the exception of the most dovish elements) appeal to the Laborites, even those who wanted to get rid of the party leadership. This factor moderated, to some extent, the attacks on the leadership, as well as the demands for a PLO role. In the meantime, Peres supported Rabin in sticking to Labor's and the government's policy of not talking to the PLO.[82] In spite of his statements that, in the absence of a Jordanian presence, "we have to talk to the Palestinians as they are," he refrained from challenging the government's position.[83] Though he aired, in March 1989, at a very low profile, a "Benelux solution," i.e., some kind of Israeli–Palestinian–Jordanian confederation, he rejected a pure PLO approach, as advocated by some doves. Finally, he supported the National Unity government's peace initiative of May 1989. While the United States was transforming this initiative into an indirect Israeli dialogue with the PLO, neither Peres nor Rabin made any objection.

Yet, Rabin's views on the PLO did not change in the slightest in the aftermath of the November–December 1988 events. After Arafat's Geneva statements in December, he remarked, "Behind the verbiage the PLO remains as it was: a murderous terrorist organization."[84] He then added bluntly, "What is there to talk about with the PLO?! . . . Agreeing to talk with the PLO means getting used to the idea of a third state between Israel and Jordan."[85] According to Rabin, in contrast to a dialogue with the inhabitants of the Israeli-ruled territories, which might possibly lead to coexistence, talks with the PLO meant also discussing the "right of return" for the Palestinian refugees. In his view, if presented with an adamant Israeli opposition, the dialogue between the United States and the PLO would peter out.[86] As noted previously, Rabin believed that an entrenched Israel would eventually revise the positions of friends and foes alike.

However, the Palestinian uprising, the PLO successes, and the erosion in the U.S. position indicated to Rabin the necessity for the continuation of the peace process. Indeed, at the end of January 1989, Rabin renewed his proposal for elections in the territories for a leadership with whom discussions could be held for an interim agreement, making a clear differentiation between Palestinians living in the territories and those outside it.[87] The defense minister hoped that this distinction would circumvent talking with the PLO, although he was aware that the local leaders needed some PLO backing. Furthermore, Rabin wanted the support of the Likud, as well as of the United States, in stressing this distinction. His Likud coalition partners accepted his plan, while the new Bush administration, still in the stages of molding its Middle East policies, did not reject this differentiation as a first step in an Israeli–Palestinian dialogue. Most of the party doves even supported Rabin's plan, whose main aspect—the elections—had actually been their idea. Rabin, together with Prime Minister Shamir, succeeded in shaping the elections proposal into the central feature of the peace initiative adopted by the National Unity government in May 1989. Rabin preferred to ignore the fact that once set in motion, this initiative would evolve into an indirect Israeli–PLO channel of communication. He probably hoped to use the PLO to legitimize a delegation of local Palestinians. Rabin was even willing to allow some Palestinians living outside the territories who were clearly associated with the PLO to participate in a Palestinian delegation, whose main mandate would be to discuss with Israel the preparations for the elections.

The hawkish Central Stream and its leader Shlomo Hillel naturally opposed talks with the PLO, and maintained that any other posture was contrary to the party platform.[88] Furthermore, they claimed that Arafat had proved his intentions were not bona fide, citing examples such as his threats against Elias Freij (Bethlehem's mayor) in January 1989 and his calls to step up the uprising. The main objection was, as Hillel put it: "Since we oppose a Palestinian state, I see no basis for talking to the PLO at this point."[89] Some hawks, for example former MK Amnon Lin, argued that the changes in the PLO were simply part of its plan to dismantle Israel in stages.[90] He was referring to the PLO "phased plan" of destroying Israel, which allowed the organization to declare its willingness to first build a state in the territories, from which Israel would be forced to retreat. The Dor Hemshech group similarly backed the Rabin–Peres insistence on denying the PLO a negotiating role. Rabin's proposal of dealing with local Palestinians was generally accepted in hawkish Laborite quarters. Yet, as noted previously, MKs Zisman and Cohen of the Central Stream heavily criticized the elections plan, on the ground that it might lead to negotiations with the PLO.[91] MK Hillel was just as adamantly against the idea of holding elections in the territories.[92] Rabin's agreement to allow Palestinians residing in Jerusalem to vote (at voting booths outside of Jerusalem) in the election particularly troubled the party hawks. More vocal criticism was directed at their dovish colleagues' eagerness to meet with PLO supporters, in the territories or elsewhere.

Initially, Bar-Lev refused to consider revising the party platform concerning the PLO, as some doves demanded at the end of 1988, since, he felt, the only thing to be discussed with this organization was a Palestinian state. In spite of the dialogue between the PLO and the United States, Bar-Lev expected the new Bush administration to attempt to revive the Jordanian option.[93] Despite his affiliation as a yonetz, on this issue Bar-Lev's heart was in the hawkish camp. Yet it did not take him long to accept that elections in the territories must inevitably lead to indirect negotiations with the PLO, since this organization's candidates would be elected.[94]

As we have seen, Gur, also a yonetz, was not against a dialogue with the PLO, though he preferred to use the term talks rather than negotiations. But he did emphasize that public contacts would probably lead nowhere because of the enormous differences between the two sides. He did not oppose a PLO party's running for the elections to be held in the territories according to the Rabin plan, but stressed that only secret talks and Israeli patience could bring about an acceptable solution in the future. Gur was not willing to deal solely with the Palestinians, and maintained that a solution had to be connected somehow to Jordan.[95] To get better results, he hoped to play the PLO against Jordan in the negotiations.

Shahal, another yonetz, criticized his party colleagues' hurry to change the party policy toward the PLO,[96] but was willing to negotiate with that organization if it unambiguously stopped using terror, recognized Israel and UN Resolution 242, and gave up the "right of return."[97] He did not see anybody else to negotiate with.[98] Simply put, he wanted a better deal. Moreover, the plan he presented, which included negotiations with the PLO, insisted on a Jordanian–Palestinian solution. While this obviously demonstrated opposition to a Palestinian state, it was also a challenge to the conventional party wisdom that the result of negotiation would be automatically determined by the identity of the negotiating partner.

Yaakobi, another yonetz at the ministerial level, also showed willingness to engage in talks with the PLO. Though skeptical about the PLO's abandonment of terrorism, he pointed out that this organization was aware that recognition of Israel's existence was a prerequisite for becoming a partner in the dialogue.[99] He actually joined Weizman in demanding a revision in the party platform.

The Rabin and Peres stance came under heavy fire from the party's doves, who regarded the revisions in the PLO as of great significance. The doves (Baram, Namir, Ramon, Beilin, Burg, Eliav, Peretz, Eban, and Tzadok) established the Labor Forum for the Promotion of Peace in December 1988 to bolster their demand for a formal party debate on the clause in the platform that excluded the PLO from the political process. Baram voiced their view of the situation as follows: "Instead of welcoming every sign of moderation among our enemies, we react negatively. . . . We should formulate a policy that will not position us as the new rejectionist front. We must adopt a policy that will bring peace, rather than follow a blind and unrealistic one."[100] Baram and his colleagues expressed their fears that an additional opportunity for resolving the conflict would be missed. Burg even called Rabin "the suppressor of peace."[101] In 1989, Ramon, then the Knesset faction chairperson, joined in the unsuccessful parliamentary moves of the left to repeal the law forbidding contacts with PLO representatives.[102] Namir regarded the PLO's statements as amounting to a recognition of Israel and a renunciation of terror, and also as equivalent to an annulment of the Palestinian National Covenant. Therefore, according to her interpretation, the party platform no longer prevented any contacts with the PLO. Yet Namir believed that only a cease-fire with the Palestinians could effect a psychological change in the Israeli public's outlook toward the PLO.[103] She even went to Paris in January 1989, together with Eliav and other non-Labor leftists, to attend a conference in which PLO representatives participated. Beilin, Burg, and other Labor doves met PLO supporters in the territories. Both these moves were heavily criticized by the party's hawks.

Some of the doves, such as Baram and Ramon, had no idealized vision of the PLO. By 1990 they still regarded it as an abominable terrorist organization. Yet they maintained that, just as Israel had negotiated with

Syria, a most brutal regime, it had to talk to the PLO.[104] Furthermore, the doves argued that since the whole world, including the United States, recognized the PLO, the battle to delegitimize the organization was lost, and Israel had to reconcile itself to the new reality. They pointed out that it was absurd for Israelis to think they could influence the appointment of Arab delegations, and that the local Palestinian leaders were, in actuality, PLO representatives. The doves also tried to undermine the assumption that talks with the PLO would inevitably lead to a Palestinan state. Finally, they argued that a Palestinian state could not possibly pose a security threat to Israel.[105]

However, the doves in the party were in an awkward position. On the one hand, they sensed a difference in the PLO and felt duty-bound to lobby for their views. On the other hand, as Burg indicated, they had "to accept the will of the majority, which is at this point to remain passive."[106] They were well aware that a revision in the party platform on the issue of the PLO meant an end to the National Unity government, a development they rather welcomed, though an unlikely one in terms of the intraparty power constellation at the end of the decade. They realized, too, that programmatic revisions were connected to changes in the leadership.

For the time being, then, most of the ministers and MKs backed Rabin and Peres, or were unwilling to precipitate a governmental or party crisis on the issue of dealing with the PLO, since no prospects for a quick and favorable agreement with the PLO and Jordan were in sight. Significant U.S. pressure was also not foreseeable in the immediate future. The United States was actually not interested in a governmental crisis, which would delay the peace process; and they were far from happy when the government fell in March 1990. Furthermore, without Rabin's support, no change in the party stance toward the PLO was seen as possible. Therefore many in the party adopted a wait-and-see posture to assess the significance of the new PLO image and of its dialogue with the United States.

Beilin and other doves were quick to point out that an indirect dialogue with the PLO was actually taking place.[107] Some Laborite doves, such as MKs Burg, Dayan, and Arad, indeed advocated indirect negotiations as a first step toward a formal Israeli–Palestinian dialogue. They hoped this course of events might gradually lower reluctance in the party, and elsewhere, toward talking to the PLO. Another virtue of the indirect approach, it was believed, was that it would prevent the sort of immediate breakdown that was seen as likely in the case of direct formal negotiation, given the divergent opening positions of the two parties.[108]

In addition, time was needed for reorganization of the party after the electoral defeats, in October 1988 at the national level and in February 1989 at the municipal one. The need to project unity before the important elections to the Histadrut (October 1989) also reduced tensions in the party. Among the hawks, the hope—or certainty—grew that with the passing of time the

PLO, with its many constituent organizations, would eventually prove its inability to change. Nevertheless, even the hawks approved proposing an amendment to the Prevention of Terrorism Act that would make it legal for an Israeli to participate in a debate at which a PLO representative was also present. The secretary-general, MK Harish, explained that the amendment did not sanction talks with the PLO; it was intended to allow Labor representatives to participate in forums at which PLO representatives were present, such as the Socialist International.[109] Technically, Harish was on sound footing. In suggesting such an amendment, however, Labor seemed also to be sending political signals. The establishment of a de facto cease-fire between Israel and the PLO in Lebanon in 1989 is also worth noting in this context.[110] While the PLO refrained from sending terrorists to Israel from South Lebanon, the IDF, under Rabin, redirected its attacks to non-PLO targets.

Nevertheless, it may take a great political effort to turn this silent dialogue into a party call for talks with the PLO. Developments in the summer of 1990 made such an about-face improbable in the near future. Following the unsuccessful PLO attempt on May 30 at a terrorist attack on several Israeli beaches, which Arafat refused to condemn, the United States formally suspended its dialogue with the PLO. The PLO's support for the Iraqi invasion of Kuwait further discredited its leadership in Washington, as well as in Jerusalem. PLO policies played into the hands of the more hawkish elements in Israel, including Laborites, who harbored deep suspicions as to whether this organization would ever desist from terror and behave moderately.

CONCLUSION

Aside from reluctance to negotiate with a terrorist organization, dealing with the PLO was regarded by Laborites as leading to only one possible outcome—a Palestinian state. (The strong and persisting opposition to the establishment of such a state in the administered territories will be analyzed in Chapter 5.) Yet the Labor Party did move gradually toward the acceptance of a greater role for the Palestinians, although it still preferred a Jordanian input in future agreements. The table on page 73, which outlines revisions in the party platform on this issue, clearly demonstrates this dovish shift. The party demonstrated willingness to accept PLO supporters in the territories as its interlocutors. Over time, opposition to meeting with the PLO has eroded, even at the ministerial level. Apprehensions over the establishment of a Palestinian state have also diminished. During the 1980s, however, the party position clearly ran counter to such a state and, though less unequivocally, to talks with the PLO.

Undoubtedly, the developments in the PLO and the subsequent U.S.

decision to hold talks with that organization created additional tension in the party between doves and hawks. The doves, who were generally reluctant to join the 1988 National Unity government led by Likud leader Yitzhak Shamir, used these developments in the PLO to question the wisdom of becoming a partner with Likud in the government. Disagreements over policy were intertwined with calls for a change in the party leadership.

The suspension of the U.S. dialogue with the PLO and the latter's alliance with Baghdad in the Gulf crisis placed additional obstacles on the Laborite road to formally accepting the PLO as a legitimate interlocutor. The widespread Palestinian support for Saddam Hussein similarly cast into some doubt the greater role the party had ascribed to them in future negotiations. Yet despite the deep disappointment and frustration with the PLO and Palestinians among Israeli doves, including Laborites, most still held to their old views about the centrality of the Palestinian issue and the urgent need to involve, as difficult as it may be, the PLO in a developing peace process. Such doves as Beilin, Burg, Eliav, Dayan, and Peretz regarded the setback to rapprochement as quite real, but temporary. They asserted that despite the mistakes of the Palestinian leadership, the conflict between Israelis and Palestinians still had to be resolved and the occupation had to be ended.[111] In contrast, the hawks regarded the policies of the PLO and the behavior of the Palestinians as conforming their higher threat perception and their view that the Palestinian issue was marginal and should be treated as such. All in all, the Iraqi threat, at least for the time being, placed greater stress on the interstate dimension of the conflict at the expense of the Israeli–Palestinian dimension.

In regard to the future, we may predict that the pragmatic nature of Labor's leadership will enable it to accommodate further revisions in its stance on the negotiating partner. If convinced that it was necessary or expedient, both Peres and Rabin could adjust their views to changing circumstances; moreover, the contenders for the leadership position are all willing to consider a PLO role under certain circumstances. The actual content of the political settlement desired by party members is discussed in Chapter 5.

NOTES

1. See Uri Bar-Yoseph, *The Best of Enemies: Israel and Transjordan in the War of 1948* (London: Frank Cass, 1987); Aaron Klieman, *Unpeaceful Coexistence: Israel, Jordan, and the Palestinians* (Hebrew) (Tel Aviv: Maariv Library, 1986); Dan Shueftan, *The Jordanian Option* (Hebrew) (Tel Aviv: Hakibbutz Hameuchad Publishing House, 1986).

2. For a sympathetic account of the efforts made by Peres, see Arye Naor, *The Writing on the Wall* (Hebrew) (Tel Aviv: Edanim, 1988), pp. 125–165.

3. *Haaretz*, August 4, 1988; Avraham Tirosh, "Interview with Peres," *Maariv*, October 28, 1988.

4. *Haaretz*, August 4, 1988, pp. 4–5.
5. Yehezkel Dror, *Crazy States* (Lexington: D.C. Heath, 1973), pp. 4–5.
6. For Bar-Lev's views, see *Maariv*, August 9, 1988; for Tzur's views, see *Haaretz*, August 16, 1988; for Weizman's views, see *Maariv*, August 2, 1988.
7. This project was ill-managed by Peres's advisors, and misfired politically.
8. *Haaretz*, March 21, 1989.
9. *Haaretz*, February 12, 1989.
10. For the Palestinian national movement, see Yehoshua Porat, *The Emergence of the Palestinian–Arab National Movement, 1918–1929* (London: Frank Cass, 1974); his companion volume, *The Emergence of the Palestinian–Arab National Movement, 1929–1939* (London: Frank Cass, 1977); William B. Quandt, Fouad Jabber, and Ann Moseley Lesch, *The Politics of Palestinian Nationalism* (Berkeley: University of California Press, 1973); Helena Cobban, *The Palestinian Liberation Organization* (Cambridge: Cambridge University Press, 1984).
11. Sunday Times, June 15, 1969. For her position on the Palestinian issue, see Amnon Sella, "Custodians and Redeemers: Israeli Leaders' Perceptions of Peace, 1967–1979," *Middle Eastern Studies* 22 (April 1986), p. 245.
12. For an analysis of its covenant, see Yehoshafat Harkabi, *Palestinians and Israel* (Jerusalem: Keter, 1974), pp. 49–69. As noted in the previous chapter, Harkabi differentiates between a grand design and policy goals.
13. Interview with Yossi Sarid; Aryeh Haas, "A New Political Platform for the Labor Party," *Bama*, February 1, 1986.
14. For a summary of the dovish position and an attempt to refute it, see Chaim Bar-Lev, "The Future of the Territories—A Compromise or a State?" *Migvan* 43 (January 1980), pp. 3–6.
15. For an academic counterargument, see Mark Heller, *A Palestinian State: The Implications for Israel* (Cambridge: Harvard University Press, 1983).
16. "The Dovecot," *Spectrum* 5 (April 1987), p. 12.
17. *Maariv*, February 17, 1988.
18. *Maariv*, October 12, 1987.
19. *Maariv*, April 28, 1987.
20. *Yediot Achronot*, October 30, 1980.
21. *Maariv*, April 28, 1987.
22. Transcript of Rabin interview on Israeli TV, January 13, 1988, *Journal of Palestine Studies* 17 (Spring 1988), p. 153. See also a similar statement in *Haaretz*, June 1, 1988.
23. "Interview with Rabin," *Migvan* 72 (August 1982), p. 6.
24. For Navon's position, see Yossi Beilin, *The Price of Unity*, p. 42; for Eliav's views, see his *Eretz Hatzvi*, pp. 141–142.
25. *Maariv*, December 23, 1987.
26. "Interview with Ezer Weizman," *Spectrum* 6 (June 1988), p. 10.
27. Yitzhak Rabin, "Middle East Chess: King's Move," p. 8.
28. Yitzhak Rabin, "Learning from History," *Spectrum* 6 (May 1988), p. 10.
29. Ibid.
30. For an elaboration of the two dimensions of the Arab–Israeli conflict, see Shmuel Sandler and Hillel Frisch, *Israel, the West Bank and the Palestinians* (Lexington: Lexington Books, 1984), pp. 1–12; and Shmuel Sandler, "The Protracted Arab–Israeli Conflict: A Temporal–Spatial Analysis," Jerusalem Journal of International Relations 10 (December 1988), pp. 54–78.
31. Naomi Chazan, "Domestic Developments in Israel," in *The Middle East:*

Ten Years After Camp David, ed. William B. Quandt (Washington, D.C.: The Brookings Institution, 1988), pp. 161-164.
32. Emile Sahliyeh, "Jordan and the Palestinians," in *The Middle East: Ten Years After Camp David*, ed. Quandt, pp. 309-312.
33. *Kol Ha'ir*, September 23, 1988.
34. *Maariv Magazine*, May 19, 1989.
35. "Interview with Yitzhak Rabin," Jerusalem Post, May 19, 1989.
36. The Platform for the 8th Knesset (Hebrew) (The Alignment, December 31, 1973), pp. 4-5.
37. See, e.g., Mapam's reaction, in *New Outlook*, vols. 16-17 (December 1973-January 1974), p. 47.
38. The Platform for the 9th Knesset (Hebrew) (The Alignment, May 1977), articles 6 and 9, p. 4.
39. The Platform for the 9th Knesset, article 6, p. 4.
40. Yitzhak Rabin, *Memoirs* (Hebrew) (Tel Aviv: Maariv Library, 1978), p. 496.
41. The Platform for the 10th Knesset, article 1, p. 10.
42. The Platform for the 10th Knesset, articles 4 and 7, p. 6.
43. *Sidra Medinit*, no. 1, Israeli Labor Party, December 1981, p. 10. (This is another publication of the party.)
44. The Platform for the 10th Knesset, article 8, p. 6.
45. See MK Michael Harish, "The Rearguard Battle," *Migvan* 42 (December 1979), p. 17.
46. *Haaretz*, August 16, 1988; interview with MK Chaim Ramon; for Beilin's claim, see *Maariv*, August 18, 1988.
47. For Rabin's opposition to the Yariv-Shemtov formula, see Yitzhak Rabin, "Against Labor's Autonomy Plan," *Migvan* 36 (May 1979), p. 6.
48. See Simcha Dinitz, "The Path to Change Goes Via the PLO," *Baavoda*, no. 10 (October 1986), pp. 1-3. *Baavoda* is a party organ.
49. Minutes of the Convention, Political-Security Affairs Meeting, March 4, 1986, p. 127.
50. Shmuel Bahat and Dr. Israel Gat, eds., *A Selection of Decisions and Conclusions of Leshiluv, A Zionist-Socialist Circle in the Labor Party*, p. 17.
51. *Yediot Achronot*, October 30, 31, 1980.
52. *The Israeli Labor Party*, no. 10 (Hebrew), December 1986, p. 9.
53. See the signatories on the declaration in *Spectrum* 5 (April 1987), inner cover page.
54. *Yediot Achronot*, October 31, 1980.
55. See Dinitz, "The Path to Change Goes Via the PLO," pp. 1-3.
56. *Maariv*, March 8, 1986.
57. *The Israeli Labor Party*, no. 10, p. 10.
58. *Maariv*, April 10, 1986.
59. See Sandler and Frisch, *Israel, the West Bank and the Palestinians*, pp. 58-70; 150-157.
60. *Maariv*, August 19, 1988.
61. The Platform for the 12th Knesset (Hebrew) (The Israeli Labor Party, October 1988), article 1.2.6, p. 10 (for the offical English version, see Appendix B); for the changes suggested after an intensive struggle between hawks and doves in a Labor subcommittee drafting the party election platform, see *Maariv*, August 19, 1988. For reports of the intraparty struggle, see *Maariv*, August 16, 18, 19, 1988; *Haaretz*, August 16, 17, 18, 1988; *Jerusalem Post*, August 16, 1988.
62. *Maariv*, August 1, 1988; *Haaretz*, August 11, 16, 1988.
63. See *Maariv*, August 2, 1988.

64. For Beilin's suggestion, see *Maariv*, August 16, 1988; for Ramon's, see *Haaretz*, August 18, 1988.
65. *Haaretz*, August 11, 1988.
66. *Davar*, May 13, 1988.
67. *Haaretz*, June 1, 1988.
68. For Beilin's and Burg's suggestion, see *Haaretz*, August 2, 1988; for Chaim Tzadok, see his "On the Negotiating Table and Beneath It," *Davar*, February 12, 1988. For Tzadok's dovish views, as early as 1971, see Beilin, *The Price of Unity*, p. 149.
69. *Haaretz*, May 13, 1988.
70. "Interview with Rabin," *Spectrum* 6 (March 1988), p. 12.
71. *Haaretz*, March 27, 1988; *Maariv*, August 1, 1988. For Weizman's willingness to talk to the PLO, see "The Dovecot," *Spectrum* 5 (April 1987), p. 12; also his statement to *Haaretz*, August 2, 1988.
72. "Never Say Never," *Spectrum* 6 (February 1988), p. 19.
73. Menachem Rahat, "Doves and Hawks Under Rabin's Wings," *Maariv*, March 25, 1988.
74. *Maariv*, March 3, 1988.
75. *Maariv*, February 5, 1988.
76. Yakir Tzur, "Interview with Peres," Davar, November 25, 1988.
77. *Haaretz*, November 17, 1988. For Navon's disappointment at the Algiers resolutions, see *Haaretz*, November 20, 1988.
78. *Haaretz*, November 18, 1988.
79. Dan Petreanu, "Labour's PLO Dilemma," *Jerusalem Post*, January 20, 1988.
80. *Maariv*, December 19, 1988.
81. *Maariv*, June 7, 1988.
82. *Maariv*, January 6, 1989.
83. *Jerusalem Post*, March 10, 1989.
84. Dan Petreanu, "Labour's PLO Dilemma."
85. *Maariv*, January 13, 1989.
86. Ibid. See also "Interview with Yitzhak Rabin," *Jerusalem Post*, May 19, 1989.
87. *Yediot Achronot*, January 31, 1989.
88. *Haaretz*, December 12, 1988.
89. Petreanu, "Labour's PLO Dilemma."
90. Amnon Lin, "PLO: All the Facts," *Maariv*, February 1, 1989.
91. See also Amos Carmel's opposition in his "No Good News," *Yediot Achronot*, February 23, 1989.
92. Interview with MK Shlomo Hillel, April 20, 1990.
93. Eti Chasid, "Interview with Bar-Lev," *Haaretz Magazine*, December 30, 1988.
94. *Haaretz*, May 12, 1989.
95. See Gideon Levi, "Interview with Gur," *Haaretz Magazine*, February 10, 1989; *Maariv*, February 17, 1989.
96. *Maariv*, January 6, 1989.
97. *Haaretz*, March 7, 1989.
98. *Maariv*, May 19, 1989.
99. Gad Yaakobi, "From Bunkers to a New Political Process," *Maariv*, January 1, 1988.
100. *Davar*, December 12, 1988. For his support for talks with the PLO, see his "There's No Alternative to a Dialogue With the PLO," *Haaretz*, June 20, 1989; "We and the Changing World," *Haaretz*, November 23, 1989.

101. *Maariv*, December 12, 1988.
102. *Maariv*, January 15, 1988.
103. Israel Landers, "Interview with Ora Namir," *Davar*, December 23, 1988; see also Aliza Walach, "Interview with Ora Namir," *Davar*, January 20, 1989.
104. See Ramon's statement to *Davar*, September 8, 1989; and Baram, "There's No Alternative to a Dialogue With the PLO."
105. For the most eloquent presentation, see Abba Eban, "Negotiate Now—From Strength," *Jerusalem Post*, February 10, 1989, and his "The 'Partner' Fantasy," *Jerusalem Post*, July 14, 1989.
106. Petreanu, "Labour's PLO Dilemma."
107. For Beilin's remarks from the Knesset rostrum, see *Spectrum* 8 (March 1990), p. 28.
108. Interviews with MKs Arad, Burg, and Dayan.
109. Elazar Hacohen, "Meetings With the PLO," *Spectrum* 8 (January 1990), p. 26. The yonetz MK David Libai initiated the amendment.
110. See Zeev Schiff, "A Hostile Cease-Fire," *Haaretz*, May 13, 1990.
111. *Haaretz*, September 19, 1990.

CHAPTER 5
The Content of the Future Agreements

In contrast to the clear move toward a dovish position concerning the Palestinians in the 1980s, the direction taken by the party on the territorial issue was less sharply defined, though dovish tendencies were discernible. Inside the party, as elsewhere, the territorial component of the desired future agreements with the Arab states was the main focus of attention. Yet how much territory to be yielded by Israel was not the only question involved in the design of the future settlement. Other questions involved the type of control to be maintained over territories retained; the political future of the territories ceded; the security measures to be sustained following an agreement; the future of Israeli settlements; the fate of the Palestinian refugees; and the political return for Israeli concessions. The party also distinguished between a permanent settlement that would incorporate a full political quid pro quo, i.e., peace, and an interim agreement with more modest political returns. The price to be paid and the element of risk involved for Israel differed according to the type of agreement. Party members also raised the possibility of unilateral Israeli steps. The character of the desired agreements, as well as the nature of the unilateral solutions, are analyzed in this chapter.

THE PERMANENT SETTLEMENT

The party was united on the principle of territories for peace, known in Israeli political parlance as "territorial compromise." Unlike the Likud, there were no signs among Laborites in the 1980s of an ideological commitment to the idea of a Greater Israel. Even Labor's hawks, some of whom, like Yitzhak Rabin, publicly proclaimed the Jewish people's right to all of Palestine, reconciled themselves, albeit with great pain, to the necessity for partition.[1] As a matter of fact, various degrees of attachment to all parts of the historic homeland were to be found in all quarters of the party, with no necessary correspondence to the degree of territorial largesse. Territories acquired in 1967 were thus to be exchanged for peace. Yet the party made it clear that peace was not to come at any cost. Border revisions were necessary for security reasons and, in the case of Jerusalem, for symbolic and sentimental considerations as well. This city evoked feelings too strong to be the subject of utilitarian discourse among most Jews. Indeed, its eastern part was annexed immediately after the 1967 war.

With the exception of Jerusalem, however, the party formally opposed any unilateral annexation of territories, even in the case of those areas it insisted on incorporating into Israel once a formal understanding with the Arabs was reached. Despite the fact that proposals for unilateral measures were aired by party members, the party remained firm on the issue of a negotiated settlement. The military deployment and administration in place in the Israeli-ruled territories was regarded as temporary, until a permanent solution agreeable to Israel and its Arab rivals was attained.

The Political Quid Pro Quo

The expected political outcome of a permanent agreement was peace, a term that members of the Labor Party, without exception, took to mean mutual recognition, full diplomatic relations, and a free movement of people and cargo. Israelis have always dreamed of breaking the wall of Arab hostility and of fully integrating into the Middle East. Because Egypt accepted Israeli demands on this issue when it signed the 1979 peace treaty with Israel, demanding the same from other Arab states was considered reasonable. The rather cool Egyptian attitude toward normalization of relations with the Jewish state educated many Israelis about the short-range limits of integration in the region, but did not influence their insistence on the formal aspects of a peaceful relationship. Furthermore, this definition of peace was supported by U.S. diplomacy, though the United States did not back other elements of the Labor-endorsed future agreement. It was expected, though not explicitly mentioned, that a settlement would include some kind of U.S. commitment to come to Israel's aid, or to allow Israel a free hand, in case the peace treaty was not fully observed by the Arab side. A discussion of the perceived U.S. role in reaching regional agreements is beyond the scope of this work, but it should be noted that the stability of a negotiated permanent agreement was not taken for granted. The perceived chances for its duration were closely related to levels of threat perception and to evaluations of the probability of peace (discussed in Chapter 3).

The Territorial Dimension

Labor's "territorial compromise" formula has been formally incorporated into party platforms since 1973. Essentially, this formula refers to major changes along the 1967 borders with Egypt, Syria, and Jordan, coupled with complementary security arrangements. The extent of the territories to be retained, what type of control they were to be under, and under what circumstances, were issues that generated a great deal of attention and debate.[2]

The disputes over the southern border in the Sinai ended, however, in March 1979, following the Knesset ratification of the peace treaty with Egypt. Thus in the 1980s the Sinai was a nonissue; the party—particularly the hawks, who had in the 1970s advocated significant border changes in the Sinai to satisfy security concerns—reconciled itself to the return to the 1967 international border with Egypt. Indeed, the party dropped from its platform any territorial claims in the Sinai.

Similarly, the determination of Israel's northern border with Syria aroused little agitation in the party. Widespread consensus prevailed in all party quarters for keeping the Golan Heights, and territorial concessions Labor leaders were ready to make there were minimal. However, though not publicized, the possibility of dismantling a few settlements close to the border was not ruled out, even by the party's hawks. Already in 1976, Rabin used the term "painful solutions" when referring to a future interim agreement on the Golan.[3] Gur, in his opposition to any territorial concession on the Golan, was an exception.[4] Yet Syria clearly showed little interest in expanding its political commitment to Israel beyond the 1974 agreement to disengage forces, negotiated after the October War. Syria's and Israel's increased involvement in Lebanon after the outbreak of the civil war (1975) opened up a new arena of competition and cooperation between the two countries, but had little effect on Syria's reluctance to abandon its fundamental position of uncompromising enmity toward the "Zionist entity." As there were no chances of a political quid pro quo for Israeli territorial concessions, any erosion in the Israeli consensus on the strategic need to retain the Golan, or at least most of it, was highly unlikely. A hawkish position of territorial maximalism in this region was also easier to sustain than in regard to the West Bank, since the Golan was clearly an indispensable strategic asset sparsely populated by non-Jews. The "demographic problem" that haunted the Laborites' attitudes toward the West Bank in the 1980s, as well as the problems connected with the occupation tasks there, did not exist on the Golan Heights. In addition, the 1981 annexation of the Golan commanded a large consensus in Israel. Since withdrawal from the Golan was not an issue, and since the southern border was a closed topic, the territorial debate in the 1980s therefore focused on Judea, Samaria, and, to a lesser extent, on the Gaza Strip.

Interestingly enough, even the most dovish elements in the party rejected the claims of a few extreme doves (the best known being Meron Benvenisti) that the massive Jewish settlement conducted by the Likud-led governments between 1977 and 1984 had created an irreversible situation in Judea and Samaria. Future partition in those areas was still considered possible.[5]

The basic concept of a territorial settlement in the east during the 1980s continued to be the Allon Plan. Yigal Allon (1918–1981), a prominent Laborite leader, submitted his plan for consideration to the government in the summer of 1967, but to prevent its rejection, no vote was taken on it. Allon presented his plan in public in 1972.[6] According to this plan, Israeli sovereignty was to be extended to several security zones, as seen in the map. These included a strip along the Jordan River reaching to the Dead Sea (the Jordan Valley Rift), with a width of 14 kilometers in the north and 24 kilometers in the south. Other areas to be annexed were Greater Jerusalem, including a new city east of it known today as Maale Adumim; the Gush Etzion area south of Jerusalem; the area south of Hebron (including the newly built city of Kiryat Arba, east of Hebron); and several kilometers of expansion northeastward in the Latrun area. A corridor from the Jordan River through Jericho and up to Ramallah was to remain in Arab hands, together with the densely populated Arab areas on the ridge of the mountains north and south of Jerusalem. Initially, Allon planned the annexation of the Gaza Strip, but as of 1972 only its southern part was to be incorporated into a security zone, in addition to the adjacent Rafiah salient in the Sinai.[7] This plan attempted to reconcile Israel's need for defensible borders—those borders providing both strategic depth and the option of absorbing the enemy's first strike—with the aim of preserving a solid Jewish majority.[8] Allon believed that an Israeli military presence along the Jordan River, and around the few passages controlling land routes toward the center of the country, was of vital strategic importance. Gradually, in the late 1960s and early 1970s, the party's center and left accepted the Allon Plan as the basic framework for a permanent solution. Prominent party doves such as Chaim Tzadok and Avraham Ofer, both ministers in Rabin's government (1974–1977), already favored the territorial compromise formula even before 1973,[9] while the party right wing preferred retaining Israeli control over all of western Palestine. Rabin favored the plan of his former commander in the Palmah, Allon, from the beginning, as did other middle-of-the-road Laborites. The explicit Allon Plan was formally adopted by the party only in 1977, but by 1990 only the party's hawks still adhered to it in its entirety.

Until 1977, the Labor Party refused either to officially adopt the plan or to specify which territories were of security importance and could not therefore be relinquished following a withdrawal. In fact, Labor-led Israeli governments refrained from using the term withdrawal at all. UN Security Council Resolution 242 of November 1967, which stipulated withdrawal to defensible borders, was only accepted by Labor-led Israel in 1970. It was argued that from a negotiating standpoint an elaboration of Israel's minimum territorial requirements was counterproductive. Furthermore, the factional nature of the Labor Party allowed its hawkish elements to prevent the public specification advocated by the doves. At that time two of the three factions in the Labor Party, Rafi and Achdut Haavodah, were hawkish. Despite the rivalry between them, and the fact that they controlled only some 40 percent of members in decision-making forums, they succeeded—with the help of hawks from the third and largest faction, Mapai—in persuading the party to adopt a rather hawkish line.[10] The government's bargaining strategy was

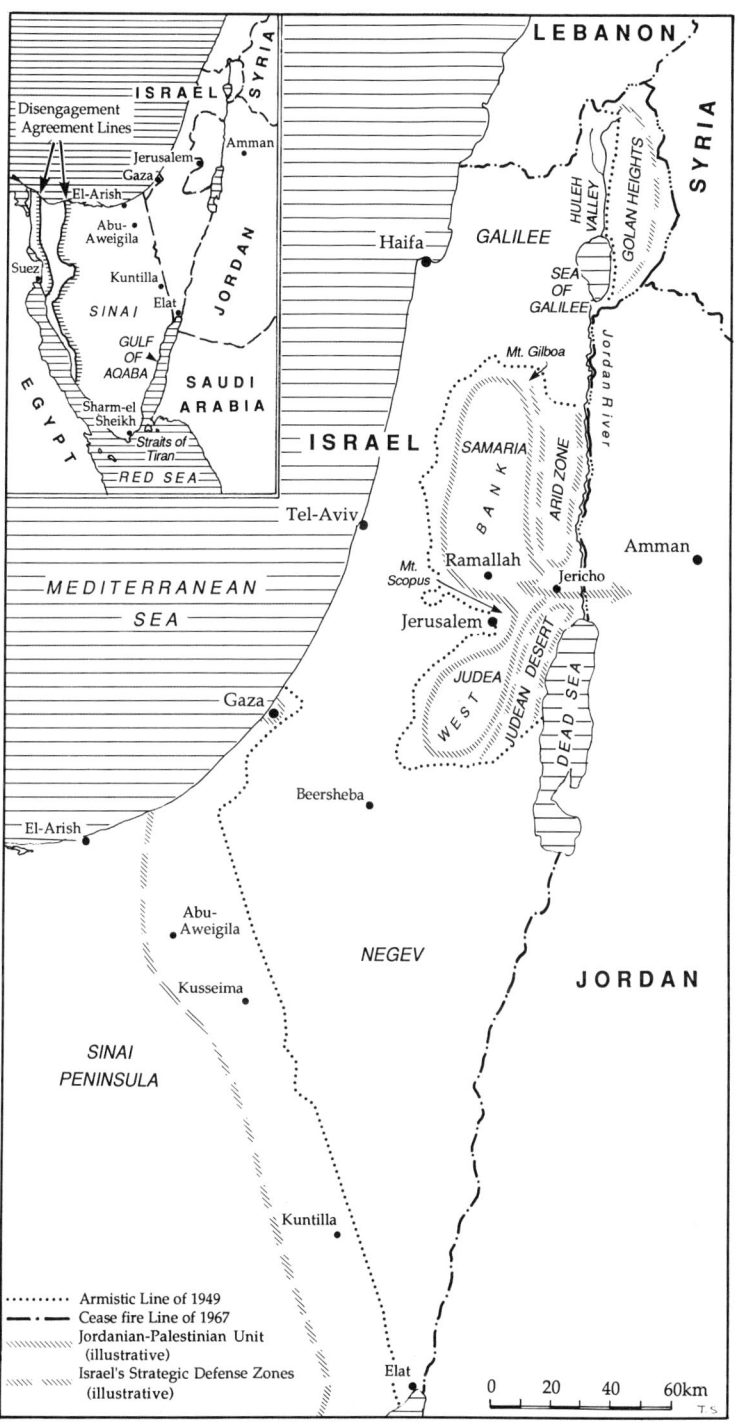

reinforced by party politics. In all fairness, however, though the party had not formally backed the territorial compromise formula, most Laborite ministers in the Labor-led governments before 1973 were tacitly in favor of it, and the settlement policy of the Labor-led governments prior to that year also conformed with the Allon Plan.

Before 1977, some of the party hawks, notably Moshe Dayan and Shimon Peres, actually advocated a functional compromise instead of a territorial one. This was a "rule-sharing" approach, which recommended that the territory of the West Bank not be divided between Israel and Jordan, but only the governmental functions in this region.[11] Its basic assumption was strategic, as it attached vital importance to the mountains in the heart of Judea and Samaria for the defense of Israel (in contrast to the Allon Plan, which placed the emphasis on the Jordan Valley Rift). Unfortunately for Israel, this area happened to be densely populated by Arabs, and annexation was therefore regarded as undesirable.[12]

Following the October War, the party leadership—primarily the premier, Golda Meir, and her defense minister, Moshe Dayan, both hawks—was discredited and a new leadership emerged. In addition, the factional regime broke down.[13] These intraparty developments, which were conected to the political upheaval following the war, allowed for revisions in the party positions, which were expressed also in the party platform. The platform for the December 1973 elections mentioned "territorial compromise" for the first time. Furthermore, following the shock of the 1973 war, the hawkish Galili Document, adopted before the outbreak of the war, was deleted from the party platform.[14] The new platform also reflected changes in regard to the Palestinian issue.

The Rabin government (1974–1977), which succeeded that of Meir, displayed territorial flexibility in the south and in the north. It implemented a limited withdrawal in the Sinai in September 1975. Furthermore, in January 1976 Rabin, bowing to U.S. pressure, agreed to consider some territorial adjustments even on the Golan.[15] Yet his government, which included Peres as defense minister, persisted in its reluctance to "draw maps," as specification of concessions was known in Israeli political parlance, although the party's left pressed in that direction.[16] Labor was then unwilling to state its minimum territorial requirements. Allon, for example, who served as foreign minister in that period, was heavily criticized in his party for publishing an article that delineated the principles of territorial compromise in accordance with his famous plan.[17] Despite reluctance to verbally "draw maps," the Rabin government continued the settlement policy according to the Allon Plan. Actually, a new area was added in Samaria. The settlements three to eight kilometers east of the Green Line (the 1967 border) were supposed to widen the narrow waist of the 1967 borders and to ensure control over the aquifers located there.[18]

The party congress in February 1977 formally accepted the defensible borders approach according to the Allon Plan, and rejected the functional compromise defended by Dayan at the congress.[19] Indeed, several months later the Allon Plan was incorporated into the party platform for the 9th Knesset (1977), which was quite explicit about the nature of the preferred defensible borders. The term "security zones" was used for the first time here. Those mentioned were the areas around Jerusalem, the Golan, the Jordan Valley Rift, the Rafiah salient, and the Sharm-el-Sheikh region (at the tip of the Sinai peninsula in the Straits of Tiran).[20] Another new feature of the 1977 platform, also in the dovish direction, was the explicit application of the principle of territorial compromise to future political settlements with Jordan, Egypt, and even Syria. Rabin's informal concession to the United States in 1976 was transformed into a formal pledge.

This greater explicitness concerning the scope of an Israeli withdrawal was viewed in the late 1960s and 1970s as a clear indication of dovish leanings. Until the mid-1970s, the Allon Plan represented a middle-of-the-road approach that most doves in the party could accept. They advocated "drawing maps," and Allon did not object. It took several years, however, before the party platform in 1977 included the explicit Allon formula for secure borders, a fact that indicated the party's adoption of stances previously advocated by its doves.

The Evolution of Party Positions After 1977

The 1978 Camp David Accords stand out as representing a drastic change in Israel's diplomatic history. The Labor Party—or at least the majority of its parliamentary faction—then in opposition, voted in favor of the accords in the Knesset despite many misgivings. As a matter of fact, Labor's support was crucial for the Knesset's approval of the accords. As pointed out, only nineteen Labor MKs voted in favor of the Camp David agreement, while four opposed it and three abstained. The MKs against the accords were Shlomo Hillel, Shoshana Arbeli-Almozlino, Amos Hadar, and Yehezkel Zakai (the last two were representatives of the moshav movement). The abstainees were Yigal Allon, Dani Rosolio (of Hakibbutz Hameuchad), and Tamar Eshel. This agreement, which committed Israel to return all of Sinai to Egypt, was in fact an abandonment of the defensible borders concept. Indeed, already by the 1970s, in the aftermath of the Yom Kippur War, looser interpretations of the concept surfaced in the strategic thinking of Laborites. Though the term "defensible borders" was still in usage, it referred to border changes to accommodate some Israeli defense needs rather than to its exact initial meaning.[21] For example, in October 1980 during the debates on the party platform for the next year's elections, Bar-Lev even suggested replacing the term "defensible borders" with less exacting appellations, such as "reasonable borders" or "good borders"; on the same occasion Eban proposed using "a territorial agreement" instead of "territorial compromise."[22] Then the dovish

"77 Circle" demanded an explicit statement that Labor wanted to return to the 1967 borders with minimal rectifications.[23] This thinking deviated from the general scheme of the Allon Plan in its willingness to take greater security risks and in its emphasis on political considerations for providing security rather than territorial factors. In other words, political agreement based on Arab acceptance of Israel was given security value.

In the 1980s, because of the party's shift to the left, supporters of the Allon Plan were identified in the party as its hawks; its doves envisioned a return to the 1967 borders on the eastern front, with slight rectifications, primarily in the Jerusalem area. Explicit public expressions in this vein by dovish senior Laborites were still quite rare, as this could estrange them from party colleagues when running for a party position. The perception that the electorate leaned toward the right also inhibited the airing of such views. Privately, however, their territorial generosity was great indeed.

In April 1986 at the party congress, the doves, in accordance with their stance of territorial minimalism, managed to get the southern Gaza Strip removed from the party's list of security zones. The security significance of that region, which in the aftermath of the Camp David Accords was designed to substitute for the Rafiah settlements as a security zone, was belittled by the doves, even by some who were not obvious doves. The most striking example of this was cabinet member Avraham Katz-Oz, then a yonetz MK.[24] Katz-Oz suggested putting an end to Jewish settlement in the midst of Arab populated areas in the Gaza strip, but advocated annexing a very limited section of the strip for security reasons. Katz-Oz voted, as mentioned, for annexing the sparsely Druze populated Golan Heights. Another amendment designating only the Jordan Valley Rift and Jerusalem as security zones failed to receive the backing of the party congress.[25] Nevertheless, all this discussion indicated erosion in party support for the original Allon Plan. Greater support was given to the retention of Jerusalem and the sparsely populated Jordan Valley Rift than to retention of the other security zones mentioned in the party platform. Hillel and other hawks wished also to include in the platform's list of security zones the Yatir region south of Hebron, a region that was part of the original Allon Plan. But they were unsuccessful in this endeavor, and after 1986 the attempt was not repeated, a further sign of the dovish power to block such a step in the party. In fact, at the preparatory committee of the 1986 congress, Peres attempted, albeit unsuccessfully, to delete explicit mention of all security zones.[26] MK Chaim Ramon placed the same amendment on the Congress agenda, but it was defeated. The decisions of the congress were incorporated into the party platform for the 1988 elections (see Appendix B).

Ironically, the hawks' opposition to map drawing in the late 1960s and early 1970s was taken up by old and new doves in the late 1980s, by which time the magnitude of territory from which doves would consider withdrawing had increased. They therefore preferred vague phraseology concerning territorial changes, so as to prevent an overly strong party commitment to the Allon Plan, which was not to their liking.[27]

Peres even decided in 1987 to stop using the Hebrew names (Judea and Samaria) for the administered territories—an obvious attempt to delegitimize Jewish claims to those areas.[28] Indeed, in the party's 1988 Plan for Peace and Security, which Peres himself drafted in April 1988, he did not name any security zones (see Appendix A). The program read: "Israel will not return to the 1967 borders and will continue to hold territories which are not populated and are important for its security." The exclusion from the party Plan for Peace and Security of explicit mention of specific security zones, and the document's silence on the matter of Israeli sovereignty in those zones following an agreement, was censured by Hillel and other hawks in the party.[29] Their criticism was directed at the informal decision-making process as well. Peres, who was not mentioned by name in their remarks, was actually being blamed for abusing his leadership position. The version that the party approved in May did cite the Jordan Valley Rift, an addition that was a gesture to the hawks.[30] Peres, however, during a tour of the Jewish settlements in the Jordan rift, refused to commit himself to any statement that this area had to stay under Israeli sovereignty.[31] The "Generals' Plan"—a proposal that the party publicized during its 1988 elections campaign, following instructions from Peres and his dovish advisors—similarly refrained both from specifying security zones and from even using the term sovereignty in reference to those areas. All this was to the hawks' chagrin. They consoled themselves that Peres was unable to change the platform.

The move toward dovish positions after 1973 was not unequivocal. From 1981 on, the platform continued to specify that the security zones should be under Israeli sovereignty, a demand disputed by party doves who preferred the term "control." This more ambiguous term was perceived as more acceptable to the Arab side. In contrast, the politico-strategic rationale advocated by the hawks demanded that those areas be under Israeli sovereignty; any other arrangement, they argued, would create a precarious situation. In addition, establishment by the IDF of "foreign bases" in the West Bank could result in future demands for termination of the Israeli military presence. Formal annexation would also mean that any entry of Arab forces into the security zones would be a breach of Israeli sovereignty justifying an Israeli military response. The security zones specified in 1981 also included the Gush Etzion area (usually regarded as part of the Jerusalem region) as well as the northern section of the Dead Sea area.

Furthermore, following the Likud-initiated Golan annexation in December 1981, the 1984 Labor party platform dropped its explicit reference to a possible territorial compromise with Syria, though even the party hawks were ready to make some territorial concessions on the Golan. As noted, Syria's unabated opposition to the Jewish state showed no sign of any change that might have warranted more conciliatory language.

In fact, some Laborite hawks were quite pleased with Likud's annexation bill, since this is what they also advocated at least as a way of buttressing Israeli claims for major adjustments along the Syrian border. In 1980 and 1981, hawkish leaders such as Israel Galili had made an unsuccessful attempt to include a demand for such annexation in the platform.[32] Despite the fact that the Labor Knesset faction, then in opposition, decided to deny its support for unilateral annexation of the Golan, eight Labor MKs voted with the coalition to pass the bill—Jacques Amir, Shoshana Arbeli-Almozlino, Tamar Eshel, Shlomo Hillel, Avraham Katz-Oz, Raanan Naim, Dani Rosolio, and Yaakov Tzur. The vote indicated the persisting influence of the hawkish perspective. Katz-Oz, for example, was a yonetz rather than a hawk. Similarly, Tzur, though moving toward yonetz positions, voted for annexation, and used this occasion to protest against full withdrawal from the Sinai.[33] Tzur displayed hawkishness on the territorial issue on another occasion as well: in 1986, he demanded that Gaza be restored to the list of security zones. Gaza was, of course, much less coveted territorially than the Golan. Indeed, in 1986 the party congress passed a resolution stating that "Israel views the Golan Heights as an area which is important to its welfare and security and will act to strengthen the settlements there." This article was incorporated in the 1988 party platform (see Appendix B). Yet this should not be construed as an abandonment by Labor of its readiness for border revisions on the Golan, a stance shared by almost all party members.

An unusual hawkish proposal was aired in 1988 by Micha Goldman, a member of the Dor Hemshech group, who became an MK at the end of that year. He called for unilateral annexation of the security zones specified in the party platform. A member of the Rabin camp, his closeness to Rabin made it necessary for the defense minister to publicly disassociate himself from the proposal. Goldman was not the only one in the party who had such thoughts, and a more limited annexation of the northern part of the Jordan Valley Rift was discussed in the United Kibbutz Movement.[34] As the party drafted its platform in August 1988, before the November elections, similar suggestions were made by the hawks, primarily to counter dovish amendments. A more serious effort, led by the Central Stream activist Zisman, was mounted to gain support for annexing the Maale Adumim area, a security zone east of Jerusalem (in the administered territories).[35] This effort was not, however, successful. In 1990, the party remained formally committed to negotiate the Allon Plan.

During the 1980s the party leadership, with the exception of the hawks, generally refrained from any detailed discussion of the territorial component of a future agreement. One of the few to go into greater detail as to the future territorial settlement was Yitzhak Rabin. He adhered to the security zones mentioned in the platform, and did not hesitate to explicitly name all of them. He stated that the Greater Jerusalem area included the town of

Maale Adumim, east of Jerusalem,[36] and specified the magnitude of the annexation: "About a third, more or less, of the territory of the West Bank and the Gaza strip must be included in the context of peace, under Israeli sovereignty."[37] Rabin was not oblivious to the Arabs living in the territories intended for annexation. In 1988 he envisioned an enlarged Israel "with an additional half million [Arabs] over and above the present 700,000."[38] As for these additional Palestinians living within Israel, Rabin was willing to offer them the choice of becoming Israeli citizens or of remaining Jordanians.[39] Hillel similarly acknowledged the fact that an additional number of Arabs would have to be absorbed into Israel in order to secure defensible borders. Such statements were made despite awareness of the "demographic problem."

Bar-Lev, like Rabin, adhered to the Allon Plan.[40] During the 1980s, however, he appeared to move leftward and even found it necessary, in the 1988 party elections for the Knesset list, to dispel rumors of dovishness. In 1988 Bar-Lev, unlike other hawks, preferred to emphasize the need to control only the Jordan Valley Rift, but insisted rather hawkishly on Israeli sovereignty there.[41] As mentioned, Bar-Lev favored a limited withdrawal on the Golan Heights under certain circumstances. In 1990, however, Bar-Lev became an unreserved hawk.

Yaakobi suggested border rectifications in the area east of the Latrun–Cfar Saba line. Regarding the Jordan Valley Rift, Greater Jerusalem, and the Golan Heights, he was satisfied with continued Israeli "control" only.[42] Shahal, in a clearly dovish manner, publicized his own peace plan, in which he demanded a united Jerusalem under Israeli sovereignty.[43] He underlined his wish to put an end to Israeli rule over more than 1.5 million Arabs, and did not hesitate to declare, "I sanctify nothing, except Jerusalem and security."[44] This was an obvious deviation from the party platform. Weizman, the newcomer to the party, had no qualms in 1987 about directly challenging the territorial clauses in the platform and belittling their importance. He demanded that the party cease adhering to the Allon Plan and stop regarding the Jordan as Israel's security border.[45] Other doves were reluctant to disassociate themselves completely from their own party's program, although they fought hard to change it. Peres, as noted, preferred not to mention any security zones, despite his occasional statements in favor of the Allon Plan.

Those who supported a territorial compromise, and who preferred Hussein as negotiating partner, argued that he could be enticed into a deal with Israel since the Gaza Strip, or most of it, would be offered to him. Bar-Lev and Hillel, for example, believed that since this offer would also give Jordan a port on the Mediterranean, it had significant attraction.[46] Furthermore, returning Gaza to Jordan could be presented as an exchange of territories, diminishing Arab resistance to the loss of part of the West Bank. Since there had been considerable slippage in the Israeli drive to control Gaza (even in Likud quarters), no electoral penalty was foreseen for territorial largesse on this issue. A similar erosion in the commitment to retain all security zones under Israeli sovereignty was displayed even in the highest party echelons—the ministerial level.

Settlements

The destiny of the Jewish settlements in Israeli-ruled territories was related to the debate over the dimensions of territorial compromise. The Allon Plan required establishing political "facts," i.e., settlements, in the areas designed to become part of Israel. Such settlements were perceived by Allon and other Laborites as having political significance, as well as an important defense role. Labor has always distinguished between those settlements that fulfill security needs and those that have other functions. Indeed, for many years Israeli border settlements were viewed as providing artificial strategic depth, and were incorporated in the "territorial defense" command of the IDF.[47] This was a system of fortified settlements located on possible routes of invasion, meant to stop or delay the enemy until the IDF completed its mobilization of reserves and concentration of forces for the counterattack. The system was designed for the purpose of gaining time; hence, the term "artificial" strategic depth, i.e., a compensation for Israel's lack of vast territories that could be converted into time in the event of an invasion. The territorial defense also freed the most highly trained military forces, since it made optimum use of individuals with no alternative battle function, such as teen-agers, women, and the aged. The party platforms have called for strengthening this territorial defense (see Appendix B).

The ongoing debate over the security value of settlements—which began with the state's establishment in 1948—continued into the 1980s. During this period, the party's doves joined ranks with those who belittled the role of armed and fortified settlements in modern warfare. This evaluation was of course quite compatible with territorial minimalism. Building settlements in the security zones was no longer regarded as beneficial in terms of security in dovish quarters. Politically, it was obviously a burden, because it made disengagement from the settled areas more difficult. The sight of Jewish settlements being dismantled in Sinai, even in return for peace, was something most Israelis found hard to take, though the doves regarded these events as an important political precedent.

All Laborites were well aware, however, that evacuating Jews from Judea and Samaria was a much more difficult task than in Sinai, which was not considered by most Israelis as a part of the homeland. Moreover, in contrast to the few thousand settlers in Sinai, the West Bank has tens of thousands of Jewish inhabitants. Labor regarded most of the settlements set up by the Likud in the 1977–1984 period as worthless from a defense perspective (in contrast to the settlements within the Allon map). Even

Rabin, a hawk, had no qualms about actually dubbing them on many occasions a "security burden." Yet they were a reality not to be easily ignored.

Furthermore, a policy of *Judenrein* (ban on Jewish presence) for any part of the land of Israel was an extremely difficult demand on a Zionist party, since the dominant tendency in Zionism regarded all of Palestine as the Jewish homeland. Even an extreme dove like Eliav favored the Jewish right to settle in all of western Palestine.[48] Settlement was an integral part of the Zionist ethos. In fact, the right of Jews to establish settlements anywhere in the homeland has never been disputed in the party, only the wisdom of exercising it in every location and at any time.

The party reconciled itself to the established presence of tens of thousands of Jewish settlers in areas of Judea and Samaria outside the perimeter of the Allon Plan. Indeed, in 1983 the party decided to allow the opening of a party chapter in Ariel, a town in the heart of Samaria. More significantly, beginning in 1984 the party platform carried an article pledging opposition to the dismantling of any Jewish settlements in the territories, and guaranteeing their safety following a political agreement. Here again, the party adapted itself to the realities created by the Likud government. At the party congress in 1986 this article was the object of dovish attacks, but to no avail. Ramon's amendment to delete this article was rejected by a majority of 279, with only 175 convention members supporting him.[49] Even Peres included it in the party's Plan for Peace and Security, which was a dovish statement deviating from the party platform. It is noteworthy that even the guidelines of the putative, Labor-led dovish government of April 1990 mentioned the duty to safeguard the settlements in Judea, Samaria, and Gaza.[50]

The party did, however, oppose any additional settlements outside of the security zones. When it was a partner in the first National Unity government (1984–1988), Labor prevented the erection of new settlements in areas outside of the Allon map. Similarly, in 1988 Labor insisted on a veto power over the building of new settlements by the second National Unity government.

Despite the party's commitment to the well-being of all settlements, even the hawks did not rule out evacuation of several Jewish settlements in the framework of a permanent agreement. A few doves, moreover, regarded the dismantling of all Jewish settlements as the inevitable price to be paid for reaching an agreement with the Arabs.[51] It was argued that the evacuation of all Jewish settlers from the Sinai by the Likud-led government set a precedent that the Arabs could not ignore. Furthermore, the Likud's action in Sinai lent legitimacy to Israeli dovish demands for similar measures to be adopted on other fronts. Abba Eban explicitly used the Sinai precedent and the Algerian example to refute the argument that an evacuation of Jews from the administered territories was not feasible.[52]

Security Measures

Although the exact nature of future security arrangements was never given much attention in the party, a general consensus prevailed to regard the Jordan River as Israel's eastern security border, excluding any Arab military presence west of it. The distinction between a security border and a political one was important, since it allowed for flexibility on the issue of sovereignty in the area between the Jordan River and the Green Line (the 1967 borders). As a matter of fact, demilitarization of any territory from which Israel might withdraw was a basic tenet of Labor, as well as of other parties in Israel that advocated some measure of withdrawal. In addition, some degree of Israeli military presence in these areas was envisioned for purposes of surveillance, for erecting an air defense system, and, in case of war, for holding back an Arab ground attack on Israel pending mobilization of the reserves. Party documents also mentioned free ground movement for the IDF in the West Bank and control of its skies, to enable the air force to perform early warning missions as well as to train.[53] Details as to the character and magnitude of such an Israeli military presence were viewed as technical problems, left to the decision of the military experts.[54]

During the 1988 elections the security arrangements proposed by the party were presented to the public as the "Generals' Plan," to confer on it the legitimacy of military expertise. Indeed, reserve generals were mobilized by the party to advertise it. This plan included the demilitarization of evacuated areas as well as two additional features: the right of pursuit, i.e., unrestricted freedom of action for the IDF, at least in areas in the vicinity of the new border; and the establishment of a fence, entailing elaborate support systems, along the newly defined political border, which was to supplant the Green Line. This fence, which would be designed to prevent infiltration, or to alert the IDF to the presence of intruders, was not to be confounded with the border along the Jordan River. The Generals' Plan referred to the Jordan River as a security border only in order to delineate the area to be demilitarized. The hawks regarded it as a political border also, since they insisted on the future annexation of the Jordan Valley Rift and its settlements. The plan made no reference to settlements and their security potential, omissions that made it a quite dovish proposal. Party hawks were effectively barred from having a say in the formulation of the electoral campaign policy, which was managed almost exclusively by Peres and his dovish entourage. Hawkish criticism of the Generals' Plan was muted, in any case, in the interest of appearing united before the impending November elections. Focusing on the dovish omissions in the plan could play into the hands of the Likud, which was already accusing Labor of excessive dovishness.

Since the doves had a lower level of threat perception, their security recommendations were less stringent. Furthermore, as noted, they were willing to take risks in order to reach an agreement with the Arabs. For example, Ramon, in a Knesset debate, prodded the National Unity government to take chances, as Begin had, to achieve a peace treaty.[55] The emphasis on political elements in regard to securing the stability of an agreement also led to more flexible definitions of Israel's security needs. A striking example of an extreme deviation from the concept of defensible borders was the formula "Secure borders are, among other things, frontiers along and inside of which peace exists," which appeared in 1988 in an officially sponsored Labor article; this was identical to the Arab interpretation of "secure borders."[56] The military component of the term was disposed of, the emphasis being only on the political elements needed for a peaceful frontier.

Even party members in governmental positions refrained from entering into detailed discussions of future military arrangements, as this, in the absence of a negotiating partner, was seen as premature. More generally, this lack of planning was typical of the Israeli decision-making process.[57]

Refugees

An issue that attracted little popular attention in the debate over solutions to the Arab–Israeli conflict was the refugee problem. Yet this element was addressed in Labor's security discussions, particularly by the hawks. It was seen as an integral part of any deal with the Arabs on the future of the West Bank, since it meant bringing an end to a human tragedy that fostered hatred against Israel and fueled the continuing conflict. Rabin and Hillel insisted on solving the refugee problem by resettlement east of the Jordan River.[58] This actually involved a population transfer of hundreds of thousands of people. In 1979, one of MK Amos Hadar's criticisms of the peace treaty with Egypt was that Egypt was not absorbing any refugees.[59] In his opinion, as long as the refugees in Lebanon and Gaza were not resettled there was no hope of "true peace."[60] At the party convention in 1986 some hawks, for example MK Tamar Eshel, made an unsuccessful attempt to include an article in the party platform calling for the refugee problem to be solved in the Arab countries.[61] The party was satisfied with a statement, which had been included in the platform since 1977, calling for a mutual effort by Israel and the Jordanian–Palestinian state to rehabilitate the refugees in the framework of a permanent settlement.

Rabin reiterated his concern about the refugee problem in January 1989 when he aired proposals for a solution of the Palestinian problem. He suggested convening an international conference to deal solely with this issue.[62] The intifada, which was fueled partly by the suffering in the refugee camps, highlighted for hawks and doves alike the need to solve the refugee problem, whose magnitude was beyond the means of the Jewish state. In contrast to the usual aversion to involving outside actors, on this topic an international interference was welcomed as a step toward raising the huge capital needed to rehabilitate the refugees. Rabin had little difficulty in incorporating this feature in the National Unity government's May 1989 peace initiative, which was a response to the intifada. He also wanted the conference to deal with the problem of Jewish refugees, that is, reparations to Jews from Arab countries who had found refuge in Israel. This demand created some symmetry in the balance of misery caused by the 1948 war. Furthermore, it highlighted the fact that in contrast to the Arab states, most of which did nothing to alleviate their refugees' condition, Israel, like other countries in the world, managed to absorb its refugees. Politically, this demand freed Israel of sole responsibility for redressing the situation.

The importance of solving the refugee problem was cited as a further argument against the establishment of a Palestinian state in Judea, Samaria, and Gaza. The small size of these areas, it was pointed out by MK Avraham Shochat, a yonetz, could not possibly accommodate the hundreds of thousands of remaining refugees.[63] Such an effort required the cooperation of several Arab countries. Resettling the refugees could also weaken the political charisma of the PLO, which encouraged their hopes of exercising the "right of return." Refusal to speak to the PLO was partly rooted in the realization that its main constituency was the refugees—a sector of the Palestinian people that was, not unexpectedly, the most anti-Israeli. In the past these arguments had strengthened the Jordanian orientation.

Peres concurred in viewing the solution of the refugee problem as part of the future deal.[64] He did not, however, include it in the party's Plan for Peace and Security. The settlement of the refugee problem, as a condition for arriving at an agreement with the Arabs, was regarded by many doves as unrealistic and as therefore constituting a barrier to peace.

A Palestinian Entity

As a consequence of the Jordanian orientation, the future of the territories to be conceded was linked to Jordan. Initially there was great opposition to the idea of a separate political entity in the West Bank, even if it were somehow linked to Jordan. But as the party veered leftward and considered greater participation of Palestinians in the peace process, adamant opposition to any Palestinian political entity substantially diminished.

Yet the establishment of an independent Palestinian *state*—a "third" state, as it was usually referred to—was still strongly rejected in 1990. Since 1973, the party platform had explicitly opposed the possibility that such a state would emerge as part of a permanent settlement. This categorical opposition was reiterated in the platforms for 1977, 1981, 1984, and 1988. Beginning in 1981, the platform specified that such a state could not serve as a solution to the conflict, but rather as "a focus of hostility and the inflammation of passions." Rabin described it in 1988 as "a cancer in the heart of the Middle East."[65] On a later occasion he called it a "time bomb."[66]

Reluctance to witness the evolution of an independent Palestinian state was shared by most party doves. Abba Eban and Yossi Sarid were the outstanding examples; they questioned the viability of such an entity. The Palestinian majority on the east bank of the Jordan was also mentioned in the argument against the establishment of a new state.[67] The Jordan River was not endowed with any political significance in regard to the Palestinian problem: on both its banks lived populations with the same nationality and language. Moreover, a small Palestinian state, it was urged, could not contribute to the solution of the refugee problem because it could not absorb them all.[68]

Yet, toward the end of the 1980s, as the party displayed a greater openness to a Palestinian negotiating role, a growing number of doves were willing to consider the possibility of a semi-independent political entity in the West Bank. Usually it was proposed in a federal package, linked somehow to Jordan (the "East Bank"), which was generally viewed as being ethnically Palestinian. Tzadok suggested self-determination for the Palestinians in the territories evacuated by Israel, but through a common political framework with Jordan, even if the Jordanians developed a separate identity. He emphasized that there were precedents for implementing this principle in federal arrangements, as in Belgium, Switzerland, Czechoslovakia, and Yugoslavia.[69] Aharon Yariv was another dove who was known to favor a Palestinian state in confederation with Jordan.[70] The term confederation usually indicated a large measure of independence for the Palestinian entity; the term federation seemed to imply less autonomy and more integration with Jordan. Laborites often, however, used these terms indiscriminately. Even a yonetz like Yaakobi accepted a Palestinian–Jordanian confederation, although what he had in mind exactly was unclear.[71]

A marginal group in the party that called itself The Confederation proposed in 1987 an Israeli–Jordanian–Palestinian confederation of three states. The Palestinian member of the confederation was to have all state attributes such as citizenship and UN membership; the only limitation would be on the possession of a military force.[72] To make this proposal of a Palestinian state more palatable, it was linked to Jordan and Israel. At the 1986 party congress an attempt had been made to include such a proposal in the platform as an additional option. It was, however, rejected by the majority of the delegates.[73] In 1989 MK Eliav again advocated a confederation between Jordan, Palestine, and Israel.[74]

Indeed, some doves were even willing to reconcile themselves to a separate Palestinian state if the Jordanian–Palestinian option proved impractical.[75] The most senior Laborite to admit this publicly was Minister Navon in March 1988. In an interview with the party's monthly he stated that, though a Jordanian–Palestinian solution was preferable, "I have no difficulty in agreeing to a Palestinian state in the West Bank and the Gaza Strip."[76] At the end of 1989, however, after having second thoughts, he rejected the possibility of an independent state and reversed his position to advocacy of a federal solution.[77] Shahal dropped his opposition to an independent Palestinian state in 1989 when he contemplated allowing the Palestinian entity to have statehood attributes such as a UN seat, though he agreed that a confederation with Jordan seemed a better solution.[78] Avigdor (Yanosh) Ben-Gal, a major general of the reserves whom the party had recruited in 1988 to allay the electorate's fears of an eventual withdrawal, also did not exclude the possibility of a Palestinian state.[79] In August 1988, Beilin and Ramon likewise proposed that the party platform express willingness to negotiate with the Palestinians for a permanent solution. This could hardly lead to anything but a Palestinian state.

Following U.S. recognition of the PLO at the end of 1988, several doves regarded a Palestinian state as a foregone conclusion. Ora Namir dared to say out loud what some doves were quietly reconciling themselves to: "A Palestinian state will eventually be established."[80] Ramon, too, no longer hesitated to accept a Palestinian state, should a Jordanian-Palestinian confederation fail to materialize.[81] Burg went even further and published an article showing why Israel had nothing to fear from a Palestinian state.[82] Abba Eban similarly mellowed his resistance and in February 1989 expressed the view that such a state did not constitute a frightening development.[83]

Peres was reluctant to use the term Palestinian state, but in March 1989 disclosed his willingness to accept a Benelux arrangement, which would include Israel, Jordan, and a Palestinian entity. The exact nature of the entity was not made clear. This proposal, despite the fact that it incorporated a Jordanian orientation, moved him further in a dovish direction, since it implied that the Palestinian entity was to be equal in status to its two neighbors.

After more than a year of intifada, and following U.S. recognition of the PLO, even Rabin was willing to consider the possibility of giving the local Arab population the option of entering into a federation with Jordan, after the completion of an interim agreement in Judea, Samaria, and Gaza.[84] This appeared to be a substantive shift from his previous aversion toward a separate political entity in the West Bank. A state was, however, something he was not willing to grant. Gur, a yonetz, also continued to oppose the establishment of a Palestinian state, although he was willing, under certain conditions, to talk to the PLO.[85] Gur did not consider a Palestinian state a grave security threat, but saw it as an inadequate solution.

The Central Stream's Zisman even criticized using the term "Palestinian entity" because it had become a euphemism for a Palestinian state.[86] The Central Stream's opposition remained strong; they maintained that there was no need to compromise on such an important issue. Indeed, the hawks pointed out that the United States was still committed to its opposition to a Palestinian state. They also believed, as we have seen, that U.S. relations with the PLO would eventually peter out. As far as they were concerned, Israel could, in the final analysis, prevent a Palestinian state if it would only be firm in opposing it. Therefore, as long as no significant erosion in the Israeli consensus against such a state was detected, the hawks refused to regard a "third" state as a component of the permanent settlement. In April 1990 their position won the day in Labor's negotiations with the leftist parties CRM and Mapam, during the attempted formation of a left-wing government; in these talks, Labor refused to include any reference to a Palestinian state in the guidelines for the coalition government they were trying to establish.

INTERVENING VARIABLES

The most important variable directly influencing a Laborite's vision of a future agreement was the level of threat perception and degree of optimism regarding chances for peaceful relations with the Arabs (an issue explored at length in Chapter 3). A high level of threat perception and the evaluation that stable peaceful relations were doubtful led to greater insistence on security arrangements that would be as foolproof as possible. Such a hawkish and skeptical perspective also tended to give higher priority to solving the refugee problem, so as to minimize sources of friction in the future. Hawkish skepticism about the changes occurring within the PLO and fears of Palestinian nationalism inevitably led, furthermore, to a continued preference for renewed Jordanian rule over whatever territories might be evacuated.

In contrast, a low level of threat perception, typical of the party's doves, was directly linked to territorial largesse. According to them, the drive for territorial expansion of the security margins of the Jewish state was less justifiable under the new circumstance of Arab benevolence toward Israel. The doves also argued that only a proposal based on significant territorial concessions could bring the Arab moderates to the negotiating table and thus finally put an end to the conflict. The doves' sense of urgency about the need to reach a settlement quickly was another factor promoting their territorial generosity. Urgency, in particular, was a new theme in the dovish way of thinking in the 1980s.

Another intervening variable, of great persuasiveness, was the "demographic problem," or the Jewish inability to match Arab population growth in western Palestine. Labor was to a large extent responsible for increased awareness of the "demographic problem," as it fought annexationist tendencies to the right of it on the Israeli political spectrum. Both hawks and doves worked together in this endeavor. Although the hawks did advocate Israeli incorporation of security zones inhabited by relatively few Arabs, they acknowledged that the addition of even a small number of Arabs was problematic given their own and their party's sensitivity to the demographic issue. But one corollary of the "demographic problem" was "foreign rule" over the Palestinians. In this view, the longer military occupation of the territories lasted the more threatening was the status quo to Israel's social fiber and even to its security. The territories were regarded not only as a bargaining asset, but as a liability. As of 1981, the Labor party platform carried a clause underlining the moral erosion resulting from the occupation. Furthermore, in the absence of a political settlement allowing Israeli disengagement from the territories, fears that a binational state might arise increased.

The Palestinian uprising, which began in December 1987, drastically increased the price of occupation. More troops were needed to police the territories, which placed an added burden on reservists and on the national budget. The rise in direct expenditures was accompanied by indirect economic costs, such as loss of tourism, a fall in output, and a reduction in sales to the territories. The Labor party stressed this increasing price for retaining the territories. Before the November 1988 elections a special pamphlet on the intifada was published, in which it was emphasized that the *daily* cost to the Israeli economy was NIS3 million ($1.875 million)—a most impressive amount, even if assumed to be somewhat exaggerated.[87] In June 1989, Peres, in his capacity as finance minister, put a price tag of NIS2 billion ($1.1 billion) on cumulative economic losses exacted by the intifada.[88] At a time of economic difficulties and budgetary cuts, the emphasis given to such figures served the argument for an urgent effort to end the status quo.

Laborites, in particular the doves, were also perturbed by damage to Israel's image overseas. The sights of repression as a result of the occupation were painful for Israel's friends abroad. A decline in support for Israel was feared. But as time went by and the international media turned their attention to other events, this argument was less effective in augmenting dovish ranks and influence. As long as the intifada could not again capture the headlines for long periods of time, the hawks could point to world indifference—a fact hardly surprising from their realpolitik standpoint.

The doves, more than the hawks, echoed the army's complaint that in the endeavor to restore law and order in the territories, the IDF was diverted from its main task of preparing for the next war. Above all, they claimed, Israelis were morally ill-equipped to suppress the hostile and violent activities Palestinian women and children were engaged in, a confrontation which had, at least initially, a devastating effect on Israeli morale. Therefore, the "demographic problem," and particularly the issues raised by the intifada, put greater pressure on the party to come up with more modest requirements in the negotiations for a permanent settlement.

Similarly, the Palestinization of the conflict—of which the intifada was one facet—strengthened the dovish cause, because it seemed as if the doves had been reading the political map better than the hawks. Indeed, they have always shown greater cognizance of the emerging political power of Palestinian nationalism—a factor that lent credibility to their other assumptions and prescriptions—although this recognition actually had little bearing on most other issues.

A further intervening factor in molding the Laborite conception of Israel's future borders was the assessment of the strategic importance of territory in the context of modern warfare in general. The doves believed that in the age of missiles the territorial component of security had lost much of its significance. Peres, for example, tried to press this point as a lesson to be derived from the missile exchanges in the Iran–Iraq war. In fact, as a rule he always paid great attention to the technological dimension in strategy: "Anybody speaking on security in terms of kilometers only . . . does not understand that geography is secondary to technology . . . "[89] At the end of the decade, Peres asked rhetorically, "Of what value is strategic depth when a modern rocket flies over mountains and rivers? Of what value is time—if the rockets swallow distances in minutes, or even seconds?"[90] Belittlement of the importance of strategic depth—an article of faith for the party's hawks—had clear territorial implications. Similarly, Abba Eban pointed out in 1988 that revisions in modern weapons technology called for a reassessment of Labor's traditional positions concerning security arrangements and, in particular, of the Allon Plan. In this speech, Eban also called for a reevaluation of the party position on the Palestinian issue.[91] In the same year, Weizman, banking on his high military rank (major general), concluded, "At the end of the 20th century it is much easier to prove that territory is less significant, from a security perspective, than when we had to depend on cannons and mortars."[92]

In contrast, Gur, a former chief of staff, pointed out in 1987 that the longer range of weapons as well as their greater precision actually enhanced the importance of territory. In other words, technology had not revolutionized the approach to war and peace. Wars were still won through the conquest of vital territory by ground forces, rather than by aerial bombing or missiles. There was no reason, according to Gur, for a drastic change in Israel's national security thinking. Relinquishing control of the Golan and the area along the Jordan River was, therefore, "unthinkable."[93] Dinitz, a hawk, admitted that security is not entirely a question of territory. But in case of war, he asserted, "It makes all the difference in the world whether your starting point is a secure border or its opposite. Not that there are absolutely secure borders anywhere, but the ability to defend a frontier with minimal losses is significant."[94] This thinking was typical of party hawks; in contrast to dovish evaluations that IDF might was sufficient to deter or overpower an Arab military attack, they believed that the IDF could face difficulties in a military encounter without certain topographical assets. Ironically, the doves within the party, like those outside it, were the ones to display greater reliance on military force alone. This was another aspect of the difference between the two schools in levels of threat perception. Although both relied on the IDF, the hawks believed that Israel's narrow security margins needed to be widened with additional territory.

The controversy over the significance of territory in the analysis of national power was also connected to Israel's nuclear dilemma. Although this issue was not the main prism through which security affairs were generally looked at, some of the doves nevertheless regarded the introduction of such weapons as annulling any advantages accruing to Israel from the maintenance of security zones. Peres's statement, cited above, exemplified such a view. In contrast, the hawks regarded territory as important even in a nuclear environment. They argued that when highly destructive weapons are used, defense and survival require dispersal, and successful dispersal depends on vast territory. Rabin, however, as we have seen, did not foresee the introduction of nuclear weapons into the Middle East in any case in the near future. All in all, the nuclear aspect was not dominant, since the sides taken in the debate over the role of nuclear weapons for Israel did not correspond to the dovish/hawkish distinction: opposition to, or support for, an Israeli nuclear force cut across the dovish/hawkish divide.

All these intervening variables also had an impact, naturally, on Labor's positions on an interim agreement, as well as on proposals for unilateral Israeli steps.

THE INTERIM AGREEMENT

An interim agreement was generally regarded in the party as a necessary stage in the process toward a peace treaty. Its main function was to de-escalate the conflict between the Middle Eastern rivals with a minimum of security risks for Israel. It was also viewed as a confidence-building measure by those, such as Rabin, who espoused the gradualist approach. The September 1975 Sinai II agreement, in which Rabin's government evacuated some territory in the Sinai, was claimed by Labor in the 1980s—ex post facto—as an interim agreement contributing to the peace process that culminated in the 1979 peace treaty with Egypt. In fact, the territorial concessions in 1975 had been aimed at preventing the re-emergence of an Egyptian–Syrian alliance, and at securing U.S. political and financial support.[95] The later developments leading to a peace treaty with Egypt came as a total surprise to Rabin and his party. Nevertheless, the Sinai II model could be emulated, though with some difficulty, on the Syrian front. Already in 1976, Rabin agreed to evacuate several settlements in exchange for a Syrian declaration of nonbelligerence.[96]

Yet the principle of limited withdrawal could not be easily implemented in the West Bank. First, the area along the border, the Jordan River, was almost unanimously regarded as a security zone, which Labor hawks even wished to annex in the framework of a permanent settlement. Second, withdrawal from any part of the West Bank was a highly sensitive issue politically. Since the mid-1970s, Labor had committed itself to bringing any proposal for a withdrawal from this region to the judgment of the voters. Popular support for a withdrawal in that area was, apparently, likely only if the quid pro quo was peace. Rabin and Peres recognized the difficulties in applying a territorial approach to the West Bank in 1974, when a plan to withdraw from Jericho in the context of an interim agreement with Jordan failed to materialize.[97] Despite the fact that Labor gradually came to accept the territorial compromise formula, and eventually incorporated it into its platform, in the case of an interim agreement with Jordan this approach was found lacking.

After the 1978 Camp David Accords, the autonomy plan—an interim agreement based on the functional approach—appeared on the political agenda. Interestingly enough, this approach, following the lines of the Camp David Accords, appealed to some doves in the party, because of its potential to serve as a point of departure for a full withdrawal, and even as the embryo for a Palestinian entity. A few doves, like Eliav and Dayan, expressed reservations about an autonomy plan because they feared that the interim phase would actually be a continuation of the status quo and would further entrench the Israeli presence in the territories. Yet they were willing to support any effort that promised ultimately to change the status quo. Once abhorred by the doves, then, this solution became increasingly attractive to them in the 1980s.

Indeed, the hawks, as well as others in the party, initially saw the plan as dangerous precisely because it opened up the possibility of a Palestinian state. Gur even cynically called Menachem Begin, who signed the accords, "Lord Balfour of the Palestinians." Every Israeli understood that Gur was implying that Begin's action constituted the beginning of international legitimacy for a Palestinian state, in a fashion similar to the role played by the 1917 Balfour Declaration for the Zionists.[98] This is one of the reasons hawkish Laborites, such as MK Rosolio, opposed the Camp David accords.[99] Yet the autonomy idea was grounded in an internationally binding document, supported by the United States, that could not easily be ignored. Therefore, by the end of 1978 the party established a committee to prepare a Labor version of autonomy. This committee became the arena of struggle between left and right in the party. The hawks succeeded in limiting the proposed autonomy to areas outside the security zones; the doves managed to commit the party to autonomy talks even without Jordanian participation. It is not clear whether Egyptian participation was regarded as mandatory for reaching an autonomy agreement in talks with an independent Palestinian delegation from the administered territories.[100]

Then, in 1979, Rabin actually rejected his own party's autonomy plan, suggesting instead an interim period of Jordanian–Israeli rule in part of the administered territories.[101] He preferred a more limited role for the Palestinians. He also ruled out an interim agreement based on a limited Israeli withdrawal like the one specified by the agreement between his government and Egypt in 1975. In the 1980s, Rabin also rejected the idea of "Gaza first," i.e., an Israeli withdrawal from that region, since neither the

Egyptians nor the Jordanians seemed to be interested in taking control of Gaza as part of an interim agreement. Rabin realized that, following Egyptian disengagement from Gaza, its destiny was linked to Judea and Samaria.[102]

Thus, hawks of the 1980s, including Rabin, found no alternative but to support a functional compromise for an interim agreement in those areas of Judea, Samaria, and Gaza that were regarded as dispensable from a strategic perspective. Rabin and others did not object to the clause in the party's 1988 Plan for Peace and Security (drafted by Peres) that mentioned an interim agreement for a duration of up to five years, along the lines of autonomy. In January 1989, in response to the continuing Palestinian uprising, Rabin even suggested the establishment of an "enlarged autonomy" (to follow elections in the territories). What he meant by "enlarged" was not specified, but Rabin was known for his insistence on Israeli responsibility even for internal security in the interim period.[103]

"Autonomy" was a subject around which national consensus could be reached, since the Likud was also committed to such an interim agreement. Indeed, Rabin was the pivot around which the second National Unity government was formed in 1988. As was discussed earlier, he emphasized the need for a broad consensus if any progress in the peace process was to be made. The May 1989 peace initiative was the result of his efforts. Its main feature was the elections plan to provide a partner with whom to negotiate an autonomy agreement. In the five-year transitional period of self-rule, suggested by the initiative, the inhabitants of Judea, Samaria, and Gaza were to conduct their own daily affairs, whereas Israel would continue to be responsible for security, foreign affairs, and all matters concerning Israeli citizens in the territories.[104]

Although the peace initiative attracted large support in all wings of the party, some hawks, for example Hillel, refused to lend support to the election plan.[105] Rabin's willingness to allow the Arabs in East Jerusalem to vote evoked criticism. Furthermore, the hawks pointed out that the government's plan deviated from the party position in that it made no distinction between security zones and other parts of the territories. Therefore, some hawks, such as Shimon Shitrit, clung to the party position and insisted that the autonomy plan was to be restricted to areas outside the Allon Plan security zones. This tended to underline the territorial compromise approach for the permanent settlement.

In contrast, Peres always favored a functional approach. The party's Plan for Peace and Security contained his views concerning an interim agreement that could be in place for up to five years. Authority to manage the lives of the Palestinians would be transferred to an autonomous administrative council, whereas security and foreign affairs would remain in Israeli hands. As expected, security arrangements such as IDF deployment, surveillance stations, and IDF land and air patrols were to be determined by the IDF. It was inconceivable that there would be more limited security arrangements in the interim stage than afterward. Peres did not specify precisely which regions would be "autonomous," despite the party's position of limiting them to areas outside the security zones. In addition, he did not mention the issue of internal security, or restrictions on the freedom to pursue antiterrorist activities—activities the hawks were not prepared to suspend.

Peres was even willing to consider a territorial interim arrangement.[106] Though its nature was left undisclosed, in the late 1980s, he occasionally expressed interest in a withdrawal from Gaza within the context of an interim agreement.[107] In 1988, he indicated that Hussein was interested in Gaza.[108] But it was far from clear that Jordan had any interest in the control of Gaza in the framework of an interim agreement. The annexation of parts of Gaza was not favorably regarded either in the party or outside it, because of the large numbers of Arabs residing in that small area. On the other hand, Peres warned of a Lebanonization of Gaza; quite probably, this was why he refrained from supporting a unilateral withdrawal.

In addition to the territorial dimension, the core difference between hawks and doves regarding the interim agreement in Judea and Samaria was the amount of authority the autonomy regime was to be allotted. The hawks favored limiting its authority; until the summer of 1988, Jordan was the preferred candidate to share rule with Israel. In contrast, the doves were willing to permit a large measure of autonomy so as to satisfy at least partially Palestinian aspirations for a political entity of their own.[109] The debate was, therefore, linked to the issue of who was to be the partner in the agreement. The hawks favored the Jordanian option because they feared that if Jordan were restricted to a limited role in Judea, Samaria, and Gaza, as advocated by the doves, a separate state might then emerge. However, by 1988 the party had finally reconciled itself to the idea of negotiating the details of an interim agreement solely with the Palestinians. In addition, the hawks wished to extend the interim agreement for the longest duration possible. The five years Peres mentioned in the party's Plan for Peace and Security appeared reasonable to them. Since this transitional period was also acceptable to the Likud, it was incorporated in the May 1989 peace initiative. As was to be expected, the pace for implementing the government's initiative was an object of disagreement. The doves, in accordance with the urgency thesis, demanded fast progress, whereas Rabin, for substantive as well as coalition reasons, displayed his typical caution. Some of his party colleagues in the cabinet let their exasperation with Rabin's slow pace be known through leaks to the media.[110]

A number of doves in the party, under the influence of more dovish elements nationally, were willing to desert the gradualist approach that insisted on an interim agreement. Extreme dovish groups outside of the party, such as those in the Citizens' Rights Movement, regarded an interim agreement as simply a ploy to perpetuate the unbearable status quo. They therefore pressed for immediate negotiations for a permanent agreement. In such quarters, an interim agreement was tolerable only if linked to a permanent settlement. Even Shahal, in April 1989, cautiously expressed his view that preoccupation with the interim agreement should not delay work on a permanent settlement.[111] As for the more dovish elements in the party that were willing not only to talk to the PLO but also to accept a Palestinian state, they had little reason to delay negotiations with the PLO that would aim toward arriving at permanent agreement.

A UNILATERAL DISENGAGEMENT

Variants of the envisioned security packages almost all excluded a unilateral disengagement from those territories not judged to be of strategic significance.[112] The 1967 conquest of the territories was considered to have created a bargaining situation, since the Arabs showed interest in retrieving these territories. In the event of Israel's returning some territory to Arab hands, a quid pro quo was expected. In the attempt to extract political concessions from the Arabs, therefore, a unilateral withdrawal made no sense, so long as the price for the Israeli occupation was not too high. Furthermore, such a step could be perceived by the Arabs as a sign of weakness and lack of resolve.

In the 1980s, however, the calculus of cost and benefit underwent a drastic change, particularly for the doves. As noted, as of 1981 the party platform carried a clause warning of dangers to the public morale and to democracy as a result of the occupation of the territories. In the latter years of the decade, and particularly since the beginning of the Palestinian uprising, such a cost-benefit analysis led a few dovish Laborites to consider unilateral solutions, on the ground that the occupation was proving too taxing on Israeli society. They no longer viewed the territories as a bargaining asset, but as a liability. Indeed, Chaim Tzadok, at a meeting of the party's doves in December 1987, called on the government to draft a plan for unilateral withdrawal from the territories.[113] The famous writer Amos Oz, in Labor's organ *Davar*, praised veteran leader Yitzhak Ben-Aharon for renewing his earlier proposal for unilateral withdrawal.[114] Beilin too at one point entertained the idea of unilateral Israeli action, a plan that was studied by a task force he organized for Peres in anticipation of the 1984 elections.[115]

The Gaza Strip was the subject of several proposals for a unilateral withdrawal toward the end of the decade. In 1987, MK Ramon demanded either unilateral withdrawal from Gaza or turning it over to the United Nations.[116] Another dove, Amir Peretz, a new MK in 1988, similarly supported international rule over Gaza instead of the Israeli presence.[117] This would mean, in fact, unilateral withdrawal without any security measures, as the United Nations could provide neither a political quid pro quo nor the desired level of security. These proposals were impelled by the Palestinian population's high level of growth in Gaza. The doves simply wanted to put as quick an end as possible to Israeli occupation over so many Arabs. Of the territories, Gaza has always had the least historical association for Israelis, and considering the demographic proportions between Jews and Arabs there, the case for disengagement from Gaza was the easiest to make.

Gradually, the formulations of the doves, who regarded a continuation of the status quo as highly threatening, infiltrated the party's official documents. The 1988 elections kit for party activists, for example, stressed that the time factor was working against Israel, while the occupation constituted an economic burden and sapped the power of the IDF. This outlook, combined with a low regard for the strategic significance of territory, a high regard for the deterrent power of the IDF, and a low level of threat perception, led to the conclusion that Israel had best cut its losses by simply getting out of the territories. The withdrawal of the IDF from most of the Lebanese territory it had once controlled was cited as an instructive example. The continuing Israeli presence in the security zone north of the border was conveniently ignored by the doves.

It was not only doves who were interested in unilateral steps. Yaakobi, a yonetz, advocated since 1982 a unilateral implementation of the autonomy plan, in the absence of progress in the peace process.[118] The basic hypothesis behind his proposal was that the status quo "harbors many dangers for Israel's future."[119] He therefore suggested that "the IDF would leave the major Arab centers, allowing the local police to take charge of internal law and order. Israeli forces would become involved only if access to Jewish settlements and their security was endangered, or if developments took place in the autonomous areas posing a threat to Israel."[120] Furthermore, Yaakobi claimed that a unilateral disengagement of this kind did not close off any options. He advocated limited withdrawal from territories densely populated by Arabs and renunciation of any responsibility for administration of local affairs in the evacuated area. In June 1989, he recognized the difficulties in implementing his plan under the circumstances at that time, but still believed it could be realized in the future.[121] Yaakobi, like others in the party, wanted no part in continued occupation of the territories. His plan was based on the hope that the Palestinians would take control of their own affairs, and that they would be sensible enough not to provoke an Israeli retaliation by terrorist attacks on Israeli targets. Both assumptions were, however, far from infallible. Furthermore, Israel could not prevent the eventual emergence of a political and military infrastructure in the evacuated area, including the establishment of a Palestinian state. Thus, even if such a unilateral withdrawal would not pose a security threat in the short run, in the long run, it appeared quite dangerous to most party leaders.

Another yonetz who flirted with the idea of unilateral withdrawal was Tzur. Already in 1986 he had called for a gradual disengagement from some of the territories. In 1988 he still thought the idea deserved greater consideration.[122] In contrast to Yaakobi, however, Tzur made no efforts to develop his idea further, publicize it, or gain support for it in the party. His closeness to Rabin probably had an inhibiting effect.

For some Israelis, the developments leading to U.S. recognition of the PLO seemed to underline the need for greater Israeli activism. Shahal, displeased at the PLO's good fortune, expressed the hope in 1988 that a unilateral Israeli imposition of the autonomy plan might possibly divest the PLO of any accrued advantages and prevent the establishment of a Palestinian state.[123] In March 1989, he suggested a unilateral withdrawal from Gaza as well. Proposing unilateral steps represented a new line for Shahal. The perception that the situation was deteriorating seemed to pressure some Laborites into looking for radical solutions, which resulted in suggestions for unilateral steps. Yet, because of the widespread opposition within the party to such measures, these propositions were not placed on the party's political agenda, although greater support for unilateral steps could be clearly detected.

The situation in the territories caused the hawks great worry as well, but they seemed to display more patience in searching for an organization, other than the PLO, willing to take over control from the Israelis. The United Nations or some other international regime could not be trusted to prevent security problems for Israel. In 1989, Rabin refused even to consider UN auspices for the elections in Judea, Samaria, and Gaza envisaged by the May 1989 peace initiative. In a speech to a Labor dovish forum in December 1987, he denigrated the idea of unilateral withdrawal, calling it "a recipe for terror."[124] The defense minister repeated his opposition to any unilateral steps in December 1988, and scorned Shahal's proposal for disengagement from Gaza in March 1989. As far as Rabin was concerned, such steps signaled weakness and fostered Arab hopes of pushing Israel out of the territories without a political quid pro quo.[125] After the beginning of the intifada, Rabin was particularly intent on not allowing the other side to gain a feeling of achievement. Peres similarly dismissed the idea of a unilateral autonomy, pointing to the need for some body that would assume responsibility for local administration.[126] As long as Rabin and Peres concurred on the impracticality of partial unilateral withdrawals, or autonomy, there was no chance of these suggestions being incorporated into the party's formal position.

Some hawks appeared to lose patience, too. In 1986 Dinitz, then an MK, discussed the disadvantages of unilateral steps, pointing out specifically that they freed the Arabs from having to give something in return. Yet he mentioned that if there were no hope of reaching an agreement, unilateral measures would have to be considered.[127] He hinted at annexing additional territories, according to the Allon Plan. Indeed, when Micha Goldman advocated unilaterally annexing parts of the territories, he was not a lone voice in the party. The main concern of the more extreme party hawks was to present a fait accompli to the world, to the Arabs, and to the Israeli doves. Still, most Labor hawks by 1990, in contrast to the doves, regarded the status quo, at least for the time being, as bearable and were in no hurry to be rid of the territories. They therefore viewed the proposed unilateral measures emanating from dovish circles as a reflection of weariness with the protracted Arab–Israeli conflict, rather than as resulting from a strategic calculus.

CONCLUSION

Following the Labor Party's acceptance of the explicit Allon Plan in 1977, it made no major revisions in the 1980s in its official platform positions concerning territorial demands. In 1981, the hawks succeeded in including their demand for Israeli sovereignty in the security zones, once a permanent settlement was reached with the Arabs. The annexation of the Golan Heights was accepted as a fait accompli with little opposition. In 1984, the party committed itself to oppose the dismantling of Jewish settlements in the administered territories. However, in 1986 the doves managed to get the Gaza Strip deleted from the list of security zones. Unofficially, many party leaders displayed much greater territorial largesse, and gradually a few minimalist demands gained acceptance in the party. Many of the party statements toward the end of the 1980s simply omitted the official formulations. Interestingly enough, explicitness concerning territorial concessions—once considered a virtue by the party doves—turned, from their perspective, into a hawkish vice. On the issue of sovereignty over the territories captured in 1967, only Jerusalem commanded the consensus of the party by 1990. The doves seemed satisfied with looser security arrangements, and did not insist on a solution for the refugee problem in the context of a permanent settlement. Despite the widespread resistance to a Palestinian state, developments in the territories such as the Palestinian uprising and Jordan's disengagement from the West Bank eroded the consensus on this issue. The doves led the struggle to revise the party position gradually on this issue as well.

In regard to the interim agreement, considerable concurrence obtained regarding a functional solution. Most apprehensions on this score, primarily among the hawks, revolved around the possibility that this approach could lead to a separate Palestinian entity, whereas some doves now reluctantly accepted such a scenario; others even actively regarded it as a good solution. Thus, an additional inversion of positions was dovish support for the functional approach, once the guiding principle of the party's hawks. The perception that the status quo was harming Israel led to increased demands for unilateral disengagement from the territories, even at the ministerial level.

NOTES

1. For Rabin's statements in this vein, see *Haaretz*, September 9, 1988, and the "Security and Peace" section in the party's 1988 elections kit for its activists ("the activists' kit"). For various types of orientation to territory, see E. Cohen, "Environmental Orientations: A Multidimensional Approach to Social Ecology," *Current Anthropology* 17, no. 1 (1976), pp. 49–70. For an analysis of Israeli politics from a territorial perspective, see Baruch Kimmerling, *Zionism and Territory: The Socio-Territorial Dimensions of Zionist Politics* (Berkeley: University of California, Berkeley, Institute for International Studies, 1983).

2. For a discussion of various patterns of control over territory, see Baruch Kimmerling, "A Conceptual Framework for the Analysis of Behavior in the Territorial Conflict: The Generalization of the Israeli Case," Jerusalem Papers on Peace Problems, no. 25 (Jerusalem: The Leonard Davis Institute for International Relations, The Hebrew University of Jerusalem, 1979), pp. 12–13.

3. Rabin, *Memoirs*, p. 496. Interview with Amos Carmel, one of the Central Stream activists. Hillel and Bar-Lev expressed basic agreement with this position; see *Yediot Achronot*, September 6, 1983.

4. See *Haaretz*, March 19, 1989; *Maariv*, March 30, 1990.

5. See Abba Eban, "We Can Still Trade Territory For Peace," *Spectrum* 2 (June–July 1982), pp. 30–31; see also "Interview with Shimon Peres," *Migvan* 71 (June 1982), p. 5. For Meron Benvenisti's argument, see his *The West Bank Data Project*. Some Likud members, on the other side of the Israeli political spectrum, fully agreed with his judgment.

6. The most detailed version is found in Yerucham Cohen, *The Allon Plan* (Hebrew) (Tel Aviv: Hakibbutz Hameuchad Publishing House, 1973); see also Yigal Allon, "Israel: The Case for Defensible Borders," *Foreign Affairs* 55 (October 1976), pp. 38–53. For an analysis of his thinking on borders, see Reudor Manor, "The Conception of Borders in Allon's Strategic Thinking," *Shorashim* 3 (1982) (Hebrew), pp. 165–190. For contemporary versions, see Shlomo Hillel, "The Allon Plan Has Come of Age," *Spectrum* (March 1983), pp. 13–15; and Chaim Bar-Lev, "The Future of the Territories: Compromise or State?" pp. 3–6. For a detailed study of territorial adjustments on broadly based criteria reaching similar conclusions, see Saul Cohen, *The Geopolitics of Israel's Border Question*, Jaffee Center for Strategic Studies Study, no. 7 (Jerusalem: *Jerusalem Post*/Westview, 1986).

7. Allon initially preferred to see the establishment of an autonomous Palestinian region, rather than a renewed Jordanian presence (Cohen, *The Allon Plan*, p. 179). In the present terminology, his orientation was Palestinian. In addition, his plan was designed on the assumption that peace with the Arabs was feasible (Yael Yishai, *Land or Peace: Whither Israel?* p. 67). On those two dimensions of the hawkish–dovish continuum, he was a dove. On other dimensions of the continuum, he displayed more hawkish positions. (See Michael Brecher, *The Foreign Policy System of Israel*, pp. 361–369.)

8. For an analysis of the Israeli conceptions of defensible borders, see Dan Horowitz, "Israel's Concept of Defensible Borders," Jerusalem Papers on Peace Problems, no. 16, 1975.

9. See Yossi Beilin, *The Price of Unity*, p. 96.

10. Beilin, *The Price of Unity*. For Israel's lack of direction in foreign policy because of internal party divisions, see Avi Shlaim and Avner Yaniv, "Domestic Politics and Foreign Policy in Israel," *International Affairs* 56 (April 1980), pp. 225–262. The debate on whether Israel shares the blame for not reaching peace before 1973 is beyond the scope of this work. Two participants in

the decision-making process in that period, Abba Eban and Mordechai Gazit, both doves, have refuted such a claim. See Abba Eban, "Truth and Legend About Peace Initiatives," *Davar*, May 23, 1982; and Mordechai Gazit, "The Peace Process 1969–1973: Efforts and Contacts," Jerusalem Papers on Peace Problems, no. 35, 1983.

11. For a discussion of various constitutional arrangements within such an approach, see the contributions in Daniel J. Elazar, ed., *Self-Rule/Shared Rule* (Lanham: University Press of America and the Jerusalem Center for Public Affairs, 1984).

12. For Dayan's views on the territories, see Yael Yishai, *Land or Peace*, pp. 63–67. The functional approach was adopted by Begin's Likud-led government, and formulated into the Israeli version of the autonomy plan. Then, the strategic considerations were of secondary importance, as the initial prime motivation for this approach was the ideological commitment to retain all of the land of Israel. Dayan served as foreign minister in this government. This concept, which was originally meant to be the final settlement, was later incorporated into the September 1978 Camp David Accords as the proposed interim agreement.

13. See Myron J. Aronoff, *Power and Ritual in the Israeli Labor Party*, pp. 145–165.

14. Beilin, *The Price of Unity*, p. 141. The document committed the party to intensifying the settlement effort, and specifically to building the city of Yamit in the Sinai, as well as to allowing tax concessions to Israeli investors in the administered territories. See Gershon R. Kieval, *Party Politics in Israel and the Occupied Territories*, pp. 76–78.

15. For developments from Rabin's perspective, see his *Memoirs*, pp. 442–496.

16. Arieh (Lova) Eliav, *Eretz Hatzvi* p. 157. Eliav, a dove, served as the party's secretary-general until his resignation in 1975. He left the party because of his dovish convictions and returned to it only in 1986. In 1988, he again represented Labor as an MK, with no alternation in his views.

17. Allon, "Israel: The Case for Defensible Borders."

18. For the Rabin settlement policy, see Efraim Inbar, "Problems of Pariah States: The National Security Policy of the Rabin Government," pp. 240–242.

19. Yigal Wagner, "Politics and Ideology in the Controversy on Greater Israel," in *State of Israel and Land of Israel*, ed. Adam Doron, p. 142.

20. The Platform for the 9th Knesset, p. 4.

21. Horowitz, *Israel's Concept of Defensible Borders*, p. 29.

22. *Yediot Achronot*, October 31, 1980.

23. Ibid. The "77 Circle" was a group of leftist intellectuals who became active following Labor's loss of power in 1977.

24. For his views on Gaza, see his "Gaza First," *Spectrum* (March 1984), pp. 14–15.

25. Minutes of the Fourth Party Congress, the Security Political Meeting, April 9, 1986, pp. 156–163. This amendment was suggested by a member of the small, dovish Arahim group.

26. Yoseph Harif, "Israel: Two States," *Maariv*, February 26, 1988.

27. For the process of commitment in international affairs, see Thomas C. Schelling, *Arms and Influence* (New Haven: Yale University Press, 1966), pp. 35–90.

28. See Eyal Erlich, "Historical Mapai," *Haaretz Magazine*, February 12, 1988.

29. See *Haaretz*, April 29, 1988; *Davar*, April 29, 1988; *Maariv*, May 2, 1988. The program, however, was approved by the informal forum of Labor

ministers, Sareinu. It is not clear to what extent hawkish ministers, such as Nehamkin, Arbeli-Almozlino, or Rabin, paid attention to the details in the document.

30. Yehoshua Bitzur, "Who Will Annex the Jordan Valley Rift Settlements?" *Maariv*, May 17, 1988.

31. Ibid.

32. Asher Maniv, "A Conversation with Chaim Tzadok," *Migvan* 57 (March 1981), p. 7.

33. See his "Why Did I Vote for the Golan Law?" *Maariv*, December 18, 1981. For the dovish position against the annexation, see Abba Eban, "A Stumbling Block on the Golan," *Maariv*, December 18, 1981; Chaim Tzadok, "A Harmful Law," *Maariv*, December 18, 1981.

34. See *Maariv*, January 3, 1988; *Davar*, February 12, 1988.

35. See *Haaretz*, August 15, 18, 1988; *Maariv*, August 15, 1988.

36. *Maariv*, August 4, 1987.

37. Yitzhak Rabin, "Middle East Chess: King's Move," p. 8.

38. "Rabin's Plan," *Jerusalem Post*, March 11, 1988.

39. Ibid.

40. For his adherence to the Allon Plan, see his "The Future of the Territories: Compromise or State"; Natan Raanan, "Interview with Bar-Lev," *Migvan* 60 (June 1981), p. 12; The Labor Party Position on the Establishment of a National Unity Government, The Labor Party, April 1982, p. 6; for his orthodox definition of secure borders, see The Minutes of the Fourth Congress, April 9, 1986, p. 146.

41. *Davar*, June 6, 1988.

42. See "Interview with Yaakobi," *Davar Magazine*, June 10, 1988.

43. *Maariv*, January 20, 1988. For a similar minimalist proposal, see Shevach Weiss, "The Real Alternatives," *Maariv*, August 17, 1988. A well-known dove, he has served as a Labor MK since 1981.

44. Menachem Rahat, "The Magic Platform of the Labor Party," *Maariv*, January 1, 1988.

45. See *Maariv*, June 16, 1987.

46. See Hillel, "The Allon Plan Has Come of Age"; for Bar-Lev's views, see *Davar*, June 10, 1988.

47. For an early exposition of the rationale of the territorial defense, see Yigal Allon, *Curtain of Sand* (Hebrew) (Tel Aviv: Hakibbutz Hameuchad Publishing House, 1968), pp. 65–68; for a more recent reformulation of the doctrine, see Danny Noy, "Territorial Defense and National Security," *Mibifnim* 39 (December 1977), pp. 243–255. *Mibifnim* is a Hakibbutz Hameuchad organ.

48. Eliav, *Eretz Hatzvi*, p. 162.

49. See Minutes of the Fourth Party Congress, the Security Political Meeting, April 9, 1986, pp. 166–167.

50. *Haaretz*, April 11, 1990.

51. Interview with Yossi Sarid.

52. See his "We Can Still Trade Territory for Peace," pp. 30–31.

53. See "Labor's Plan for Peace and Security," *Haaretz*, April 29, 1988. For the English version, see Appendix A. See also "the activists' kit" (1988).

54. For a detailed study of the minimum required security arrangements on the eastern border from a dovish perspective, see Arye Shalev, *The West Bank: Line of Defense* (New York: Praeger, 1984). See also *The West Bank and Gaza: Israel's Options For Peace*, Report of a JCSS Study Group (Jerusalem: *Jerusalem Post*, 1989), pp. 161–175.

55. *Haaretz*, January 18, 1990.

56. Sh. Ari, "The Concern for the Future of the State and Its Inhabitants: Labor's First Priority," *Haaretz Magazine on Israel's First Forty Years*, May 1988, p. 3.

57. For Israeli decisionmaking on national security issues, see Lewis Brownstein, "Decision Making in Israeli Foreign Policy: An Unplanned Process," *Political Science Quarterly* 92 (Summer 1977), pp. 259–280; Yehudah Ben-Meir, *National Security Decision Making: The Israeli Case* (Jerusalem: Jerusalem Post, 1986).

58. Hillel, "Allon's Plan Has Come of Age," p. 15; "Rabin's Plan," *Jerusalem Post*, March 11, 1988.

59. Amos Hadar, "With No Illusions," *Migvan* 42 (December 1979), p. 13.

60. *Maariv*, September 19, 1978.

61. See Zisman, "At Maale Efraim."

62. *Haaretz*, January 31, 1989.

63. See, inter alia, Israel Landers, "Interview with Avraham Shochat," *Davar Magazine*, February 24, 1989. As mentioned, Shochat was a yonetz, a member of the Rabin camp.

64. For Peres's view, see *Haaretz*, March 9, 1988.

65. Yoseph Harif, "Rabin Suggests Waiting Period," *Maariv*, October 10, 1988.

66. Amnon Abramovitch, "Interview with Rabin," *Maariv*, February 10, 1989.

67. Interview with Yossi Sarid; Abba Eban, "Israel and the Palestinians," *Spectrum* 1 (December 1982), p. 13; see also "Interview with Abba Eban," *Migvan* 69 (April 1982), p. 5.

68. Haim Zadok, "A Small Step in a Long Journey," *Davar*, November 17, 1989.

69. Ibid.

70. Moshe Amirav, "What Should We Get Rid Of to Prevent the Next War?" *Haaretz*, August 22, 1988.

71. "Interview with Yaakobi," *Davar Magazine*, June 10, 1988.

72. See Arye Haas, "A Confederative Solution for the West Bank and Gaza," *Baavoda*, May 3, 1987, p. 4.

73. See Minutes of the Fourth Party Congress, the Security Political Meeting, April 9, 1986, pp. 151–156.

74. See Arie Lova Eliav, "Back to the Future," pp. 10–11.

75. Interview with Yossi Sarid.

76. *Spectrum* 6 (March 1988), p. 10.

77. Shalom Yerushalmi, "Political Text," *Kol Ha'ir*, December 22, 1989.

78. *Maariv*, September 17, 1989. For his opposition to a Palestinian state at the beginning of 1989, see *Maariv*, January 31, 1989.

79. *Maariv*, June 2, 1988.

80. *Maariv*, December 19, 1988; see also Israel Landers, "Interview with Ora Namir," *Davar*, December 23, 1988.

81. Chaim Baram, "Interview with Chaim Ramon," *Kol Ha'ir*, January 27, 1989.

82. Avraham Burg, "Who Is Afraid of a Palestinian State?" *Haaretz*, January 27, 1989.

83. Dan Shilon, "Interview with Abba Eban," *Haaretz*, February 10, 1989.

84. *Jerusalem Post*, January 20, 1989.

85. See Gideon Levi, "Interview with Gur," *Haaretz Magazine*, February 10, 1989.

86. Immanuel Zisman, "Tell the Truth," *Haaretz*, August 21, 1989.

87. "Mivzak" (an eloction pamphlet), no. 4, Israeli Labor Party, August 17, 1988. See also Gad Yaakobi, "Not All Is Well on the Economic Front," *Spectrum* 6 (September 1988), p. 18.
88. *Haaretz*, June 6, 1989.
89. Shimon Peres, "Futurology and Foresight," pp. 93-94. On this occasion he was also referring to the advent of nuclear technology.
90. Shimon Peres, "The Middle East in a Brave New World."
91. *Maariv*, August 1, 1988.
92. "Interview with Ezer Weizman," *Spectrum* 6 (June 1988), p. 10.
93. Mordechai Gur, "The Point of Change," *Maariv*, September 23, 1987.
94. "Interview with Dinitz," *Spectrum* 7 (May-June 1989), p. 12.
95. See Inbar, *Problems of Pariah States*, Parts 2, 3.
96. Rabin, *Memoirs*, pp. 495-496.
97. For this failure, see Saadia Touval, *The Peace Brokers* (Princeton: Princeton University Press, 1982), pp. 259-261; and Inbar, *Problems of Pariah States*, pp. 123-128. For Rabin's views, see his *Memoirs*, pp. 435, 495-496. For Peres's views on the negotiations with Jordan in 1974, see Matti Golan, *Peres* (Hebrew) (Jerusalem: Shocken, 1982), pp. 160-161.
98. For Gur's opposition, see *Emda Medinit*, no. 1, The Israeli Labor Party, December 1981, p. 14.
99. For Dani Rosolio's opposition, see *Maariv*, September 19, 1978.
100. For the struggle between hawks and doves in the autonomy committee, see Yossi Beilin, "A Dominant Party in Opposition: The Israeli Labor Party, 1977-1981," *Middle East Review* 17 (Summer 1985), pp. 37-44; the version was incorporated in The Platform of the 10th Knesset, p. 6.
101. Yitzhak Rabin, "Against Labor's Autonomy Plan," pp. 3-7.
102. *Maariv*, October 10, 1987; *Maariv*, January 15, 1988.
103. See Rabin, "Against Labor's Autonomy Plan."
104. For the English version of the peace initiative, see *Jerusalem Post*, May 15, 1989.
105. Interview with MK Shlomo Hillel, April 20, 1990.
106. "Interview with Peres," *Migvan* 71 (June 1982) p. 6.
107. See *Maariv*, December 12, 29, 30, 1987; January 12, 1988.
108. *Maariv*, July 14, 1988.
109. For a greater extent of authority than the Likud is willing to allow, see Bar-Lev's remarks at the party center, in "The Labor Position on the Establishment of a National Unity Government," *Israeli Labor Party* (April 1982); Ezer Weizman, "Before War," *Yediot Achronot*, January 12, 1988.
110. *Haaretz*, September 25, 1989.
111. *Haaretz*, April 24, 1989.
112. An early proposal for unilateral withdrawal was aired in February 1973 by Yitzhak Ben-Aharon, a dovish Laborite leader. See Kieval, *Party Politics in Israel and the Occupied Territories*, pp. 71-72.
113. *Maariv*, December 27, 1987. For his views on this matter, see Chaim Tzadok, "On the Negotiating Table and Under It," *Davar*, February 12, 1987; and his "From a Bargaining Card to a Millstone," *Davar*, August 12, 1988.
114. Amos Oz, "The Activist," *Davar*, August 26, 1986. The idea resurfaced in Ben-Aharon's recently published book *Occupation Corrupts: The End of the Road* (Tel Aviv: Hakibbutz Hameuchad), 1988.
115. See *Haaretz*, August 26, 1988.
116. *Maariv*, October 20, 1987. For a realistic analysis of such a proposal, see *The West Bank and Gaza: Israel's Options for Peace*, pp. 119-134.
117. *Maariv*, August 11, 1987.

118. See his reiteration of such a proposal to *Haaretz*, December 12, 1988.
119. Gad Yaakobi, "Autonomy Now," *Spectrum* 5 (May 1987), p. 22.
120. Ibid.
121. Gad Yaakobi, "Lebanon or Cyprus," *Yediot Achronot*, June 18, 1989.
122. "Interview with Tzur," *Kol Ha'ir*, September, 23, 1988.
123. *Haaretz*, December 18, 1988.
124. *Maariv*, December 27, 1987.
125. Abramovitch, "Interview with Rabin."
126. Israel TV, December 18, 1988.
127. Chaim Maman, "Interview with MK Simcha Dinitz," *Bama*, February 1, 1986.

CHAPTER 6
The Use of Military Force

One obvious aspect of Israeli national security is the recurrent use of force, regarded by all, doves and hawks alike, as a continuing possibility in the region. The violent conflict between Jews and Arabs has become part of Israel's social routine.[1] In the 1960s Rabin coined the term "dormant war" to describe the Israeli reality. The Arab–Israeli conflict has occasionally erupted in spurts of violence. The levels of violence engaged in by the rivals have varied from low-intensity raids to wars of attrition to large-scale wars. A total war, such as the Six Day War in 1967 or the October War of 1973, in which there was a feeling that the state's existence was at stake and in which all the reserves had to be called up to confront the danger, did not occur in the 1980s. Yet in those years the IDF was engaged in commando raids, in artillery exchanges with the Palestinians, in a long war in Lebanon, in "surgical" air strikes against Arab targets close to and far from Israel's borders, and in quelling a popular uprising in Judea, Samaria, and Gaza. Thus military force essentially remained part of an existential reality, despite the fact that a peace treaty had been signed with Egypt at the end of the previous decade.

In the 1980s, then, Laborites had ample opportunities to discuss the issue of the use of force. After 1973, there was less hesitation about publicly discussing military affairs. Not surprisingly, there was no consensus in the Labor Party over either the contingencies warranting or the scope of a military response. As we saw in Chapter 2, the doves displayed greater reluctance to use force and minimized its contribution to the advancement of political goals, whereas the hawks showed greater respect for military measures as tools in the service of foreign policy. This chapter focuses on Laborite attitudes toward the use of force. First, I shall assess the cultural and personal background of members of the party leadership with respect to the issue of military force. I shall then discuss the role they ascribed to force in the resolution of conflict. Subsequently, I shall analyze attitudes toward the two main levels of conventional military violence—war and limited use of force—and, finally, the perceived side effects of war will be reviewed.

CULTURAL AND PERSONAL BACKGROUND

The Israeli Labor Party, in contrast to European socialist parties, has never displayed any pacifist tendencies.[2] In fact, the Zionist movement, of which Labor was the main component, regarded the organized use of force as one of the positive changes it had introduced in the long history of Jewish passivity in the Diaspora. Breeding a new kind of Jew, as Zionist ideology advocated, meant the inculcation of martial qualities and the determination to fight back, in contrast to the stereotype of the helpless Diaspora Jew.[3] Reinforced by the necessity of using force—to defend the Zionist enterprise during its early days and, after 1948, to protect the Jewish state from violent Arab opposition—this ideology led to the prevalent view of military force as an acceptable and common type of interaction in world politics. Among Israeli politicians—and Laborites were no exception—there existed no principled opposition to the use of force, nor any advocacy of disarmament. The might of the IDF is still viewed, in the final analysis, as the best guarantee for Israel's security. Even the party doves, who display a rather low threat perception and who attach great significance to political variables for the country's defense, recognize the importance of military power for its security.

Nevertheless, within Israeli political culture, a tendency to regard the use of force as something imposed on Israel, rather than as an instrument of policy, to some extent inhibited clear thinking on the issue.[4] Many statements, particularly by inexperienced backbenchers in all parties, constituted ritualistic expressions of sorrow at the loss of human life, and were intended to place the moral responsibility for the ongoing violence on Israel's foes.

In Israel, where all males are mobilized into regular service and then serve for many years afterward in reserve units, knowledge about weapons and military affairs is widespread. In addition, the various military activities in which the IDF has engaged have, to some extent, sensitized the public and its political representatives to the problems involved in warfare. As a matter of fact, a significant proportion of Labor's leadership in the 1980s, including party members at the highest national level, had rich military experience. In the case of several of Labor's first-rank leaders, involvement in party affairs and national politics constituted a second career after long service in the military. Yitzhak Rabin, Chaim Bar-Lev, and Mordechai Gur each attained the highest possible military rank in Israel, IDF chief of staff. Ezer Weizman, a major general in the reserves, had a distinguished career in the Israeli Air Force (IAF) and also served as the IDF's chief of operations. Later on, as politician, he returned to dealing with national security affairs by serving as defense minister under Begin from 1977 to 1980. Rabin served as prime minister (1974–1977) and defense minister (1984–1990); Shimon Peres, following a long career in the defense establishment, became defense minister (1974–1977), prime minister (1984–1986), and foreign minister

(1986–1988). Abba Eban, Israel's most famous diplomat, was for years part of the high policy elite on national security affairs. He and Yitzhak Navon, who worked in Ben-Gurion's close entourage for many years, have both held the position of chairperson of the Knesset Foreign Affairs and Defense Committee. Israel's president, Chaim Herzog, before becoming a Labor MP, ended his career in the IDF as chief of the intelligence branch, with a rank of major general. For a long period he held the prestigious post of Israeli ambassador to the United Nations, and he also became a prolific and authoritative commentator on Israel's wars. Similarly, Simcha Dinitz reached the Knesset after serving for many years as close political advisor to Prime Minister Golda Meir, and later as Israel's ambassador to the United States (1973–1978). Other party leaders, like most Israeli politicians, could hardly avoid devoting thought to the issues involved in employing military force, especially since the violent conflict between Jews and Arabs has become part of Israel's social reality. Overall, senior Laborites usually had a good grasp of the intricacies involved in the use of force.

THE USE OF FORCE AND THE RESOLUTION OF THE CONFLICT

Being well acquainted with the use of force did not always lead to unanimity of opinion. Yet no Laborite believed that the Arab–Israeli conflict could be ended by military means alone. As Peres wrote in 1978, "The power relations and the military balance cannot ensure Israel a decisive and final military victory that would force the Arabs to make peace on Israel's terms."[5] In the same vein, Bar-Lev stressed in 1978 that a war could not solve Israel's political problems: "Such a war is not possible, because in Israel's special geostrategic situation . . . [it] lacks the ability to force the Arab world to accept unconditional surrender."[6] Rabin often voiced his opposition to the idea of a military solution that would take the form of "a war once and for all."[7] He was frequently critical of the Likud's greater tendency to use force and to attach great weight to military factors in altering fortunes in the Arab–Israeli conflict.[8]

Thus, military superiority was not regarded as a sufficient condition for putting an end to the Arab–Israeli conflict. But although the IDF could not force the Arabs to make peace, its ability to overpower any Arab coalition on the battlefield was considered a necessary condition for this political goal. Rabin claimed in 1988 that the IDF's first politico-military objective was to divert the resolution of the conflict from the battlefield to the negotiating table, under optimum conditions for maximizing Israeli gains in this process.[9] He reiterated on many occasions that the Arabs had to be taught that violent means would not yield any political concessions from Israel; thus the IDF was seen as instrumental in lowering Arab political expectations in the conflict. In Rabin's eyes, there was a clear linkage between military force and political ends.

The limited political use of military power was generally accepted also in the case of the antiterrorist campaign mounted by Israel. Rabin insisted that no amount of military effort could put an end to terror, and that its total elimination was an illusory goal. The goal of the security organs was, therefore, to minimize its effectiveness. Rabin's views on this subject were representative of the party leadership. Similarly, once he grasped the significance of the intifada early in 1988, Rabin categorically rejected all claims that a military solution for ending the uprising was possible. Only a political approach accompanied by a combination of administrative and military measures could, in his opinion, quell the intifada. The proportions in the mix of political and coercive means were a source of controversy in the party, as we shall see.

Constant emphasis on the limitations of the use of force clearly contributed to a more sophisticated attitude toward military measures. At the same time, the insistence that only political solutions could ultimately eradicate violence underlined the fact that in the absence of political change, violence in the region was endemic. Laborites recognized that, although military exchanges constituted one avenue of "dialogue" with the Arabs— sometimes the one most often used—only political measures could bring about a reduction in the level of hostility between the protagonists. (The range of expectations accorded to such measures was reviewed in Chapter 3.) All in all, a party consensus believed that the Arab–Israeli conflict could not be solved by force.

Yet, as noted, a real difference existed between doves and hawks concerning the degree of force each advocated in the conduct of the country's foreign policy. On the one hand, the doves were aware of the linkage between the use of force and political ends and of the fact that Israel's demonstrated military superiority was one of the factors effecting change in the Arab positions toward the Jewish state. On the other hand, the doves saw such demonstrations of force, justifiable in the past, as increasingly counterproductive, as they could raise the level of threat perception in Arab quarters—a development that in turn stiffened the Arab negotiating position. In contrast, the hawks, with a higher threat perception, had fewer qualms about the occasional use of force, which in their view, among other things, enhanced Israel's power of deterrence. They continued to fear that the Arabs still entertained the notion of putting an end to the conflict through force, i.e., defeating the IDF and destroying Israel.

One clear constraint on the use of force was the international environment. The doves were more responsive to world public opinion and to foreign governments' reactions to Israeli military measures. As noted, they feared in particular that Israeli violence could put unbearable strains on relations with Egypt. The "American factor" was taken into consideration by all, hawks and doves alike, when considering employing the IDF. Indeed, this heightened sensitivity to the United States was characteristic of Israeli foreign policy in general. There were occasional differences in the estimations of the latitude Israel had vis-à-vis U.S. interests and wishes. Hawks usually felt that Israel had greater leeway than the doves perceived. This also strengthened their predilection to use force.

Hawks and doves alike professed to subscribe to a realpolitik outlook, although doves were more inclined to voice moral considerations. In addition, some doves pointed out the changing nature of national power, somewhat belittling the importance of military prowess. Peres, for example, in a speech to a group of scientists in 1989, claimed that it is not the size or the strength of its army that determines a country's power, but rather its scientific and technological achievement. Peres also stressed, "It is a world in which the economy is more important than strategy."[10] At the end of that year, in reaction to the developments in Eastern Europe, he was even more explicit about the depreciation of military power. He noted that weapons had become so expensive that their purchase could be economically destructive. Furthermore, "Nearly everything which is important today is not attainable through military means—most of what armies would achieve has lost much significance."[11] On the same occasion, Peres observed, "No wonder that statesmen have concluded that the best thing today is gradually to dismantle the armaments, or most of them, and to establish relations between nations on a basis of demilitarization and economic cooperation." Arguments in such a vein were new in the Labor Party, particularly when applied to the situation in the Middle East. Such dovish argumentation was in accordance with lower levels of threat perception.

WAGING WAR

A most significant event in the area of national security in the 1980s was the Lebanon War, which broke out on June 6, 1982. Israel's extended, massive involvement in Lebanon until the end of the war in May 1985 left a lasting imprint on the mood and thinking of the Israeli public.[12] The sensitivity of the political leadership to public dissent and protest during wartime was significantly increased. Since the IDF relies on reserve units, making Israel into essentially a nation in arms, Israeli politicians realized that the government's freedom of action was curtailed in the event of a lack of consensus.[13] Indeed, the Labor party platforms for 1984 and 1988 included an article on taking into consideration the national consensus in case of military use of the IDF (see Appendix B, article 1.6.2.). This was, however, a careful formulation allowing considerable leeway for interpretation at the political level. As a matter of fact, there was no fundamental change in the Israeli public's perceptions regarding the appropriate use of force after the war in Lebanon.[14]

The range of Laborite reactions to the Lebanon War was indicative of more general attitudes in the party on the issue of waging war, which also to a great extent reflected hawkish/dovish variations. Initially, the party Knesset faction supported the Likud government's decision to intervene militarily in Lebanon, though three dovish Laborites were conspicuously missing from the no-confidence ballot in the Knesset proposed by the Arab–Jewish communist party Hadash. Leftist Mapam MKs similarly expressed their lack of enthusiasm by their absence. As a matter of fact, the hawkish MKs' demand to impose party discipline on the no-confidence vote was rejected by Peres.[15] Peres, then the party chair as well as opposition leader, issued a statement that referred to the IDF incursion into Lebanon as "a purely defensive action."[16] On June 25, 1982, a few weeks after the beginning of the war, Eban, then a leading party dove, asserted, "We should give our fullest backing to our forces on crucial objectives, as stated by the Prime Minister."[17] At this stage, the IDF was besieging Beirut.

Less than a month later, Eban was critical of the Laborites' praise of the government for reaching Beirut, and for striking against the Syrians. He went on to attack *Davar*, Labor's daily, for "leaving its pages wide open to the neorevisionism [i.e., Jabotinsky–Begin ideology] within our midst."[18] The popular consensus in favor of the war gradually disintegrated after the August bombings of Beirut, and particularly following the September massacres perpetrated by Israel's allies, the Christian Phalangists, in the Sabra and Shatilla refugee camps.[19] By then, Laborites, primarily the doves, had increased their criticism of the war. Among the party's doves, MK Yossi Sarid was the only one to speak out consistently against the war from the beginning. The belated criticism by others in the party, when the price for continuing the war became increasingly higher, was explained later by the claim that the party leadership was not originally aware of the ambitious goals of the Peace for Galilee Operation. This contention was, however, far from convincing.

In fact, the leaders of Labor, most with links to the security establishment, had excellent sources of information. For example, the opposition's prior knowledge of the secret preparations to attack the nuclear reactor near Baghdad (see the next section) clearly discredited claims of ignorance. Furthermore, Israel's plans to invade Lebanon were public knowledge. Military correspondents, Israeli and foreign, frequently reported on the preparations for the coming war. Indeed, Rabin admitted that the Labor Party was in possession of "authoritative information about the two schools of thought in the government as to the scope of the military action."[20] He was referring to the two contingency plans in readiness: a minimalist operation with a forty-kilometer range, and an invasion on a much larger scale, with Beirut and the highway from that city to Damascus as its targets.

On January 14, 1982, Labor's Executive Bureau (Lishka) was already discussing the conditions warranting IDF action in Lebanon. In the case of a war of attrition by the terrorists, the Labor Party decided that military action was necessary, "with the aim of removing the terrorists and their bases from areas where shelling is possible, in order to ensure that the northern border is not violated from within Lebanon, and to set conditions which prevent the possibility of their returning to and consolidating in those areas."[21] The Executive Bureau then recommended avoiding a confrontation with the Syrian forces that were in Lebanon. The Israeli–PLO artillery exchanges in the summer of 1981 ended in a cease-fire, but underlined Israel's inability to sustain an attrition war successfully along its northern border. Labor recommended, therefore, a limited escalation in the use of force. Unquestionably, most Laborites at that point preferred an enlarged version of the March 1978 Litani Operation, which was characterized by modest political goals, a limited territorial scope, and avoidance of contact with the Syrians.[22] The choice of escalation, which was a deeply rooted disposition, was typical of the Israeli response to the security dilemmas the country faced.[23]

The discussions in the Executive Bureau and its subsequent recommendations were not academic, but were clearly a response to the rumors of an imminent, large-scale Israeli invasion of Lebanon. Such an escalation appeared to be uncalled for. Indeed, most of the later criticism, which was well taken, focused on the unattainable goals of the war beyond the forty kilometers, which included ousting the Syrians from Lebanon and establishing a strong and friendly regime in Beirut.[24]

But the belatedness of party criticism was not connected to the hawks' influence in the party, nor to the latent attitudes toward the use of force. A concatenation of motives reinforced Labor's early reluctance to raise objections to the Likud's war in Lebanon.[25] First, the initial stage of the war appeared to be a great success and that was difficult to argue with. The party did not want to repeat its July 1981 performance after the successful air raid on the Iraqi nuclear reactor, when its muted criticism was portrayed as irresponsible partisan politics.[26] Second, despite some misgivings, the United States was perceived by all in the Israeli political system as lending support to the Begin government's aims in Lebanon.[27] Labor leaders were disinclined to criticize a U.S.-backed policy. Finally, when the Israeli presence in Lebanon began to appear more problematic, Labor leaders were inhibited from pointing out the growing difficulties of the Lebanon adventure because of the continuous engagement of the IDF in military action. As Rabin put it unequivocally in August 1982, "In the midst of the fighting there is no place for public debate."[28] A year earlier, he had shown a greater reluctance than his party colleagues to criticize publicly the raid on the Baghdad reactor.[29] Even lower-ranking Laborites accepted such a norm. For example, the secretariat of the Leshiluv group decided on June 20, 1982 "that the time to elaborate on the present critique has not yet come."[30]

The tendency to refrain from berating the government during wartime, but rather to foster consensus, was seen as a necessary condition for the achievement of victory and is typical of societies at war.[31] During the war, the extent of legitimate dissent was an issue that generated heated discussion in the Israeli public and in the party. Undoubtedly, the mere existence of this debate curtailed public criticism.[32] On the other hand, the hawks were certainly more inhibited in this regard. A hawkish exception was MK Shlomo Hillel, who believed that it was his duty to voice his criticism, even during the war.[33] In contrast, doves such as Sarid and yonetz Yaakov Tzur (then an MK, and since 1984 a cabinet member) were unrestrained in their condemnation of the war from its early stages.[34] Peres, who initially refrained from any criticism, changed his mind three weeks later, and then welcomed free debate.[35] This meant, of course, a free hand to attack the Likud-led government for its military involvement in Lebanon.

Yet some hawks in the party, for example veteran Israel Galili and MK Nachman Raz, had no reservations about the war's far-reaching goals, particularly getting to Beirut and expelling the PLO.[36] Chaim Herzog, a future president and then a hawkish Labor MK, claimed at the end of July 1982 that the war was inevitable, adding that "the government's timing and its political calculations about the U.S. and Syrian responses were correct and it would serve the opposition best to admit this."[37] Dani Rosolio, a hawk, also argued that the war was inevitable.[38] Other hawkish Labor MKs who supported the government throughout the war were Shoshana Arbeli-Almozlino, Aryeh Nehamkin, Raanan Naim, and Tamar Eshel. Even a yonetz like Dov Ben-Meir adopted a similar noncritical stance.[39]

All the critics in the party agreed that the political goals of the military intervention were beyond reach. Some emphasized normative problems, while others concentrated on utilitarian considerations. At issue was the matter of "war of no choice" or "war of choice," which, in the culture of Israeli politics, had the normative connotation of either a just or unjust war.[40] Tzur, one of the early critics of the war, maintained that military force was justified "only for the real and urgent security needs of Israel."[41] Furthermore, he claimed that a national consensus was needed when going to war; in his judgment, a majority was not sufficient.[42] This was one of the most extreme statements to the effect that the war was not legitimate. Yet neither Tzur nor anyone else in the party ever endorsed the position of some marginal leftist circles, outside of Labor, that advocated disobeying orders on the ground that the war was illegitimate. The party even included an article in its 1984 platform denouncing any refusal to serve in the IDF.[43]

Despite Tzur's professing to support only defensive wars, he included in this category preemptive strikes as well.[44] Bar-Lev also denied the war's legitimacy. He viewed the war objectives as "desirable, but not as justifying the use of force."[45] His criticism was that fulfillment of the war's goals was not "a vital need for the existence of Israel."[46] In the same speech, however, he described free navigation to Eilat, which was one of the goals of the 1956

Sinai Campaign, as a vital interest. This lent some flexibility to the notion of vital security needs. In their discussion of the war goals, both Tzur and Bar-Lev primarily discussed the normative dimension, which was a rather dovish emphasis. Yet their definition of "just war" was broad enough to allow plenty of room for the waging of war under many circumstances.

Rabin distinguished between two types of goals: "one group of goals relates to the direct security of Israel's citizens, its interests, and borders, while the second group of goals, though desirable, is neither directly related to, nor has a direct influence on the security of the state."[47] Rabin, in contrast to Tzur, Bar-Lev, and others in his party, refused to deny the legitimacy of objectives of the second type, although he expressed deep reservations about the effectiveness of employing force to attain them. In Rabin's opinion, the issue was never the justness of Israel's wars; the cardinal question was whether they were "worthwhile, necessary, or desirable."[48] Indeed, he admitted his dislike of the term "war of no choice."[49] The war in Lebanon was unquestionably legitimate in his judgment; it was its wisdom that he was skeptical about. He preferred, in other words, a calculus of utility rather than of normative deliberations.

Rabin's approach was attacked primarily by the party doves. His businesslike criticism and occasional advice to the Likud on how to run the war evoked resentment—for example, in Chaim Ramon.[50] Gur, despite his more critical posture, also occasionally gave his counsel. It was difficult for both Gur and Rabin, who were once involved in the highest levels of decisionmaking, not to be in the center of things. Rabin's attitude that Israel had to make the most of an uncomfortable situation, and his mere presence in Lebanon next to Ariel Sharon, the Likud defense minister, were regarded by party doves as bestowing a mantle of legitimacy on the war conducted by the Likud government. The dovish wing of the party, in particular, being more concerned with the normative aspect of Israel's presence in Lebanon, wanted to delegitimize Israel's involvement there. Dovish Laborites also wished to capitalize on the increasing obviousness of the failure of the war so as to score points in the political battle with the Likud.

Despite the party consensus that the Arab–Israeli conflict could not be solved by force, and the fact that the Lebanon War had underlined the limits of military might (limits that were understood by Labor leaders long before 1982), the search for political solutions did not exclude military means. But there was disagreement on the appropriate scope of force to use and on the degree of its effectiveness. The doves displayed, in general, greater reluctance to rely on military means, on both strategic and moral grounds. For example, the massive use of firepower during the siege of Beirut disturbed them, while the hawks were convinced that only a resolute demonstration of force could convince Arafat and his men to leave the city. The hawks preferred a utilitarian approach, with limited regard for normative objections.

Following the war in Lebanon, the Labor Party, as well as other sectors of the Israeli body politic, became more hesitant in advocating massive use of force. In fact, in the period immediately following the 1973 war, Labor had already displayed a tendency to employ less force,[51] which became somewhat more marked in the aftermath of the Lebanon War.

In 1984, after seven years in opposition, where it could influence national security policies only marginally, Labor was back in the government—this time together with the Likud and again in a position to formulate policy. The grand coalition was re-established in 1988, though with less advantageous terms for Labor. In this latter government the posts of prime minister and foreign minister were allotted to the Likud, with no rotation, while Peres was given the Treasury portfolio, a way of limiting his involvement in foreign affairs. Yet Rabin, the defense minister in the 1984–1988 National Unity government, continued to serve in the same capacity, as he was well regarded by Likud leaders.

With Rabin at the helm, Israel disassociated itself from some of the policies pursued by the Likud. Rabin and his Labor colleagues in the government were largely responsible for the government's decision to withdraw from Lebanon in May 1985, a decision that reflected the realization that massive use of force could not achieve the goals of the previous Likud-led governments. The August 1987 resolution to cancel the ambitious Lavi aircraft project, despite strong Likud opposition, was another example of disengagement from the Likud past. Even Peres, a long-time supporter of the country's defense industries, voted in favor of Rabin's recommendation to terminate the project. Rabin had always maintained a measured attitude toward the Israeli defense industry. His skepticism about the wisdom of investing in large-scale projects such as the Lavi was well known, and one of the sources of friction with Peres.[52] Possibly it was the merits of the alternatives to the Lavi, or U.S. opposition to continuing the development of this airplane, that convinced Peres. His reluctance to enter into a confrontation with Rabin, which could renew the feud between them, was also, needless to say, a powerful argument.

Under Rabin, Israel seemed to have adopted a cautious defensive strategy. In a programmatic speech at the 1986 party congress, the defense minister pointed out to his Laborite colleagues that there was no prize in the region, either military or territorial, that could make the waging of a large-scale operation a worthwhile enterprise. The test of success for Israel's national security policy, therefore, was its ability to prevent war.[53] This constituted a policy of deterrence. In 1988, Rabin emphasized that his policy would continue to be defensive, with little room for preventive or preemptive strikes, just as he had advocated in the immediate post-1973 period.[54] Neither in the 1970s nor in the 1980s did Rabin see any political goal as worth the risk of war. He added, furthermore: "Any future war will not be easy or painless. The quantity and quality of available weapons and existing firepower have grown considerably."[55] Taking into account the characteristics of the future Middle East battlefield—including enormous firepower and huge quantities of weapons—Rabin preferred to conserve his forces. His opposition to an Israeli-initiated war was practical rather than principled.

Indeed, under certain circumstances, an Israeli initiative was envisioned; this could augment deterrence. Despite his preference for a defensive posture, the defense minister insisted that "the IDF must be ready for a preemptive strike should it be felt that war is imminent."[56] However, he refused to enunciate a specific set of *casi belli*.[57] The circumstances were left vague, so as to increase uncertainty on the Arab side, but in fact the scenarios for preemptive action were rather limited. Furthermore, the IDF was still to retain the ability to transfer the war rapidly into the enemy's territory, which was a basic element of Israel's national strategy. Such preparations, however, were not in conflict with reluctance to initiate war. Gur also shared an aversion to specifying the situations that warranted Israeli use of force. Yet he was more inclined than Rabin to stress preemptive action. In reaction to calls to increase reliance on defensive measures, primarily from academic circles, Gur pointed out the dangers of adopting a purely defensive posture and maintained that victory in a future war would be assured by offense and conquest of territories.[58]

Hawks and doves alike agreed with Rabin's limited list of situations in which massive use of force was warranted. However, some doves, such as Baram, Eliav, and Peretz, seemed more intent on refraining from preemptive strikes; others were less hesitant. A position favoring defensive wars only was also found at the dovish ministerial level. For example, in the winter of 1989, when several high officers, including the chief of staff, mentioned the need for a future preemption on the Syrian front, Yitzhak Navon criticized their statements. He argued that there was no government decision authorizing such a strike, and that any expressions in this vein were dangerous. It was the escalatory potential of their remarks that Navon feared.[59] Even Peres took a stance opposing preemptive strikes.[60]

The increasing supply of long-range missiles to Middle East protagonists in the last years of the 1980s, as well as the developing Arab capacity to produce chemical and biological weapons, introduced new dangers for Israel. Reports in 1988 about Israeli plans to preempt originated in the prime ministerial offices, which were staffed by Likud people.[61] Neither Rabin nor Peres, then foreign minister, engaged in such threats. But neither did they belittle the new risks. On the contrary, Peres, in a parliamentary debate in May 1987, expressed grave concern about reports of the manufacture of chemical weapons in Arab countries, and about the supply of missiles and advanced weaponry to Israel's regional rivals. Rabin displayed similar concern over these changes in the Arab arsenal. As we have seen, however, they did not concur on the political conclusions to be drawn from these developments.

In the 1980s, the IDF increased its efforts to prepare its troops for surviving and fighting in a chemically affected battleground. Since the late 1980s, the civilian population has been similarly trained on how to react to attack by chemical warheads. In March 1990, the chief of staff disclosed that a decision had been reached to provide gas masks to the entire population in case of an emergency.[62] But passive defensive measures, however effective, were obviously not sufficient to prevent a great number of casualties. The Israeli ability to employ active defensive measures was likewise limited. Therefore, on several occasions, Rabin threatened terrible consequences for those daring to use chemical weaponry against Israel,[63] but he refrained from mentioning preemptive actions. He seemed to prefer enhanced defenses and increased deterrence, by means of escalation dominance (i.e., the advantage of escalating beyond the enemy's capability),[64] to coercive diplomacy. Again, Gur supported such a policy. Addressing the issue of missiles and nonconventional weapons in the hands of Arab countries, he advocated deterrence, rather than military action to eliminate such threats.[65] However, the ability to dominate the escalation process was increasingly problematic as Israeli civilian centers had become more vulnerable to an Arab attack than they had been previously. An increased Arab destructive capability contributed to a higher level of threat perception, primarily among the hawks, but not to any policy change.

Some of the doves in particular were not overly concerned. Weizman's nonchalant attitude toward chemical weapons has already been mentioned; we have also noted the belief that higher destructiveness was actually positive in the sense that it forced the parties to make peace.

Despite the apparently growing pressure to reconsider Israel's conventional doctrine in the face of increasing Arab capacity to exact a considerable price in a military exchange, there were no public demands in the party for a nuclear deterrent. On this issue, even more than on other national security topics, the Labor Party, as such, refrained from discussion. The dovish argument, made already in the mid-1970s, that an overt Israeli nuclear posture could allow Israel safely to disengage from the administered territories and thus solve the "demographic problem" had no clearly felt impact.[66] As noted, deliberations on whether to go nuclear, which rarely received publicity, were conducted in both dovish and hawkish quarters. Rabin's clear preference for a conventional environment was well known. In September 1975, for the first time, Rabin's government consented to the establishment of a Nuclear Weapons Free Zone.[67] In January 1988, when the specter of chemical weapons in the Middle East was very visible, Rabin, in a lecture to a delegation of the European Parliament, proposed the inclusion of chemical weapons in an arms control treaty.[68] At the UN Conference on Chemical Warfare convening in Paris at that time, the Arab countries insisted on just such a linkage—in order to negate Israeli superiority in the area of nuclear technology. Despite the transparency of Arab motivations, Rabin responded positively. He was apparently interested in strengthening the conventional threshold, which could be eroded through the use of chemical weapons. Similarly, Gur, in a rare public statement on this topic, stressed in 1989 that the political process had priority over the development of nuclear weapons.[69] The introduction of weapons of massive destruction was not regarded as beneficial for Israel, particularly in the case of large-scale war.

LIMITED USE OF FORCE

Various forms of military force were used by Israel in the 1980s. This variety is not new in Israeli history. While the Lebanon War involved large-scale use of force, low-level violence was practiced by Israel both before and after that conflict.[70] Israel's leaders, including Laborites, were not strangers to the lower rungs in the violence ladder. Targets within Lebanese territory, even after the withdrawal in 1985, continued to be attacked. However, although the Syrian army was engaged in the Lebanon War, Syrian territory remained untouched. Indeed, during the 1980s Israel refrained from infringements on the territorial integrity of other Arab countries, with two exceptions: the June 1981 air strike on the Iraqi nuclear reactor near Baghdad, and the October 1985 air raid on PLO headquarters in Tunis. In this section I shall discuss Laborite positions on all these instances of the limited use of force.

Following the daring Israeli strike against the Iraqi nuclear reactor in June 1981, a few weeks before the general elections, Peres and Rabin, Labor's leaders in the opposition, congratulated the Israeli Air Force (IAF) for its fabulous achievement, but refrained from praising Begin's government.[71] Playing down the government's role in successful military operations was typical of Israeli parties in opposition.[72] Obviously, the Labor Party was not happy with the timing of the air raid, which was regarded as an election ploy to win support for the Likud. Even a hawk like Chaim Herzog, who then served as Labor's propaganda director for the elections, criticized its timing.[73] Yet it was not only the timing of the raid that was problematic for Labor. Several of the Labor opposition leaders knew about the operation well in advance, and were all opposed to it regardless of its timing.

Begin's government did not share the details of the planned raid with senior members of Labor, although a general briefing on the possibility of such an action was given. But the ultrasecret preparations were leaked in various quarters. Weizman, for example, who then held no governmental or party position, having resigned a year earlier from Begin's government, was still well informed about the government's plans. In general, Labor leaders, even when in the opposition, had independent sources of information within the security establishment, and possessed a rather sound knowledge of security planning.

In fact, the threat to Israel's security resulting from Iraq's nuclear progress was not taken lightly. In the mid-1970s the Labor-led government, in which Rabin was the premier and Peres his defense minister, had attempted to prevent further Iraqi progress in this direction, and had resorted to sabotage, among other means. Nevertheless, Peres attempted to exert his influence to prevent the 1981 air strike.[74] A careful analysis had led him to the conclusion that it would take many years for Iraq to overcome the technical problems it faced in acquiring a nuclear weapons option; therefore, he saw no urgency about destroying the Iraqi reactor.[75] Such an action would also focus international attention on Israel's nuclear program—in Peres's view, a most undesirable effect. Furthermore, it would increase Arab motivation to produce nuclear weapons; and it could have the further negative consequence of increasing Israeli isolation. Following consultations with Rabin, Bar-Lev, Eban, Gur, and Dinitz, Peres sent an urgent letter to Prime Minister Begin, explaining his objections to the air raid and urging him to cancel the operation.[76] Neither Rabin, who was probably the best-informed Laborite on this affair, nor Bar-Lev favored a military solution to the problem.[77] Gur, who had served as chief of staff under Begin, also tried to convince the prime minister to cancel the operation;[78] he believed that every possible political means should be exhausted first.[79]

Weizman also tried to prevent the raid by engaging in intensive lobbying; he met with several cabinet members in an attempt to dissuade them from supporting the planned strike. As a former IAF commander, Weizman was less concerned about a possible failure; confident that Israel's pilots could do the job, he feared that the attack could severely damage Israel's relationship with Egypt.[80] In his view, a deterioration in relations with the only Arab country that had signed a peace treaty with Israel was too heavy a price. This great sensitivity to the effect Israeli actions might have on the peace process was, of course, typical of dovish attitudes.

Thus the Labor leadership was united in its opposition to the air strike. As noted, Labor's attitude toward the use of force was in general more restrained. Peres and Bar-Lev were risk averters, and Rabin, in particular, was known for his great caution. On paper the IAF plan looked, to many, like a very risky adventure. Yet it was difficult to argue with a military success. Politically, the price paid for eliminating an existential threat seemed to be minimal. Therefore, attacking this military accomplishment appeared partisan, and hurt the party at the polls. Electoral factors further muted the criticism, which was deemed to be unpatriotic.

The success of the air raid and the lack of serious international repercussions caused some Laborites, such as Gur, to admit later to being wrong. Even Eban, who was usually critical of Likud policies, considered the action to be a great achievement that enhanced Israel's power of deterrence.[81] Some hawks in the party, in particular, were dissatisfied with the party's failure to back the raid unequivocally.[82] It had, after all, eliminated a potential nuclear threat, something hawks had no qualms about. Furthermore, many considered the "occasional show of muscle" as necessary to enhance deterrence.⁸³ Others in the party, however, viewed the boldness of the IAF's strike against a target 1,000 kilometers away as bordering on adventurism. After the fact, many misgivings disappeared. Yet the unexpected success of the military action in Baghdad reduced the level of apprehension about the feasibility of spectacular feats in Beirut a year later.

In the 1980s, with few exceptions, Lebanon was the only theater in which the IDF was employed in battle. Excluding the Syrians in 1982, Israel did not engage in fighting any Arab military forces other than Palestinian organizations and, occasionally, irregular forces in Lebanon. Again, with the exception of the Lebanon War, Israel used mostly low-level violence against these targets. The announcements of IDF spokespersons about air raids, artillery barrages, and commando attacks received little attention, unless they resulted in Israeli casualties. The unabated campaign against terrorism was, in most Israeli minds, merely a routine military activity.

Laborites did not challenge such a view. The endless attacks on Palestinian objectives were recognized, however, as incapable of bringing an end to terror. Time and again Rabin emphasized that there was no military solution to the persistent violence perpetrated by Palestinian organizations. Even the party hawks acknowledged the political roots of the terrorist activity. Yet both hawks and doves agreed that Israel was obliged to use force to defend itself. Ora Namir, known for her dovish views, did not hesitate to defend Rabin even for initiating the October 1985 air raid against PLO headquarters in Tunis. In the parliamentary debate following the government's announcement after the raid, she said, "We have to say to the PLO's leader, Arafat, that Israel will not turn the other cheek; will not wave an olive branch; Israel has to react to terror. . . . "⁸⁴ The acceptable reaction was counterviolence.

Indeed, the long-range air strike against PLO targets in Tunisia—2,400 kilometers away from Israel—clearly exemplified the determined Israeli policy of retaliation, no matter how distant the targets, despite awareness that terrorism was not a major security problem. Rabin, in explaining the government's decision to act in Tunisia, emphasized that terror was not the main security threat: "It hurts, it annoys, it disrupts, but it does not constitute an existential threat to the state."⁸⁵ The Arab armies, increasing in size and sophistication, were seen as posing the gravest threat to Israel.⁸⁶

Nevertheless, terror was hardly to be ignored. Moreover, in October 1985, Rabin initiated a response with a clear escalation potential. Tunisia was one of the more moderate Arab countries, which had agreed to host the PLO headquarters following their forced evacuation from Beirut in 1982 only under heavy pressure from other Arab states and the United States. At the time of the raid, Israel was engaged in delicate discussions with Egypt over the destiny of the small Taba enclave, while contacts with Jordan seemed to be yielding some progress. The negotiations with Egypt and Jordan did not restrain Rabin, however. He believed that the PLO hardly enjoyed the sympathy of these two countries, and that their behavior toward Israel accorded with their own national interests, which would be affected only marginally by Israel's military actions against the Palestinians. Such an outlook was typical of the hawkish wing, which minimized the importance of the Palestinian issue in the Arab–Israeli conflict. Actually, the raid was also seen as a warning to Hussein not to allow a free hand to the PLO military presence in his territory, re-established as a result of the February 1985 Jordanian–PLO agreement.[87] Indeed, attacking PLO bases in Jordan was one of the options considered by the inner cabinet of the National Unity government before it approved Rabin's proposal for an air raid in Tunisia. Hitting a target within Jordan, however, was seen as potentially more destabilizing than an action in faraway Tunisia. Furthermore, the air strike was also intended to enhance Israel's deterrent power. The evening after the action, Rabin issued warnings to Syria not to engage in a military adventure against Israel. Though directed primarily at hindering terrorist activity, the raid thus had other motives as well.

With the exception of Ezer Weizman, all the Laborites in the inner cabinet—Peres, Bar-Lev, and Navon—voted in favor of Rabin's proposal. Weizman voted against the raid because—as he later explained—he feared that the timing of such a spectacular military action could hurt chances for improving relations with Egypt and interfere with progress in relations with Jordan. He also expressed his preference for quietly eliminating those responsible for the terror, which was less embarrassing politically.[88] The leftist opposition parties criticized the air raid on these same grounds.[89] Despite his official vote, Peres was probably not happy with the air strike either; reports about his hesitations and misgivings leaked out.[90] Yet other doves in the party backed Rabin's policy. Both Namir and MK Shevach Weiss attacked the leftist parties' positions on the raid in the parliamentary debate.[91] Incidentally, both were members of the Rabin camp in the party. Abba Eban, the chair of the Knesset Foreign Affairs and Defense Committee, expressed similar support for the raid: "I favor the government's decision."[92] The warm support of the hawkish Laborites, for example MKs Shoshana Arbeli-Almozlino and Amnon Lin, came as no surprise.[93]

Israel also used low-level military force, this time in a more sustained fashion, in the security zone along the Lebanese side of the border that was established following the Israeli withdrawal in 1985. On this issue, Laborites displayed even greater support for Rabin's policy. In fact, the party was united behind this approach, which was advocated by the party leadership and had already been clearly enunciated in the 1984 elections platform. This united position helped the party representatives in the National Unity government to extricate Israel from the Lebanese imbroglio in May 1985, when the large-scale Israeli presence in Lebanon finally ended. Actually, Israel then returned to the policy of the Rabin government in the pre-Likud period, which was based on the establishment of a security zone in southern

Lebanon to be controlled and defended by Lebanese elements. Israel trained and financed the South Lebanese Army (SLA), and lent economic and humanitarian assistance to the residents of the security zone. In addition, a limited Israeli military presence remained to aid the SLA and to enhance the security of Israeli settlements along the northern border. As defense minister, Rabin was instrumental in adopting and implementing this approach.

All party members opposed the criticism that came from the right (particularly before the 1988 elections), which demanded a widening of the security zone, i.e., increasing Israel's involvement in Lebanon. The regular military activity beyond the security zone, of varying scope and level, was not disputed. Occasional actions, particularly in the vicinity of the Syrian presence, were, however, questioned because of their escalation potential. In this context, Weizman was the most outspoken among Labor's ministers.[94] As long as the security zone approach, which included limited military activity in Lebanon, did not exact a high price politically and in terms of casualties, the party went along with the policy of the Labor defense minister.

This did not mean a carte blanche in other areas, however. The April 1988 assassination of the PLO leader Abu Jihad in Tunisia, for example—not officially ackowledged as an Israeli feat—evoked criticism in the party. Doves Weizman and Navon, members of the inner cabinet, spoke out against the assassination, and Peres took a similar stance.[95] The opposition was motivated not only by reluctance to use force, but also by the target's identity. Increasing willingness among doves to deal with the PLO created greater inhibitions about eliminating PLO senior personnel, even if engaged in terror. Weizman did not hesitate to remonstrate publicly against the assassination, claiming that it hindered the peace process.[96] Although in 1985 he had advocated "a quiet elimination," he appeared now to have changed his mind. Rabin and Bar-Lev were reported to have joined the Likud ministers in approving the operation.[97] Yaakobi made a point of emphasizing that he did not object to the assassination.[98] It is noteworthy that in the 1970s, similar actions against PLO leaders engaged in terrorism raised no objections in the party. This was another indication of the leftward shift in positions. Another example where limited force evoked some Laborite criticism was the kidnapping of the Shiite sheikh Obeid in July 1989. He was abducted in the hope of bringing about an exchange of prisoners with Shiite extremists. Shahal, however, had opposed the idea in the inner cabinet.[99]

Another bone of contention, in the party and outside it, was Rabin's military policy in Judea, Samaria, and Gaza from the beginning of the Palestinian uprising. As defense minister, he was the most crucial decisionmaker in the formulation of Israel's policy in the territories. The goal was to break the civil resistance; initially, it was believed that force could do the job. Shooting at rioters with live ammunition was discouraged, except in situations where the troops' lives were in danger. Beatings were allowed for a short time, but only in the act of quelling a riot. The IDF gradually introduced various measures of riot control, but the intifada—although its intensity decreased after several months—was not brought to an end.[100] Rabin's perception of the situation in the administered territories was that it required a limited show of force. Methods of "bloodbath," used quite effectively in several places in the world, were never even considered. Rabin aimed to maneuver between the necessity to demonstrate a resolute use of force and the need to avoid antagonizing the Palestinian population, so as to enable a return to normalcy.[101]

As the intifada continued unabated, albeit at a low level, Rabin and others in the party felt uncomfortable with responding only by military means and administrative pressure. Therefore, Rabin and Peres offered in October 1988, before the impending Israeli elections, a plan for elections in the Israeli-ruled territories that would produce a partner with whom to negotiate an interim agreement on the features of autonomy. This idea became the basis for the May 1989 peace initiative of the National Unity government. As long as the Palestinians were not willing to go along with his plan for elections and, subsequently, autonomy, Rabin felt fully justified in using force against them.[102] Generally, the amount of force used depended on the type of provocation, and the distinctions made by local commanding officers. In addition to force (beatings, shootings, and demolitions of houses), the government utilized administrative measures to force the cooperation of the civilian population. Deportations were used in a limited number of cases. Overall, after the attempt to quash the uprising rapidly through force failed, a patient attrition approach of limited use of force was adopted, in the hope that the local population would realize the increasing price they were paying for their course of action. Rabin explained to his party colleagues in March 1988 the guidelines for his policy in the territories: "I believe that the problem cannot be solved in one go. What will bring the violence to an end is a cumulative process of physical and economic fatigue and the disruption of the frameworks of daily life."[103]

Although Rabin believed that a purely military approach could not solve the situation in the Israeli-ruled territories, he emphasized that Palestinian violence had to be met with limited force by Israel so as to "prove to them that nothing can be achieved through violence."[104] Use of force had to complement the political process. Rabin became even more convinced of this when he realized that the uprising had dangerous, wide-ranging political implications (as discussed in Chapter 3). In December 1989, Rabin described the intifada as a new war of attrition "which would last another two years."[105] He, like other hawks, was reconciled to the idea of a lengthy military struggle.

Political circles right of Labor deplored "the lack of determination" in the IDF's treatment of the uprising, which meant a preference for greater use of force. Occasionally, party hawks such as Hillel joined in the demand for harsher measures. To the left of Labor, Rabin was regarded as using excessive force. In particular, the initial policy of beatings (adopted to minimize the use of firearms) drew censure. The more outspoken doves in the party joined in the attacks of the Left. MKs Ramon and Namir, for example, remonstrated against the government's policy; it was felt that Rabin was putting too much emphasis on his "strong-hand" policy and on appearing at least as firm as his Likud predecessors.[106] Not all doves were upset by this, however. MK Shevach Weiss, a dove and a member of the Rabin camp in the party, had no objection as long as he was convinced that Rabin was also searching for a political solution to the problem.[107] Tzadok, moreover, pointed out that Israel had a legal obligation, as an occupying power, to restore law and order. Reasonable use of force was, therefore, justified in this capacity. Rejecting unilateral withdrawal, Tzadok then reasoned that force was necessary to pacify the territories.[108]

Criticism of Rabin's policies was not limited to Labor backbenchers. At the ministerial level, Weizman pointed out as early as December 1987 that sticks were not enough; what was needed, in his opinion, was a "wise arm" rather than a strong one.[109] In March 1988, Navon, also a government member, expressed in a party organ his distress at the harsher elements of the policy implemented in the territories: "I disapprove of both the policy of deportations and that of beatings."[110] In this interview, he suggested that "there should be a defensive policy of keeping law and order." On the other hand, Bar-Lev, Gur, and Yaakobi did not hesitate to support Rabin. Peres, though not publicly critical, distanced himself from the defense minister's policy. As the November 1988 elections drew closer, the doves became gradually more inhibited in their criticism so as to allow Labor to appear united and to avoid projecting an overly dovish image to the public.

However, after the elections the criticism surfaced in an unrestrained fashion. It was tied also to Rabin's refusal to talk to the PLO after U.S. recognition of this organization in December 1988. It was in that context that the new MK Avraham Burg, a Peace Now activist, called Rabin "the peace suppressor." MKs Baram and Ramon attacked Peres as well, claiming that the two Labor leaders were not much different from those of Likud.[111] The more vocal discontent among several of Labor's doves was also a consequence of the more organized opposition to Rabin's policy in circles left of Labor. In addition, dovish discontent was also fueled by opposition to the partnership with Likud in the National Unity government, which Rabin strongly supported. Yet most of the party stood behind Rabin, who was considered to be the only one capable of extracting the necessary support from Likud, Labor's coalition partner, for a mutually acceptable government policy leading to a political solution. Micha Harish, Labor's new secretary general (as of February 1989) and a yonetz, reflected the general positions of the hawkish and yonetz leaders. At the beginning of 1989, he pointedly refused to criticize Rabin, stating, "I share the opinion that a political solution can be reached only from a position of strength."[112]

SIDE EFFECTS OF THE USE OF FORCE

As we have seen, the party, especially its doves, feared that a prolonged occupation would have a corrupting effect on Israeli society, particularly because of the recurrent need to employ force. Since the war in Lebanon, political circles left of Labor had expressed greater concern than before about the effects that routinization of the use of force were having on Israeli society, and such concerns were shared by some Labor members. Ora Namir was one of the most outspoken Laborites on this issue. In 1983, in the midst of the war in Lebanon, she bemoaned the tragic situation in which Israelis had to live: "It has been very difficult to be brought up in the last thirty-five years in the atmosphere of six big wars and a few smaller ones, and not to see in any one of them, unfortunately, not even the Lebanon War, the last. . . . Such an atmosphere means worship of force, of weapons, of the army."[113] In the same speech, Namir expressed sorrow that this situation was also leading to a growing tendency toward intolerance, and to the creation of a new generation that "believes in the power of naked force as an alternative to dialogue, and as the only way to resolve disagreements." Brutalization of Israeli society was feared. She concluded by demanding that the Knesset "consider what is happening to us from a moral perspective: how the reality of wars corrupts the basics of our beliefs; how vital peace is to enable us to return to our cultural and moral sources, back to our human image." She later responded in a similar fashion, as noted in Chapter 2, to the nature of Israeli attempts to suppress the intifada. The occupation and the military struggle against the Palestinian uprising had, in her view, a severely corrupting effect on the Israeli social fabric.

It was not only doves like Namir who had such thoughts. During the war in Lebanon, Tzur, a yonetz, similarly expressed his concern about possible damage to Israel's moral image.[114] Even MK Nachman Raz, a hawkish kibbutz member who supported the war, wrote in an article that appeared in a kibbutz-movement organ in the fall of 1982, "I fear that for many the crucial distinction between force as a necessary means and the worship of force as a goal has been blurred."[115] In a Knesset debate on the intifada, Gur expressed similar worries: "Our soldier . . . returns either feeling nauseous about the job which he must perform, or viewing the Arabs as 'two-legged beasts.' . . . The continued occupation is a breeding ground for Kahanism and racism."[116] In this speech he expressed awareness that this predicament is part of the educational dilemma of a nation in a protracted conflict. Commenting on the intifada, Bar-Lev pointed out the growing intolerance fostered by the situation.[117] Rabin too recognized the moral dilemmas his soldiers in the territories faced, but he also expressed pride at their high moral sensitivity.[118]

Rabin, however, had other concerns as well. He was worried about the sagging national morale; in his view, victory could only be gained by the side displaying a stronger national will. Protracted conflict required steadfast resolution and patience. He did his best to dispel notions that there are quick solutions and shortcuts in the long military and political struggle to entrench the Jewish state as a stable and secure reality in the Middle East. In his speech to the graduating class of the Military College for Staff and Command he said: "We have to foster perseverance and the ability to withstand the burdens of more than one war . . . as in the past, future victories will be achieved through determination and fortitude."[119]

Raz expressed similar dismay at the loss of determination, adding that the debates over the war in Lebanon reflected "deterioration in the sense of the justness of the path chosen, and in confidence. . . ."[120] The soldiers' doubts and lack of faith in their normative base constituted, in his opinion, a grave danger, because they led to weariness of the long conflict. The many wars, he feared, had taken their toll on the people's readiness to make sacrifices for the vital interests of the state. Indeed, many Israelis felt that there had been an erosion in Zionist resolve as a result of the seemingly unending wars. Such a perspective was typical of circles to the right of Labor; they regarded the importunateness of the Left's demands for resolving the Arab–Israeli dispute, and the great concessions advocated, as the result of weariness. Labor's hawks were quite receptive to such arguments.

War was regarded, however, as having some positive effects as well. Gur, for example, pointed out what he called "the bitter truth—that the preparations for waging war were directly related to prosperity."[121] All Laborites who supported the development of Israel's military industries similarly pointed to the tremendous spin-off effects of producing weapons. The Heraclitian thesis, however, that war is the source of all progress, was not voiced in Labor, as it was in circles outside the party.[122] The advantages indirectly resulting from war were, even when appreciated, usually seen as issuing from an undesirable situation. Furthermore, among Laborites there is no glorification of heroism or idealization of war.

Certain party members in fact, particularly the doves, regarded the regular use of force as a waste of valuable and scarce resources, thus impeding economic growth. As finance minister, Peres ascribed a heavy price to the Palestinian uprising. Weizman also emphasized the economic losses caused by the intifada; he summarized his position with the remark, "As long as we beat up children in Gaza we will be unable to increase exports."[123] Among the Laborite ministers, Yaakobi was the most attentive to the economic price of the intifada. On several occasions he lamented the lack of economic growth, which he attributed to expenses involved in suppressing the uprising.[124]

CONCLUSION

The employment of force was, in Labor's eyes, an accepted tool of Israel's foreign policy. The party leadership, most of which was intimately acquainted with strategy, displayed a rather cautious approach to military actions. Differences of opinion were for the most part not phrased as questions of principle, but rather dealt with the degree of force required. Even the "choice/no-choice" debate concerning the legitimacy of the war in Lebanon was not devoid of politico-strategic considerations. The doves, as expected, were more skeptical about the wisdom of using force. At the ministerial level, Weizman, followed by Navon, represented the minimalist dovish sentiment. Peres was not far behind them, but was more cautious in his relations with Rabin. Peres and Weizman, in fact, exemplified the changes that had taken place in the party. Both formerly hawks, in the 1980s they were more reserved about the wisdom of utilizing military power in the region. The younger or less senior doves, such as Baram, Burg, Namir, and Ramon, were even more critical. Overall, the greater reluctance in the party to employ military actions was part of a more general phenomenon that became more pronounced in Israeli society in the early 1980s. The doves were more inclined to point out the economic costs of waging war than the hawks, who tended to see these costs as the necessary price to be paid in the struggle for an independent and secure Israel. Doves also tended to be more sensitive to the potential corrupting effect of the routinization of the use of force. In contrast, hawks feared an erosion in the ability of Israelis to endure a protracted conflict.

NOTES

1. See Baruch Kimmerling, "Making Conflict a Routine: Cumulative Effects of the Arab–Jewish Conflict Upon Israeli Society," *Journal of Strategic Studies* 6 (September 1983), pp. 13–45.
2. For European socialist pacifism in the past, see Michael Howard, *War and the Liberal Conscience* (New Brunswick, N.J.: Rutgers University Press, 1978); John F. Naylor, *Labor's International Policy* (London: Weidenfeld & Nicolson, 1969); Paul U. Kellogg and Arthur Gleason, *British Labor and the War* (New York: Garland Publishing Inc., 1972).
3. For early Zionist attitudes toward the use of force, see Anita Shapira, *Visions in Conflict* (Hebrew) (Tel Aviv: Am Oved, 1988), pp. 23–71.
4. Efraim Inbar, "Attitudes Toward War in the Israeli Political Elite," *Middle East Journal* 44 (Summer 1990), pp. 431–445.
5. Shimon Peres with Hagai Eshed, *Tomorrow Is Now* (Hebrew) (Jerusalem: Mabat, 1978), p. 249.
6. Chaim Bar-Lev, "The War and Its Objectives in Light of the IDF's Wars," *Maarachot* 266 (October–November 1978), p. 3.
7. See, inter alia, *Maariv*, October 29, 1986.
8. For the greater tendency of the Likud governments to use force, see

Efraim Inbar, "Israeli Strategic Thinking After 1973," pp. 45–53; for the revisionist preference for the use of force in changing history, see Yaakov Shavit, *The Mythologies of the Zionist Right Wing* (Hebrew) (Beit Berl: Beit Berl and The Moshe Sharett Institute, 1987), pp. 225–228; Ehud Luz, "The Moral Price of Sovereignty: The Dispute About the Use of Military Power Within Zionism," *Modern Judaism* 7 (February 1987), pp. 64–69.

9. Yitzhak Rabin, "The IDF's Objectives."

10. For the transcript of his speech see *Haaretz*, June 2, 1989. For an elaborate argument about the changing nature of power, see Seyom Brown, "The Changing Essence of Power," *Foreign Affairs* 51 (January 1973), p. 286–299.

11. Shimon Peres, "The Middle East in a Brave New World."

12. For its influence on internal developments, see S. N. Eisenstadt, "The Internal Repercussions of the Lebanon War," *Policy Papers* 17 (Jerusalem: The Leonard Davis Institute for International Relations, The Hebrew University of Jerusalem, August 1986).

13. Dan Horowitz, "Strategic Limitations of 'A Nation in Arms,'" *Armed Forces and Society* 13 (Winter 1987), pp. 289–290.

14. Asher Arian, Ilan Talmud, and Tamar Hermann, *National Security and Public Opinion in Israel*, JCSS Study, no. 9 (Jerusalem: *Jerusalem Post*/Westview Press, 1988), pp. 31–32.

15. Yael Yishai, "The Israeli Labor Party and the Lebanon War," *Armed Forces and Society* 11 (Spring 1985), p. 381.

16. *Davar*, June 7, 1982.

17. *Jerusalem Post*, June 25, 1982.

18. *Davar*, July 16, 1982.

19. For the gradual erosion of the national consensus, see Shai Feldman and Heda Rechnitz-Kijner, *Deception, Consensus and War: Israel in Lebanon*, JCSS Study, no. 27 (October 1984); and Dan Horowitz, "Israel's War in Lebanon: New Patterns of Strategic Thinking and Civilian–Military Relations," *Journal of Strategic Studies* 6 (September 1983), pp. 85–88.

20. "Interview with Rabin," *Migvan* 72 (August 1982), p. 3. Ariel Sharon claimed that both the government and the opposition knew about the ultimate goals of the war. See his "The 40 Kilometers Fable," *Maariv*, August 21, 1987. Yossi Sarid, at the other end of the Israeli political spectrum and an unrestrained critic of Sharon, lent support to this claim. See his "Labor's Position During the War in Lebanon," *Haaretz*, August 21, 1987.

21. "Labour on War," *Spectrum* (December 1982), p. 22.

22. For the Litani Operation, see Avner Yaniv, *Dilemmas of Security: Politics, Strategy and the Israeli Experience in Lebanon* (Oxford: Oxford University Press, 1987), pp. 71–75; Efraim Inbar, "Israel and Lebanon: 1975–1982," *Crossroads* 10 (Spring 1983), pp. 50–52.

23. See Avner Yaniv, *Deterrence Without the Bomb: The Politics of Israeli Strategy*, pp. 223, 244.

24. For Rabin's criticism, see his "In the Aftermath of the War in Lebanon: Israel's Objectives," in *Israel's Lebanon Policy: Where To?* ed. Joseph Alper, JCSS Memorandum, no. 12, August 1984; his *The War in Lebanon* (Hebrew) (Tel Aviv, 1983); and his "Political Illusions and Their Price," in *The Lebanon War: Between Protest and Compliance* (Hebrew) (Tel Aviv: Hakibbutz Hameuchad Publishing House, 1983); for Bar-Lev's, see his speeches in the Knesset, KM, p. 3424, August 9, 1982; p. 3502, August 12, 1982; p. 3624, September 8, 1982; for Peres's, see KM, pp. 2173–2174, May 11, 1983.

25. See Sarid, "Labor's Position During the War in Lebanon."

26. Interviews with Amos Carmel, MK Nachman Raz, MK Edna Solodar, and MK Raanan Cohen.
27. See Zeev Schiff, "Green Light, Lebanon," *Foreign Policy* 50 (Spring 1983), pp. 73–85.
28. "Interview with Rabin," *Migvan* 72 (August 1982), p. 8.
29. Shlomo Nakdimon, *Tammuz in Flames* (Hebrew) (Jerusalem: Edanim Publishers, 1986), p. 292. Similar statements in which criticism was alluded to but not made explicit were voiced by Peres, Eban, and Yaakobi. For Peres's, see KM, June 8, 1982, p. 2738; KM, June 29, 1982, p. 2941; for Eban's, see KM, July 19, 1982, p. 3219; for Yaakobi's, see KM, June 16, 1982, p. 2818.
30. Shmuel Bahat and Dr. Israel Gat, eds., *A Selection of Decisions and Conclusions of "Leshiluv," A Zionist–Socialist Circle in the Labor Party*, p. 14.
31. Pitrim A. Sorokin, *Man and Society in Calamity* (Westport: Greenwood Press, 1973), p. 88.
32. For an analysis of the dissent during the Israeli wars, see Gad Barzilai, "Democracy in War: Attitudes, Reactions and Political Participation of the Israeli Public in the Processes of Decision Making" (Hebrew) (Ph.D. dissertation, The Hebrew University, 1987).
33. See KM, July 19, 1982, p. 3239.
34. See Sarid, "Labor's Position During the War in Lebanon."
35. See KM, June 29, 1982, p. 2939.
36. See Israel Galili's piece in *Davar*, July 15, 1982; Nachman Raz, "Checking Basics in Light of the War," *Mibifnim* 44 (October 1982), p. 227. *Mibifnim* is a Hakibbutz Hameuchad organ.
37. *Jerusalem Post*, July 24, 1982.
38. See *Colloquium on Historic Affairs and Basic Problems* 34 (Hebrew) (Yad Tabenkin, October 1982), p. 23.
39. Barzilai, *Democracy in War*, p. 196.
40. For a discussion of the public debate concerning this term, see Efraim Inbar, "The 'No Choice War' Debate in Israel," *Journal of Strategic Studies* 12 (March 1989), pp. 25–28.
41. Yaakov Tzur, "The Essence of the Debate," in *The Lebanon War: Between Protest and Compliance*, p. 165. The following discussion draws heavily on Efraim Inbar, "The Outlook on War of the Political Elite in the Eighties," Policy Papers 23 (Hebrew) (Jerusalem: The Leonard Davis Institute for International Relations, The Hebrew University, February 1988), pp. 16–22.
42. Tzur, "The Essence of the Debate," pp. 167–168.
43. *The Platform for the 11th Knesset* (Hebrew) (The Alignment, Israeli Labor Party–Mapam–Independent Liberals, July 1984), article c, p. 15.
44. Tzur, "The Essence of the Debate," p. 169.
45. KM, p. 3502, August 12, 1982.
46. KM, p. 3424, August 9, 1982.
47. Rabin, *The War in Lebanon*, p. 45.
48. Ibid.
49. "Interview with Rabin," *Migvan* 72 (August 1982), p. 3.
50. Interview with MK Ramon.
51. For Labor's tendency to use less force in the post-1973 period, see Barzilai, *Democracy in War*, pp. 178–181. For the Rabin government's (1974–1977) preference for a defensive posture, see Inbar, "Israeli Strategic Thinking After 1973," pp. 38–45.
52. See his *Memoirs*, pp. 111–112.
53. The Minutes of the Fourth Congress, May 15, 1986, p. 87.

54. Yitzhak Rabin, "Learning from History," p. 11. For his policies in the 1970s, see Inbar, "Israeli Strategic Thinking After 1973," pp. 38–45.
55. Rabin, "Learning from History," p. 11.
56. Ibid.
57. *Davar*, August 18, 1989.
58. *Haaretz*, June 6, 1989. His remarks were made at a seminar held at the Jaffee Center for Strategic Studies. The seminar discussed the Hebrew version of Ariel Levite, *Offense and Defense in Israeli Military Doctrine*, JCSS Study, no. 12 (Jerusalem: *Jerusalem Post*/Westview Press, 1989).
59. *Maariv*, March 22, 1989.
60. Interview with Shimon Peres, July 24, 1990.
61. A close aide to Prime Minister Shamir reacted to the sale of Chinese CSS-2 surface-to-surface missiles to Saudi Arabia by raising the possibility of a preemptive strike. See "Talk of Israeli Raid on Saudi Missiles Concerns US," *Washington Post*, March 23, 1988.
62. *Maariv*, March 4, 1990. For reports of preparations against chemical attack on civilian centers, see, inter alia, *Haaretz*, June 16, November 25, 1988; *Maariv*, July 26, 1988.
63. See, inter alia, *Maariv*, April 8, 1986; January 12, 1988; *Hatzofe*, June 22, 1988.
64. For a discussion of this term, see Herman Kahn, *On Escalation: Metaphors and Scenarios* (Baltimore: Penguin Books, 1968), p. 290.
65. *Haaretz*, December 14, 1989.
66. For a review of the debate in the 1970s, see Efraim Inbar, "Israel and Nuclear Weapons Since 1973," pp. 62–63. For the most comprehensive dovish pronuclear argument, see Shai Feldman, *Israeli Nuclear Deterrence: A Strategy for the 1980s*.
67. See Inbar, "Israel and Nuclear Weapons Since 1973," pp. 64–73.
68. *Voice of Israel*, January 10, 1989.
69. *Haaretz*, February 5, 1989.
70. For gradations in the use of force, see Thomas C. Schelling, *Arms and Influence*; Alexander L. George, David K. Hal, and William R. Simmons, *The Limits of Coercive Diplomacy* (Boston: Little, Brown, 1971).
71. *Haaretz*, June 9, 16, 1981.
72. See Barzilai, *Democracy in War*, p. 64.
73. Nakdimon, *Tammuz in Flames*, pp. 214–215.
74. Ibid., pp. 174–175.
75. Ibid., p. 283. For the technical obstacles the Iraqis faced in building a nuclear device, see Yair Evron, *Israel's Nuclear Dilemma* (Hebrew) (Tel Aviv: Yad Tabenkin, Hakibbutz Hameuchad, 1987), pp. 33–34.
76. Nakdimon, *Tammuz in Flames*, p. 175; see also *Haaretz*, June 16, 1981.
77. Nakdimon, *Tammuz in Flames*, pp. 161–162.
78. Ibid., p. 180. See also Begin's testimony in *Haaretz*, June 23, 1981.
79. Interview with Gur, in which he admitted that it was only later that he learned that Begin's government had done its best at the political level.
80. Nakdimon, *Tammuz in Flames*, pp. 97, 105, 173–174. For Weizman's opposition, see also Rafael Eitan, *A Soldier's Story* (Hebrew) (Tel Aviv: Maariv Library, 1985), p. 185.
81. Nakdimon, *Tammuz in Flames*, p. 299.
82. See Amos Hadar's remark in the October 22, 1981 Party Center, *Sidra Medinit*, no. 1, Israeli Labor Party, December 1981, p. 11.
83. Interview with Raanan Cohen, January 13, 1988. He was one of the new Laborite hawks in the 12th Knesset (1988).

84. KM, October 21, 1985, p. 100.
85. KM, October 21, 1985, p. 75.
86. Ibid.
87. For a report on Rabin's briefing to the Knesset Committee on Security and Foreign Affairs, see *Maariv*, October 3, 1985; for the problematic relations between Jordan and the PLO during that period, see Emile Sahliyeh, "Jordan and the Palestinians," in *The Middle East: Ten Years After Camp David*, ed. William B. Quandt, pp. 298–301.
88. See *Maariv*, October 2, 4, 1985.
89. For the negative reactions of Mapam and the Citizens Rights Movement, see *Maariv*, October 2, 1985.
90. Amnon Abramovich, "The Long Arm; The Short Memory," *Maariv*, October 2, 1985.
91. KM, October 21, 1985, pp. 92–95.
92. *Maariv*, October 3, 1985.
93. See KM, October 21, 1985, pp. 90–91; *Maariv*, October 3, 1985.
94. See, inter alia, *Haaretz*, May 6, 9, 1988.
95. *Jerusalem Post*, April 22, 1988.
96. *Maariv*, April 20, 1988.
97. *Jerusalem Post*, April 22, 1988.
98. "Interview with Gad Yaakobi," *Davar Magazine*, June 10, 1988.
99. *Haaretz*, August 1, 1989. For the support given by Peres, Gur, Bar-Lev, and Tzur, see *Maariv*, August 2, 1989.
100. For an analysis of the intifada, see Zeev Schiff and Ehud Yaari, *Intifada* (Hebrew) (Tel Aviv: Shocken, 1990); Arye Shalev, *The Intifada: Causes and Effects* (Tel Aviv: Papyrus, 1990).
101. *Maariv*, December 23, 1987. See also Rabin's interview on Israeli TV, January 13, 1988. For the English transcript, see *Journal of Palestine Studies* 17 (Spring 1988).
102. *Hadashot*, February 14, 1989. See also Menachem Shalev and Yoram Kessel, "Interview with Yitzhak Rabin," *Jerusalem Post*, May 19, 1989.
103. Yitzhak Rabin, "We Have Our Priorities," *Spectrum* 6 (April 1988), p. 11.
104. Rabin's interview on Israeli TV, January 13, 1988. See also Gabi Cohen, "Interview with Rabin," *Davar*, September 29, 1989.
105. *Jerusalem Post*, December 8, 1989.
106. For Ramon's views, see Eyal Erlich, "Historical Mapai"; for Namir's views, see *Spectrum* 6 (February 1988), p. 13; and *Maariv*, March 25, 1988.
107. Menachem Rahat, "Hawks and Doves Under Rabin's Wings," *Maariv*, March 25, 1988.
108. Haim Tzadok, "A First Step in a Long Journey," *Davar*, November 17, 1989.
109. *Maariv*, December 23, 1987.
110. "Interview with Navon," *Spectrum* 6 (March 1988), p. 9.
111. *Haaretz*, December 19, 1988.
112. Shlomo Genosar, "Interview with Micha Charish," *Davar*, January 27, 1989.
113. KM, May 16, 1983, pp. 2203–2204.
114. Tzur, "The Essence of the Debate," p. 166.
115. Nachman Raz, "Checking Basics in Light of the War," p. 229.
116. See the transcript of his speech in *Spectrum* 6 (February 1988), p. 17.
117. Natan Roi, "Interview with Chaim Bar-Lev," *Davar*, July 21, 1989.
118. TV interview with Rabin, January 13, 1989. Transcript, p. 157.

119. *Davar*, September 1, 1989.
120. Raz, "Checking Basics in Light of the War," p. 232.
121. Mordechai Gur, "Military Power and National Security," *Davar*, March 6, 1981.
122. Inbar, "The Outlook on War of the Political Elite in the Eighties," pp. 27–28.
123. *Davar*, July 14, 1989.
124. See, inter alia, *Haaretz*, March 12, 1989.

CHAPTER 7
The Move to the Left: An Evaluation

As we have seen, a gradual increase in the dovish representation in the Labor parliamentary faction facilitated the party's move in the dovish direction on several dimensions of the hawkish–dovish continuum. The hawks became a minority in the party, but were far from being in danger of extinction. As for the level of threat perception of the party leadership, a clear reduction has been discernible ever since the 1979 peace treaty with Egypt, a tendency that was characteristic of the Israeli political elite as a whole. Laborites, particularly the doves, felt that a fundamental change had probably occurred in Arab aims concerning Israel. Obviously, the longer such a view held sway, the greater effect it had in lowering apprehensions of Arab enmity. Indeed, the threat of politicide was increasingly viewed as a thing of the past. The conciliatory declarations of the PLO at the end of 1988 accentuated this process. As a result of this changed image of the Arabs, peace became a less distant possibility. Again, such cognitive changes were strongest among the party's doves, and it was they who encouraged them in others.

A further dovish development occurred in regard to the desired partner in an agreement over Judea, Samaria, and the Gaza Strip. Labor-led Israel, since the late 1960s, had viewed King Hussein as the correct address for reaching an agreement on the question of the eastern border. In 1990 a Jordanian role in the permanent settlement was still regarded as indispensable, despite Jordan's disengagement from the affairs of the West Bank and Gaza. Yet the Palestinian national movement came to be recognized as a factor that had to be given a greater voice in molding regional arrangements. Officially, the PLO was still outside the political pale. However, in the 1980s the party gradually adopted formulations, demanded earlier by its doves, that gave a role to Palestinian negotiators. In 1988, even an independent Palestinian delegation for negotiating an interim agreement, without Jordanian participation, became acceptable. Following the changes in PLO tone and the subsequent U.S. decision to enter into a dialogue with the PLO in December 1988, dovish pressure to rescind the party ban on talks with the PLO increased. Statements in favor of negotiations with the PLO, once issued mainly off the record, were now voiced in public. Yet under the impact of the PLO support for Iraq's invasion of Kuwait, demands for a PLO role became less vocal.

A similar dovish development occurred, though mostly before 1980, in the party's territorial demands with respect to a future agreement. The principle of territorial compromise, together with the explicit Allon Plan, was incorporated into the party platform in 1977, when the party firmly rejected the functional approach for attaining a permanent agreement. On this issue, the party platform did not change much after that date. Informally, however, the doves of the 1980s displayed a territorial largesse significantly greater than that which might be inferred from a study of the platform. Insistence on sovereignty in the security zones was also dropped. Although most of the party had gradually become reconciled to the need for dialogue with the Palestinians, the hawks were less conciliatory on real estate issues. Indeed, in regard to the content of the permanent agreement, there was no softening in the hawkish position, despite their decreasing numbers. To what extent the new dovish territorial minimalism will have the upper hand in party platforms in the 1990s remains to be seen. Another long-held party position that was challenged in the late 1980s was opposition to the establishment of a Palestinian state. Yet by mid-1990, there had been no such revision in the formal party position, which was easily controlled on this issue by an alliance between hawks and middle-of-the-road members. However, the intensity of the opposition weakened. Whereas such a state was once depicted by most in the party as a highly threatening development, toward the end of the decade some regarded it as just "a bad solution."

In regard to attitudes toward the use of force, slight changes occurred. First, a greater reluctance developed concerning use of the IDF in large-scale military operations. Preemptive strikes, once an article of faith in Israeli strategic thinking, became less acceptable than in the past. Second, the employment of limited force, particularly in maintaining law and order in the occupied territories, became increasingly problematic. Third, concern was expressed about the influence of increasingly routine use of force upon Israeli society. These dovish tendencies regarding the use of force were part of a trend occurring in Israeli society at large.

Although the party's move toward dovishness regarding military force was understandable in this context, the overall move to the left was intriguing, considering that the electorate was largely regarded as moving in the opposite direction.[1] Downs's classic analysis of party behavior, which presumes that political organizations in a competing system adjust their platforms to suit the electorate's taste, would lead one to expect a hawkish turn.[2] Yet some Laborites, Ramon for example, went to great lengths to disprove the view that Israeli politics had taken a turn to the right.[3] The doves obviously had a stake in such a refutation. However, the results of several past elections clearly indicate a slight, but steady, decline in the power of the Left in Israel. The rather slow erosion in Labor's political power helps doves like Ramon to evade the truth and to continue to hold convenient misperceptions.

Only the future can tell whether this trend will continue. Yet the literature on voting behavior points to a complexity that allows the political elite great latitude in formulating their positions and policies.[4] Furthermore, public opinion is known to be less influential generally on foreign policy and national security issues than on other subjects of public policy,[5] and this is so in Israel, too, where public opinion often goes along with elite actions rather than influencing them. For example, the decisions to withdraw from Sinai, partially in 1975 and fully in 1979, went against public sentiment. After the fact, however, the government's decision received the support of the majority.[6] As a matter of fact, there is little expectation on the part of the Israeli public to have any impact on decisions in the area of national security.[7] Some doves in the party were well aware of this, and felt it underlined their role as an agent of change; in fact, they viewed this matter in the context of the requirements of political leadership.

Indeed, hawkish MKs, despite their admonitions against deviation from the electorate's preferences, viewed the essence of political leadership in Burkeian terms identical to those used by the doves. Leaders have to be sensitive to the wishes of the people, they believed, but the final decision was theirs in this view. Thus, the shifts in Labor positions were little connected to the changing composition and attitudes of the Israeli electorate; the main variables affecting the movement of Labor along the hawkish–dovish continuum were the preferences and perceptions of the party leadership. Many of those new in leadership positions were doves, even extreme ones, as noted in Chapter 2. Furthermore, the older leadership displayed changes in conviction, and Peres was the most salient example of this.

As a result of the Likud's shift toward the center, which was expressed primarily by Begin's acceptance of the 1978 Camp David Accords and by his success in attaining a peace treaty with Egypt a year later, the Labor Party had to move left of its original positions. The Likud actually abandoned the annexation option and opted for the functional approach. And once it entered the National Unity government with Labor in 1984, the policy of massive settlement in all parts of Judea, Samaria, and Gaza was abandoned in favor of settlement according to the Allon Plan.[8] The Likud, in other words, became a centrist party. To some extent, then, Labor positions were adopted by the Likud-led government. A move leftward was thus necessary in order to stress the difference between the two parties and to provide a raison d'être for Labor's existence as a separate party. The more competitive the political system, the more the need for ideological clarity, in contrast to a multiparty system with one dominant political party.[9] Before Labor lost its dominance in Israeli politics, it could afford to present an ideological supermarket to the voters. After 1977, there was a greater need to clarify its positions. The doves were attempting to lead the party in this direction of greater ideological clarity. For them, the term ideological clarity became a euphemism for indubitable dovishness.

Indeed, many doves in the party criticized the hawks precisely on this electoral calculus. A "Likud B" party, they argued, could not succeed electorally because "Likud A" had better chances of attracting the votes of those preferring hawkish positions. Flirting with hawkish positions was asserted to be counterproductive. This was also a reply to the hawkish claim that the move to the left cost the party dearly at the polls. For example, when Baram parted from the post of party secretary general in March 1989, he warned his colleagues that unless they adopted a clear dovish message, the party would continue to decline.[10] At the root of the dispute were conflicting views about the direction the Israeli electorate was taking. Both sides preferred self-serving forecasts.

Following the 1977 electoral debacle, Peres succeeded in maintaining the cohesion of Labor partly by moving it to the left on foreign and security issues.[11] The need for a more distinctly dovish platform was a consequence not only of Likud's moderating trend but also of the greater similarity between the two parties on social and economic issues— in particular, as Labor gradually lost its socialist orientation and moved toward a market orientation long advocated by Likud. Moreover, in the latter part of the 1980s, under the prodding of Peres, Labor made efforts not to fall too far behind the Likud even on religious affairs.[12] Indeed, in 1988 the party altered several articles in its platform so as not to offend religious voters and potential religious coalition partners. Thus, as the differences between Labor and Likud on social, economic, and religious affairs narrowed, national security became the main bone of contention in Israeli politics.

The fact that Likud's move toward the center occurred while Labor was in opposition further facilitated Labor's shift to the left. When in opposition, the dovish component within Labor, the wing of the party more sharply differentiated from the Likud, was more vocal and conspicuous. In the absence of governmental responsibility, this oppositional element became the moving force behind the gradual revision of the party positions, as we have seen. For example, ideological reluctance to subjugate a foreign people overshadowed the security imperatives for holding onto the territories. Ideological purity can more easily be maintained in opposition, when there is less need to make difficult choices. The best illustration of this was the high profile Yossi Sarid succeeding in gaining as a Labor MK while Labor was in opposition. He admitted that serving in the opposition best suited his talents.[13]

A further contributing factor to the changes within Labor was, simply, that the most rightist elements in the party simply left it. This is of course part of the process toward greater ideological cohesion. Already by 1973, most Laborites within the Movement for a Greater Israel (the annexationists in the party) had joined the Likud.[14] Those remaining in the party formed the militant Ein Vered circle in 1976, which withered away following the

Likud's ascent to power.[15] Moshe Dayan left the party in 1977 to join the Likud-led cabinet (from which he resigned, however, in 1979). Another hawkish Laborite who left the party on the eve of the 1977 elections was Mordechai Ben-Porat. In 1981, as the number two person in it he joined the Telem movement, established by Dayan, which attracted primarily Labor people. Eventually, however, he became a minister in the Likud government. Both Dayan and Ben-Porat shared a Rafi past, and another prominent former Rafi member to serve in the Likud government was Yigal Hurvitz. In 1968, Hurvitz refrained from returning with Rafi to the newly established Labor Party, preferring to stay with Ben-Gurion and establish the State faction. Thus the Laborite hawks of the 1960s, annexationists and functionalists, had to find other political organizations in the 1970s and 1980s that conformed with their views. The new hawks-by-default in the party (once at its center) lacked the great power of the hawkish factions of the past, which could effectively threaten to leave the party and turn the reins of power over to the Likud. As was discussed in Chapter 2, the breakdown of the factional regime in 1975 also strengthened the doves in the Labor Party.

But the party lost some of its doves as well. Lova Eliav, a former secretary-general, left in 1975 to become active in more leftist organizations. In 1984, Yossi Sarid could not bring himself to vote for the National Unity government, which included the Likud, and instead joined the Citizens Rights Movement, a party to the left of Labor founded in 1973 by former Laborite Shulamit Aloni. For the same reason, some of the remaining members of the 77 Circle, which was by then defunct, made a demonstrative exit from the party after the formation of the National Unity government. This group consisted mainly of dovish intellectuals who had joined Labor in an attempt to inject new life into the party after its electoral defeat in 1977. The group's hopes of influencing the party, however, were not realized, and most of its members left in the early 1980s, finding Labor's reaction to the war in Lebanon totally inadequate.[16] Interestingly enough, Eliav, without having changed his political stance, returned to the party in 1986—a clear indication that he found there a climate amenable to his dovish views, once considered extreme. Furthermore, as mentioned in Chapter 2, he received an enthusiastic welcome and was given tremendous backing for his successful attempt to join the Labor Knesset contingent in 1988.

Another reason for the increased dovishness may have been peer-group pressure. Political groups left of Labor (but not too far to the left), both in Israel and outside it, constituted a reference group for the more educated among the Laborites. Their advocacy of dovish positions seemed to pull some party activists in their direction. For example, senior Laborites participated regularly in the Socialist International—a body that over time became less friendly toward Israel. Furthermore, in the 1980s the Israeli media and the intellectuals as a whole tended to display leftist inclinations, and they no longer played the role of mobilized intellectuals that had served the party in the past. Party leaders, Peres in particular, revealed a sensitivity to the intellectual elite.

The reduced threat perception of the party leadership in the Arab–Israeli context was an additional, more crucial, factor in the party's move toward the dovish pole. Since many Laborites now no longer regarded politicide as the operative goal of the Arab governments, there was no longer a right-to-life issue at stake. It was therefore easier to adopt more accommodating positions toward the Arabs. Even the threats of Saddam Hussein and his aggressive policies, though they increased threat perception, were not taken as typical of all Arab states. Even many hawks viewed the struggle as essentially a contest over the characteristics of a future agreement. Others, particularly the doves, regarded the end of the conflict as within easy reach, if both sides would only overcome the psychological barriers and make some concessions.

Begin's precedent of returning all of Sinai for a peace treaty further bolstered dovish arguments in favor of territorial largesse. The treaty in fact turned out to be less fragile than the doves had anticipated, so that stability in relations with Egypt lent unexpected support to their thesis that lasting peace was not a utopian concept.

Decreased territorial appetite was also linked to increased awareness of the "demographic problem." The party was successful in placing this issue on the Israeli political agenda. The gradual realization that the Zionist dream of the ingathering—the return of all Jews to the land of Israel—had practical limitations rendered Israeli colonization efforts dubious. A Jewish immigration so massive that it could alter the demographic picture in Palestine had failed to materialize. In the 1967–1973 period, the waves of immigration (mostly from the Soviet Union) were strong enough to sustain the dream of large-scale settlement and to justify hopes for preserving a Jewish majority at least in the security zones designated by the Allon Plan. But after 1973, immigration dwindled. Consequently the Arab demographic threat became more salient, encouraging a greater inclination toward territorial concessions. Nor did Labor expect the 1990 wave of immigrants to change the demographic balance.

Viewed from this perspective, the occupation duties of the IDF became more problematic in the 1980s. The status quo, considered in the party as temporary, had begun to acquire a threatening permanence. On the one hand Israelis feared an evolution toward a binational state, and on the other hand concerns were raised about the corrupting influence of occupation. The Palestinian uprising, which broke out in December 1987, increased the burdens of occupation and unsettled many about the continuation of the status quo. Doves in the Labor Party capitalized on the general feeling that change was needed. The notion that this need was urgent seemed more persuasive than before the uprising.

Increased dovishness was also linked to the leadership's perception that the Jews in Israel were tired of continuous conflict. Such weariness had clear policy implications. The awareness that in the polarized polity there were growing numbers of people who questioned the leadership's sincerity, its ability to capitalize on those occasions that had the potential for tension reduction, pushed Labor into a more dovish direction. More conciliatory policies were therefore necessary to guarantee the needed social cohesion in the event of another war.

The decline in the Labor hawks' strength was also related to their failure to devise an acceptable alternative to the dovish position. The doves called attention to the clearly emerging limitations of the Jordanian orientation, and to the fact that they had correctly appraised the developing Palestinian nationalism. In claiming that the differences with the Arabs could be bridged, they also projected some optimism. The hawkish position, which advocated firmness and patience and counseled skepticism about a short-range solution, carried implications of continuing conflict that were psychologically difficult to accept. This was true, of course, of right-wing parties in Israel as well.

Finally, the Labor leadership has always displayed sensitivity to outside constraints. Despite the close relationship with the United States that had evolved since the mid-1970s, Israel has in this period faced international difficulties and even isolation.[17] Labor's rather pragmatic outlook took into consideration growing international acceptance of the PLO and worldwide displeasure at the Israeli military presence in Judea, Samaria, and Gaza. Most significantly, Laborites heeded U.S. policy. Since 1973, the United States has made unprecedented efforts to mediate between Israel and its neighbors.[18] The successes of U.S. diplomacy in the Middle East—the September 1975 Sinai II agreement, the October 1978 Camp David Accords, and the March 1979 peace treaty with Egypt—were paved with Israeli concessions. Even though both proposals included elements not to its liking, the Labor Party accepted the Reagan Plan of September 1982 and the Shultz initiative of winter 1988. The need to maintain good relations with the United States was considered by the Laborite leadership to be of paramount importance. The May 1989 Israeli peace initiative emanated from widespread perceptions, in the party and elsewhere, that Israel had to produce a plan capable of maintaining U.S. support. U.S. Secretary of State James Baker's suggestions for breaking the impasse confronting the Israeli election initiative were also welcomed by most in the party. Thus, the move to the left on the hawkish–dovish continuum was also a result of cumulative external pressure.

The 1980s witnessed a considerable mellowing in Labor's stances on national security. This process was connected to personnel changes at the elite level. Among those more adept at party machinations, the doves happened to be in greater numbers. Fewer hawks in the party proved to have the necessary qualities to enter the decisive MK class, despite the fact that there were clear indications that the composition of party forums such as the Central Council (Merkaz) or Congress (Veida) was more hawkish than the parliamentary faction. The simmering power struggle over leadership positions again came out into the open in 1990. The outcome will certainly have a bearing on the party's course in the future. As this book goes to press, Rabin—a hawk—appears somewhat hesitant to challenge Peres again for the leadership of the party. Peres, though a skillful political survivor, will probably be challenged from other quarters, much less hawkish, in the near future. Indeed, the new contenders for the leadership positions—Baram, Gur, Shahal, and Yaakobi—are not hawks. The impact of these factors on the Israeli political system and on the Arab–Israeli conflict is not yet clear. To some extent, the move leftward in the 1980s reflected a basic lack of consensus in Israel on what to do with the territories. Changes in the Arab world were also significant. Most recently, the revisions in the PLO positions by the end of 1988 seemed to spark off a new process of soul-searching on both sides. However, considering the complexity of the geopolitical factors and the positions of many Israelis right of Labor, an Israeli–Palestinian agreement is an extremely difficult goal to attain. Even some of Labor's doves recognize this fact. Moreover, the Palestinians' behavior during the 1990 Gulf crisis was a setback to their cause. The crisis emphasized the interstate, rather than intercommunal, dimension of the conflict, strengthening both manifest and latent hawkish dispositions.

The role that Labor will play in the formulation of national security policies in the 1990s remains to be seen. It is quite clear that there has been an increase in the Israeli public's desire to disengage from the Arabs of the territories. It is often forgotten that Labor's prescription for a permanent settlement—a territorial compromise—is the one that attracts the largest following in the public and in the Knesset. Annexation, a functional solution, and total withdrawal, the alternative approaches, are all less popular.[19] Labor, despite its decline and continuous internal struggles, is still a major political force in Israel with a potential to lead it in war and peace. Much depends on its success in attracting enough votes.

NOTES

1. See Introduction, note 13.
2. Anthony Downs, *An Economic Theory of Democracy*.
3. Interview with Chaim Ramon.
4. For the complexity of voting patterns, see Richard G. Niemi and Herbert F. Weisberg, eds., *Controversies in Voting Behavior*, 2nd ed. (Washington, D.C: Congressional Quarterly Inc., 1984); Benjamin I. Page and Calvin C. Jones, "Reciprocal Effects of Policy Preferences, Party Loyalties and the Vote," *American Political Science Review* 73 (December 1979), pp. 1071–1090; Gregory B. Markus and Philip E. Converse, "A Dynamic Simultaneous Equation Model of Electoral Choice," *American Political Science Review* 73 (December 1979), pp. 1055–1070.
5. See Gabriel Almond, *The American People and Foreign Policy* (New York: Praeger, 1960); Bernard C. Cohen, "Political Systems, Public Opinion and

Foreign Policy: The United States and the Netherlands," *International Journal* 33 (Winter 1977–1978), pp. 195–212. For a review of the literature see Asher Arian, Ilan Talmud, and Tamar Hermann, *National Security and Public Opinion in Israel*, pp. 3–10.

6. See Amnon Sela and Yael Yishai, *Israel the Peaceful Belligerent, 1967–1979* (London: Macmillan, 1986), pp. 168–171; Naomi Keis, "The Influence of Public Policy on Public Opinion in Israel, 1967–1974," *State, Government and International Relations* 8 (Hebrew) (September 1975), pp. 36–53. For the Israeli fluid voting on national security issues, see Yadin Kaufman, "Israel's Flexible Voters," *Foreign Policy* 61 (Winter 1985–1986), pp. 109–124.

7. Some 62 percent of the public responded that they have no influence whatsoever on these matters. See Arian, Talmud, and Hermann, *National Security and Public Opinion in Israel*, p. 106.

8. The contention that Likud has moderated its positions over time is not supported by the literature. It is based on the Likud's acceptance of the Camp David Accords and its policies in the National Unity governments (1984–1990). For a detailed argument, see Efraim Inbar and Giora Goldberg, "Is Israel's Political Elite Becoming More Hawkish?" *International Journal* 45 (Summer 1990).

9. Arian and Shamir, "The Primarily Political Functions of the Left–Right Continuum," pp. 269–270.

10. *Haaretz*, March 3, 1989.

11. Shlomo Aronson, "Israel's Leaders, Domestic Order and Foreign Policy, June 1981–June 1983," *Jerusalem Journal of International Relations* 6, no. 4 (1982–1983), pp. 15–16.

12. See, inter alia, Akiva Eldar, "On Torah and Labor," *Haaretz*, March 30, 1988.

13. Interview with Yossi Sarid.

14. For the Laborite sources of the Movement for a Greater Israel, see Rael Jean Isaac, *Israel Divided*, pp. 46–49, 53–68.

15. For this circle, see Yael Yishai, *Land or Peace: Whither Israel?* pp. 85–86.

16. See Zeev Sternhell, "Intellectuals and Politics," *Spectrum* 5 (April 1987), 16–17.

17. For Israel's isolation and its consequences, see Efraim Inbar, *Outcast States in the World Community*, Monograph Series in World Affairs (Denver: Denver University Press, 1985).

18. For the American mediation efforts, see Saadia Touval, *The Peace Brokers*, pp. 225–320.

19. See Efraim Inbar, "War and Peace, Hopes and Fears in the 1988 Elections."

APPENDIX A
A Plan for Peace and Security

The Labor Party's Foreign Affairs and Security Council adopted the following document in May 1988 as a platform to work for peace and Israel's security:

A. Goals

1. The attainment of a stable comprehensive peace between Israel and its neighbours.
2. Guaranteeing permanent security for the state of Israel.
3. Guaranteeing the Jewish and democratic character of the state.

B. First Step: Opening negotiations with a Jordanian–Palestinian delegation

Opening direct peace negotiations with a Jordanian–Palestinian delegation without the Palestine Liberation Organization, by means of an opening international conference, in accordance with the London document, which will not have the authority to impose a solution or dictate conditions for negotiations.

C. Second Step: Interim agreement

The interim agreement (which will last for up to 5 years) will be attained through direct negotiations.
Principles of the agreement:

a. Transfer of the powers to administer the lives of the Palestinian inhabitants into the hands of a self-administration council.
b. Foreign affairs and security issues will remain in Israeli hands.
c. Security arrangements, such as the deployment of the Israel Defence Forces, early warning systems, patrols, air reconnaissance, etc. will be determined by the IDF.

D. Third Step: Permanent peace

This agreement will be based on the security needs of the State of Israel and on the following principles:

a. The peace agreement with Jordan will include diplomatic relations, economic and trade relations, joint economic and tourist enterprises.
b. Israel will not return to the 1967 borders and will continue to hold territories which are not populated and are important for its security, such as the Jordan Valley Rift.
c. The Jordan River will remain the security boundary. The IDF will ensure that no foreign army cross it. The existing settlements will remain intact.
d. Jerusalem, the capital of Israel, will remain united and under Israeli sovereignty.
e. A Palestinian state will not be established between Israel and the Jordan River.
f. The skies will be open to the Israeli Air Force.
g. Areas with a dense Arab population in Judea, Samaria and the Gaza Strip will be handed over to Jordanian–Palestinian control, while their demilitarization will be guaranteed.

E. Referendum

In order to preserve the national unity, the following means of decision will be laid down:

a. In the 1988 elections the people will decide whether to embark on the peace process which will be conducted according to the three steps described above.
b. The results of the negotiations in each of the two stages (interim agreement and the permanent agreement) will be brought to the people for their approval in a referendum or elections.

This document appeared in *Spectrum* 6 (June 1988), p. 20.

APPENDIX B

The Labour Party Platform on Foreign Affairs and Security for the 12th Knesset

Central Goals

The central goals of the Labour Party are security, peace and the preservation of a democratic-Jewish state with a large Jewish majority maintaining full equality for all its citizens.

A. A government led by the Alignment will persevere in furthering and developing the State of Israel, and will act to realize the Zionist goals on the basis of the unquestioned right of the Jewish people to return to its country, to found its sovereign state in its historical homeland, and to maintain it in security and peace.

B. A government led by the Alignment will consider the constant striving for peace as a central goal and a vital national interest. The central political and security goals of the Alignment will be the furtherance of the peace process with Jordan and the Palestinians, the reinforcement of the peace with Egypt and the improvement of relations with it, the extension of the peace process to other Arab countries and measures to ensure the state's security and the welfare of its citizens. A principal goal of a government led by the Alignment will be to break the political deadlock which has persisted since the Likud undermined the peace initiatives of Shimon Peres. Renewal of a process of negotiation with Jordan and the Palestinians will occur only if a government headed by the Alignment can be formed.

A continuation of the political deadlock will convert Israel into a binational, Jewish–Arab state without peaceful coexistence.

C. The considerations which will guide the position of the Israeli government regarding the permanent boundaries shall be: the security requirements of the State of Israel; the preservation of its Jewish national character based on a large and stable Jewish majority; the consolidation of the state as an enlightened democratic society whose citizens will enjoy equal rights. The withdrawal from territories which are inhabited by a large Arab population within the framework of peace agreements, would be a significant contribution to the security of the State of Israel. A Jewish majority in most of the territory is preferable to the whole territory with the loss of the Jewish majority.

D. The permanent boundaries will be defensible borders, which will reduce the dangers of aggression, and will enable Israel to defend itself effectively with its own forces. The State of Israel will not return along its eastern border to the June 4th, 1967 lines, and will retain areas such as the Jordan Rift and other security areas, which are vital for its security and are not populated densely by Arabs.

Demilitarization and security provisions, which will be included in the peace agreements will supplement the permanent boundaries and will not replace them.

E. A government led by the Alignment will take pains to increase the power of the IDF and to strengthen its ability to resist any combination of Arab military threats. It will act with determination against Arab and PLO terrorism.

F. The Labour Party fully supports the IDF forces and the security services who are contending with the difficult situation in the territories. We support the policy of Minister of Defence Yitzhak Rabin of restoring order, stopping violence and ending the attempts to disrupt the normal course of life of the inhabitants of Israel and of the administered territories.

A government headed by the Alignment will simultaneously strive to renew political moves, for the solution to the Palestinian problem can only be a political solution.

G. A government led by the Alignment will be prepared to negotiate for peace without preconditions, on the basis of Security Council resolutions 242 and 338.

H. A government headed by the Alignment will renew the momentum of political initiative by means of peace negotiations to resolve the Palestinian problem with representatives of Jordan and the Palestinians, as well as by means of interim agreements and arrangements for a transitory period with Jordan or with a Palestinian representation from the territories, as well as by means of additional measures which Israel will take at its own initiative. These measures will correspond with its vital security requirements and will further the peace process.

1.1 Jerusalem

1.1.1 Jerusalem, the capital of Israel, will remain united under Israeli sovereignty.

1.1.2 The rights of all its inhabitants, irrespective of religion, nationality and citizenship, will be respected and upheld.

1.1.3 The special religious status of the places holy to Islam and Christianity will be guaranteed under self-administration.

1.1.4 Freedom of access to the holy places and freedom of religious worship will continue and be guaranteed.

1.2 Israel's Policy for Peace with Jordan and the Palestinians

1.2.1 Israel's goals in peace negotiations are:

a. Preserving the State of Israel as a democratic Jewish state with a large and stable Jewish majority, whose citizens, whether Jewish or non-Jewish, shall enjoy full equality of rights.
b. (i) The establishment of defensible borders which, once peace is established, will leave a defence deployment of the IDF forces and the settlements in the Jordan Rift, the north-west of the Dead Sea, Gush Etzion and the areas around Jerusalem as part of the sovereign territory of Israel. The Jordan will be Israel's security border. The territories which will be evacuated by Israel will be demilitarized.
Security arrangements vital to Israel will be concluded and no Arab or foreign army will cross or be found west of the River Jordan.
(ii) Jewish settlements in the areas to be evacuated will be enabled to remain in their place, and the welfare and security of the settlers will be assured.
c. The resolution of the Palestinian problem within a Jordanian–Palestinian political framework, which will also comprise the areas with a dense Palestinian population in Judea, Samaria and the Gaza Strip, and will lead to a solution of the refugee problem.
d. The rejection of the establishment of an additional separate state in the area between Israel and the Jordan. A separate Palestinian state will not solve the conflict and could constitute a focus of hostility and the inflammation of passions.
e. The termination of Israeli rule over the one and a half million Palestinian Arabs who are inhabitants of Judea, Samaria and the Gaza Strip.
f. The assurance of freedom of movement and passage across the border in accordance with agreements to be concluded in the peace treaty.

1.2.2 The Labour Party supports the energetic continuation of the initiatives of Shimon Peres and the Labour ministers for talks with Egypt and a Jordanian–Palestinian delegation with the goal of furthering the peace process. These initiatives began when Shimon Peres was Prime Minister of Israel and also continued systematically when he served as Deputy Prime Minister and Minister of Foreign Affairs. The Labour Party denounces the loss of opportunities for furthering the peace process which were the result of the rejectionist and immobile policy of the Likud and especially of Yitzhak Shamir.

1.2.3 The Labour Party supports the continued involvement of the United States in furthering the peace process in the spirit of the 1987 initiative of Secretary of State George Shultz, the failure of which was caused by the Likud's obstinacy.

1.2.4 A government headed by the Alignment will renew, as a top priority the promotion of talks and negotiations with Jordan in partnership with a Palestinian representation in order to arrive at peace along the eastern border and a settlement of the Palestinian problem. In order to open negotiations with a Jordanian–Palestinian delegation, Israel will be willing to participate in an international conference which will not have the authority to dictate the conditions for negotiations, to impose a solution or to suspend any agreement which might be reached among the parties. Its task will be to enable the opening of direct, bilateral negotiations. The Labour Party supports the conditions for holding the conference as agreed to in contacts among Israel, Jordan and the United States (in the London document) of April 1987.

The negotiations will take place without preconditions, and will be conducted on the basis of Security Council resolutions 242 and 338.

Every delegation will be able to raise its own proposals, and every delegation will be able to relate to the proposals which will be raised by the other side.

1.2.5
  a. In accordance with its aspiration to put an end to the Arab–Israeli conflict, the Alignment will be willing to hold talks with Palestinian personalities and bodies who will recognize Israel, denounce terrorism and accept Security Council resolutions 242 and 338.
  b. The PLO, as based on the Palestine Covenant, and any other organization which rejects Israel's right to exist and the national existence of the Jewish people, or which uses terrorist means, cannot be partners to such negotiations.

1.2.6 On the road toward peace Israel will also initiate interim arrangements and will discuss any proposals for interim arrangements which might be proposed to it. Israel will be willing to negotiate with Jordan and the Palestinians; or with authorized representatives of the inhabitants of Judea, Samaria and Gaza about interim arrangements, even if Jordan will not participate in the negotiations. Within the framework of a possible interim agreement Israel will hand over broad spheres of responsibility and powers of self rule in municipal and civil issues to local authorities and to civilian bodies in these areas. Israel will concentrate primarily on maintaining security and preventing subversion and terror.

1.2.7 The outbreak in December 1987 of disturbances in the territories—disturbances which continue to the present day—was caused largely by the political paralysis imposed by the Likud on the Government. The IDF and the security services will continue to act decisively to restrain the disturbances in the territories, to prevent violence and to assure order and the welfare of the inhabitants.

1.2.8 Until the completion of the peace negotiations, Israel will act in Judea, Samaria and the Gaza Strip on the basis of the following principles:

a. Normal public order will be preserved, and measures will be taken to ensure permanent and continuing security. Israel will resist manifestations of incitement, violence and terror used against it and against the Palestinian population.
b. Israel will strengthen Jewish settlement in the vital security and settlement areas.
c. Israel will prevent additional Jewish settlement in areas with a dense Palestinian population in Judea, Samaria and the Gaza Strip, and will stop the populating of these areas and investment by the Government of funds allotted for this purpose—both in rural and urban areas. In this way the distortion or order of priorities laid down by the Likud since 1977, will be rectified.
d. Israeli law will not be applied to Judea, Samaria and the Gaza Strip.
e. Israel will take, at its own initiative, additional measures and will hand over the broadest possible spheres of responsibility in civilian matters to local authorities and civilian Arab bodies in areas with a dense population.
f. Israel will maintain the policy of open bridges, and will assure freedom of movement and contacts with the Arab world for the inhabitants.
g. Israel will encourage initiatives for economic development and the creation of sources of employment in the territories.
h. Israel will safeguard the protection of the individual rights of the inhabitants, the rule of law and the equality of the inhabitants before it under the law and will act in accordance with the principles of international law.

1.3 Israeli–Egyptian Relations

1.3.1 The peace treaty between Israel and Egypt constitutes a political and historical breakthrough in the Middle East, after decades of wars and a state of belligerency under which the Arab world was united in rejecting the sovereign existence of Israel. The peace agreement between Israel and Egypt opened new horizons of peace and cooperation to the benefit of both states, and both peoples as well as of all the peoples of the whole of the Middle East.

Israel will continue to fulfill—in accordance with the rules of international law and on the basis of reciprocity—the international obligations which it undertook in the Camp David Accords and the Peace Treaty with Egypt, including the 1982 agreement for arbitration over the Taba issue.

1.3.2 A government led by the Alignment will continue to view Egypt as a central partner in the effort to further peace in our region.

1.3.3 The Labour Party considers the consolidation and development of the peace with Egypt an Israeli interest of the first order, and will act to ensure the full implementation of the peace treaty, including the clauses concerning trade, touristic and cultural relations. The Labour Party calls upon the government of Egypt to act together with the government of Israel to create a positive mutual atmosphere in public opinion in general and in the media in particular, in order to contribute to the advancement of friendship between the two peoples.

1.3.4 The Labour party will initiate contacts and discussions with the Democratic National Party in Egypt, and will act to extend the ties between public bodies in the two countries.

1.4 Israeli–Lebanese Relations

1.4.1 Israel aspires to reach a peace treaty with Lebanon on the basis of the existing boundary between the two countries.

1.4.2 The security and welfare of the northern settlements and their inhabitants, the avoidance of strategic dangers, and the prevention of terrorist acts from Lebanon are the goals which guide Israeli policy towards Lebanon.

1.4.3 The Labour Party viewed the termination of the war in Lebanon and the withdrawal of the IDF from Lebanon as a political and security goal and an achievement of the first order.

The Party supported the initiative of Shimon Peres, in his previous post as Prime Minister, Yitzhak Rabin as Minister of Defence and the Labour Party ministers in the Israeli government, to bring about the withdrawal from Lebanon while consolidating the security zones in the south.

The achievement of the withdrawal from Lebanon is especially significant against the background of stubborn opposition shown towards this move by most of the Likud ministers.

1.4.4 Israel will continue to maintain the security zones by means of local forces with the backing of the IDF as long as this is necessary to preserve security and check hostile acts against the northern settlements.

Israel has no interest in Lebanese land or Lebanese waters, or in being involved in the internal politics of Lebanon. Israel will respect an independent and peaceful Lebanon.

1.4.5 In order to maintain security, preserve the peace of the inhabitants and prevent acts of terror Israel will reserve freedom of action against terrorists in Lebanon in the air, on sea and on land.

1.4.6 The government under the leadership of the Alignment will assure the economic consolidation of the northern settlements, which is a vital condition for the preservation of their social fortitude and power of resistance.

1.5 Israeli–Syrian Relations

1.5.1 The Government of Israel will be willing to negotiate peace with Syria without preconditions.

1.5.2 Israel will continue to respect the (1974) Disengagement Agreement with Syria on a basis of reciprocity.

1.5.3 The growing strength of the Syrian army, the war threats pronounced by Syrian leaders and the encouragement of terror constitute a continuously growing threat to Israel. These developments oblige the government and the IDF to remain on a suitable level of vigilance and preparedness.

1.5.4 Israel views the Golan Heights as an area which is important to its welfare and security, and will act to strengthen the settlement there, to consolidate its economy, and its social fortitude.

1.5.5 Until the attainment of peace Israel will act to reach understandings and talks with Syria with the goal of preventing escalation and the danger of war, and in order to pave the way for peace negotiations.

1.6 Defense Policy

1.6.1 The goal of Israel's defence policy is to guarantee the existence of the state, to prevent war, and to provide maximal protection for the state and its citizens.

Israel's defence policy will serve Israel's peace policy and will provide the government with enhanced scope for political action.

1.6.2 The IDF will be used only in order to secure the existence, defence, and security of the State of Israel, and the welfare of its citizens. In any government decision to use the force of the IDF, the need for national approval will also be taken into account.

The IDF must be kept out of the inter-party debate.

1.6.3 The Israel Defence Force is subject to the absolute jurisdiction of the elected civilian authority of the state.

1.6.4 Israel will do whatever is necessary to preserve and develop the IDF's power of deterrence, warning and rapid decision-making capability in face of any combination of possible military threats.

1.6.5 The growing military power of the Arab states and their hostility requires Israel to maintain a quantitative military force with a qualitative edge over the Arab armies.

Our superiority must manifest itself in the quality of the individual fighting man, his spirit, training and conduct and in the quality of the equipment, organization, doctrine, planning and preparedness of the army and the rear.

1.6.6 Israel will maintain its military power with the goal of inducing hostile Arab states, and violent Palestinian elements to recognize their inability to defeat Israel by force of arms, or to disrupt the normal life in the country. The aim is to influence our neighbors to prefer negotiations for political agreements and a solution to the Arab–Israeli conflict. This conflict can be resolved by political means and not by force of arms.

1.6.7 In face of the disturbances in the territories, the task of the IDF and the security services is to bring about, rapidly and with determination, the enforcement of order and tranquility in Judea, Samaria and the Gaza Strip.

1.6.8 The IDF—the army of all ranks of the people—is unique in its pioneering dimension. Only by raising our moral and qualitative edge to its maximum will our army fulfill its goal in the preservation of the state's security. The nurturing of the value of volunteerism and the consciousness of national responsibility and mission amongst recruits for regular service, reserve forces and especially volunteers for career service—will continue to be a vital element in the structure of the IDF.

1.6.9 It is important to act in order to nurture volunteering for the regular army. Such service, which must be viewed as a unique national mission, is designed to ensure the qualitative superiority of the IDF. In accordance with its long tradition of responsibility for Israel's security, the Labour Party calls the best manpower in the cities and villages, in the development towns and the labour settlements to volunteer and to continue to serve in the regular army, and to contribute to the reinforcement of the IDF's strength.

1.6.10 The attributes and quality of the fighting man are the pillar of Israel's security. Therefore, the IDF must insist on suitable conditions of service for the fighting man as an individual, while paying maximal attention to his ability and needs.

1.6.11 The IDF will continue to maintain and nurture the Nahal as an entity which embodies the pioneering element in it, and the strong ties between settlement and security. The IDF will also take pains to develop and strengthen the territorial defence as a vital component in the state's security.

1.6.12 The obligatory enlistment of women, as of men, is one of the foundations of citizenship, and of the security of the state. The effort to enlist as many women as possible for service in the IDF will continue, as will the important operation of integrating them in a wide range of duties.

1.6.13 The IDF and the other security services will insist that in all their activities the purity of arms shall be upheld and high standards of fighting morality preserved. Educational and disciplinary measures will be taken to prevent diversions from these basic principles in the activities and operations of the IDF. A constant educational effort will also be implemented to strengthen the values of democracy in the consciousness of those serving in the IDF.

1.6.14 Israel will grant high priority to independent research and development in the spheres of security and to expanding the self-manufacture of weapons and modern and sophisticated military equipment with the goal of raising the quality of the IDF and strengthening its steadfastness in the foreseeable trials. Special emphasis will be placed on the realization of the alternatives to the "Lavi".

The government of Israel headed by the Labour Party will concentrate on a policy of independent development and production without damaging the other power components of the national security.

1.6.15 Israel will act tirelessly on the ideological and political level to harness other states to the struggle against terror, and to prevent the legitimation of the terrorist organizations and those who aid them.

Israel will simultaneously fight against terrorism and subversion by means of all the security services in order to stop the terrorist organizations and subversive bodies from attaining their goals. This campaign will assume both a defensive and initiatory character, and the government of Israel will consider itself free to choose the place, method, means and timing. The struggle against terrorism and subversion will be conducted within the framework of Israel's overall strategic and political needs.

1.6.16 The government of Israel headed by the Labour Party will act to prevent the massive delivery of quality weapons to the Arab states— deliveries which endanger the peace in the region. Special emphasis will be placed on preventing the development of a strategic assault capability by the Arab states with ground-to-ground missiles, chemical implements of warfare, quality airplanes and air-to-ground missiles. The government of Israel will struggle against the legitimation of the use of chemical weapons, and will act to overcome international apathy on this issue.

1.6.17 The Labour Party offers its encouragement to all those serving in the various defence services in current security tasks, in preparedness and alertness.

Bibliography

Akzin, Benyamin. "The Role of Parties in Israeli Democracy." *Journal of Politics* 17 (November 1955).
Allison, Graham T., Carnesale, Albert, and Nye, Joseph S., Jr. *Hawks, Doves and Owls*. New York: W. W. Norton, 1985.
Allon, Yigal. *Curtain of Sand* (Hebrew). Tel Aviv: Hakibbutz Hameuchad, 1968.
Allon, Yigal. "Israel: The Case for Defensible Borders." *Foreign Affairs* 55 (October 1976).
Almond, Gabriel. *The American People and Foreign Policy*. New York: Praeger, 1960.
Arian, Asher, ed. *The Elections in Israel—1977*. Jerusalem: Jerusalem Academic Press, 1980.
Arian, Asher, ed. *The Elections in Israel—1981*. Tel Aviv: Ramot, 1983.
Arian, Asher, and Shamir, Michal. "The Primarily Political Functions of the Left-Right Continuum." In Asher Arian, ed., *The Elections in Israel—1981*. Tel Aviv: Ramot, 1983.
Arian, Asher, Talmud, Ilan, and Hermann, Tamar. *National Security and Public Opinion in Israel*. Jaffee Center for Strategic Studies, Study No. 9. Jerusalem: *Jerusalem Post*/Westview Press, 1988.
Aronoff, Myron J. *Power and Ritual in the Israel Labor Party*. Assen/Amsterdam: Van Gorcum, 1977.
Aronson, Shlomo. "Israel's Leaders, Domestic Order and Foreign Policy, June 1981–June 1983." *Jerusalem Journal of International Relations* 6, 4 (1982–1983).
Bahat, Shmuel, and Gat, Israel, eds. *A Selection of Decisions and Conclusions of "Leshiluv," A Zionist Socialist Circle in the Labor Party* (Hebrew). Tel Aviv: Labor Party, 1986.
Ball, George W. "How to Save Israel in Spite of Herself." *Foreign Affairs* 55 (April 1977).
Bar-On, Mordechai. *Peace Now* (Hebrew). Tel Aviv: Hakibbutz Hameuchad, 1985.
Barzilai, Gad. *Democracy in War: Attitudes, Reactions and Political Participation of the Israeli Public in the Processes of Decision Making* (Hebrew). Ph.D. dissertation, The Hebrew University of Jerusalem, 1987.
Beilin, Yossi. *Sons in the Shade of Their Fathers* (Hebrew). Ramat Gan: Revivim, 1984.
Beilin, Yossi. "A Dominant Party in Opposition: The Israeli Labor Party, 1977–1988." *Middle East Review* 17 (Summer 1985).
Beilin, Yossi. *The Price of Unity* (Hebrew). Tel Aviv: Revivim, 1985.
Ben-Meir, Yehudah. *National Security Decision Making: The Israeli Case*. Jerusalem: *Jerusalem Post*, 1986.
Benvenisti, Meron. *The West Bank Data Project: A Survey of Israel's Policies*. Washington, D.C.: American Enterprise Institute, 1984.

Brecher, Michael. *The Foreign Policy System of Israel*. London: Oxford University Press, 1972.
Brecher, Michael, Steinberg, Blema, and Stein, Janice. "A Framework for Research on Foreign Policy Behavior." *Journal of Conflict Resolution* 13 (March 1969).
Brown, Seyom. "The Changing Essence of Power." *Foreign Affairs* 51 (January 1973).
Brownstein, Lewis. "Decision Making in Israeli Foreign Policy: An Unplanned Process." *Political Science Quarterly* 92 (Summer 1977).
Carr, E. H. *The Twenty Years Crisis, 1919–1939*. London: Macmillan, 1946.
Chazan, Naomi. "Domestic Developments in Israel." In William B. Quandt, ed., *The Middle East: Ten Years After Camp David*. Washington, D.C.: Brookings Institution, 1988.
Cobban, Helena. *The Palestinian Liberation Organization*. Cambridge: Cambridge University Press, 1984.
Cohen, Bernard C. "Political Systems, Public Opinion and Foreign Policy: The United States and the Netherlands." *International Journal* 33 (Winter 1977–78).
Cohen, E. "Environmental Orientations: A Multidimensional Approach to Social Ecology." *Current Anthropology* 17, 1 (1976).
Cohen, Saul. *The Geopolitics of Israel's Border Question*. Jaffee Center for Strategic Studies, Study No. 7. Jerusalem: *Jerusalem Post*/Westview Press, 1986.
Cohen, Yerucham. *The Allon Plan* (Hebrew). Tel Aviv: Hakibbutz Hameuchad, 1973.
Coplin, William. "Domestic Politics and the Making of Foreign Policy." *Introduction to International Politics*. Chicago: Markham, 1974.
Dallin, Alexander. "The Domestic Sources of Soviet Foreign Policy." In Seweryn Bialer, ed., *The Domestic Context of Soviet Foreign Policy*. Boulder: Westview Press, 1981.
Downs, Anthony. *An Economic Theory of Democracy*. New York: Harper & Row, 1957.
Dror, Yehezkel. *Crazy States*. Lexington, Mass.: D.C. Heath, 1973.
Duverger, Maurice. *Political Parties*. New York: Wiley, 1965.
Eban, Abba. *The New Diplomacy*. London: Weidenfeld & Nicolson, 1983.
Eisenstadt, S. N. "The Internal Repercussions of the Lebanon War," Policy Papers, No. 17. Jerusalem: Leonard Davis Institute for International Relations, The Hebrew University, August 1986.
Eitan, Rafael. *A Soldier's Story* (Hebrew). Tel Aviv: Maariv Library, 1985.
Elazar, Daniel. J., ed. *Self-Rule/Shared Rule*. Lanham: University Press of America and the Jerusalem Center for Public Affairs, 1984.
Eldersveld, Samuel J. *Political Parties: A Behavioral Analysis*. Chicago: Rand McNally, 1964.
Eliav, Lova. *Eretz Hatzvi* (Hebrew). Tel Aviv: Am Oved, 1972.
Evron, Yair. *Israel's Nuclear Dilemma* (Hebrew). Tel Aviv: Yad Tabenkin, Hakibbutz Hameuchad, 1987.
Feldman, Shai. *Israeli Nuclear Deterrence*. New York: Columbia University Press, 1982.
Feldman, Shai, and Rechnitz-Kijner, Heda. *Deception, Consensus and War: Israel in Lebanon*. JCSS Study, No. 27. Tel Aviv: Jaffee Center for Strategic Studies, October 1984.
Gazit, Mordechai. "The Peace Process 1969–1973: Efforts and Contacts."

Jerusalem Papers on Peace Problems, No. 35. Jerusalem: Leonard Davis Institute for International Relations, The Hebrew University, 1983.
George, Alexander L., Hal, David K., and Simmons, William R. *The Limits of Coercive Diplomacy.* Boston: Little, Brown, 1971.
Golan, Matti. *Peres* (Hebrew). Jerusalem: Shocken, 1982.
Goldberg, Giora. *The Parliamentary Opposition in Israel: 1965–1977* (Hebrew). Ph.D. dissertation, The Hebrew University of Jerusalem, 1980.
Harel, Aharon. "Messianism and Realism." In Adam Doron, ed., *The State of Israel and the Land of Israel* (Hebrew). Beit Berl: Beit Berl College, 1988.
Harkabi, Yehoshafat. *Fedayeen Action and Arab Strategy.* Adelphi Papers, No. 53. London: IISS, 1969.
Harkabi, Yehoshafat. *Palestinians and Israel.* Jerusalem: Keter, 1974.
Harkabi, Yehoshafat. "Main Features of the Arab–Israeli Conflict" (Hebrew). Policy Papers, No. 22. Jerusalem: Leonard Davis Institute for International Relations, The Hebrew University, January 1988.
Heller, Mark. *A Palestinian State: The Implications for Israel.* Cambridge: Harvard University Press, 1983.
Horowitz, Dan. "Israel's Concept of Defensible Borders." Jerusalem Papers on Peace Problems, No. 16. Jerusalem: Leonard Davis Institute for International Relations, The Hebrew University, 1975.
Horowitz, Dan. "Israel's War in Lebanon: New Patterns of Strategic Thinking and Civilian–Military Relations." *Journal of Strategic Studies* 6 (September 1983).
Horowitz, Dan. "Strategic Limitations of 'A Nation in Arms.'" *Armed Forces and Society* 13 (Winter 1987).
Howard, Michael. *War and the Liberal Conscience.* New Brunswick, N.J.: Rutgers University Press, 1978.
Howard, Michael. "The Forgotten Dimension of Strategy." In Douglas J. Murray and Paul R. Viotti, eds., *The Defense Policies of Nations.* Baltimore: Johns Hopkins University Press, 1982.
Inbar, Efraim. *Problems of Pariah States: The National Security Policy of the Rabin Government 1974–1977.* Ph.D. dissertation, University of Chicago, 1981.
Inbar, Efraim. "Israeli Strategic Thinking After 1973." *Journal of Strategic Studies* 6 (March 1983).
Inbar, Efraim. "Israel and Lebanon: 1975–1982." *Crossroads* 10 (Spring 1983).
Inbar, Efraim. *Outcast States in the World Community.* Monograph Series in World Affairs. Denver: Denver University Press, 1985.
Inbar, Efraim. "Israel and Nuclear Weapons Since October 1973." In Louis Rene Beres, ed., *Security or Armageddon.* Lexington, Mass.: Lexington Books, 1986.
Inbar, Efraim. "The Outlook on War of the Political Elite in the Eighties" (Hebrew). Policy Papers, No. 23. Jerusalem: Leonard Davis Institute for International Relations, The Hebrew University, February 1988.
Inbar, Efraim. "The 'No Choice War' Debate in Israel." *Journal of Strategic Studies* 12 (March 1989).
Inbar, Efraim. "Attitudes Toward War in the Israeli Political Elite." *Middle East Journal* 44 (Summer 1990).
Inbar, Efraim. "War and Peace, Hopes and Fears in the 1988 Elections." In Daniel J. Elazar and Shmuel Sandler, eds., *Israel at the Polls: The Elections of 1988–1989.* Detroit: Wayne State University Press, in press.
Inbar, Efraim, and Goldberg, Giora. "Is Israel's Political Elite Becoming More Hawkish?" *International Journal* 45 (Summer 1990).

Isaac, Rael Jean. *Israel Divided: Ideological Politics in the Jewish State.* Baltimore: Johns Hopkins University Press, 1976.
Jervis, Robert. *Perception and Misperception in International Politics.* Princeton: Princeton University Press, 1976.
Kafkafy, Eyal. "From Wisdom to Sagacity." *State, Government and International Relations* (Hebrew) 27 (Winter 1987).
Kahn, Herman. *On Escalation: Metaphors and Scenarios.* Baltimore: Penguin Books, 1968.
Kaufman, Yadin. "Israel's Flexible Voters." *Foreign Policy* 61 (Winter 1985–86).
Keis, Naomi. "The Influence of Public Policy on Public Opinion in Israel, 1967–1974." *State, Government and International Relations* (Hebrew) 8 (September 1975).
Kellogg, Paul U., and Gleason, Arthur. *British Labor and the War.* New York: Garland Publishing Inc., 1972.
Kieval, Gershon R. *Party Politics in Israel and the Occupied Territories.* Westport, Conn.: Greenwood Press, 1983.
Kimmerling, Baruch. "A Conceptual Framework for the Analysis of Behavior in the Territorial Conflict: The Generalization of the Israeli Case." Jerusalem Papers on Peace Problems, No. 25. Jerusalem: Leonard Davis Institute for International Relations, The Hebrew University, 1979.
Kimmerling, Baruch. "Making Conflict a Routine: Cumulative Effects of the Arab–Jewish Conflict Upon Israeli Society." *Journal of Strategic Studies* 6 (September 1983).
Kimmerling, Baruch. *Zionism and Territory: The Socio-Territorial Dimensions of Zionist Politics.* Berkeley: University of California, Berkeley, Institute for International Studies, 1983.
Klieman, Aaron. *Unpeaceful Coexistence: Israel, Jordan, and the Palestinians* (Hebrew). Tel Aviv: Maariv Library, 1986.
La Palombara, Joseph, and Weiner, Myron. "The Origin and the Development of Political Parties." In Joseph La Palombara and Myron Weiner, eds., *Political Parties and Political Development.* Princeton: Princeton University Press, 1966.
Levite, Ariel. *Offense and Defense in Israeli Military Doctrine.* Jaffee Center for Strategic Studies, Study No. 12. Jerusalem: *Jerusalem Post*/Westview Press, 1989.
Lustick, Ian. "Israeli State-Building in the West Bank and the Gaza Strip: Theory and Practice—A Review Article." *International Organization* 41 (January 1987).
Luz, Ehud. "The Moral Price of Sovereignty: The Dispute About the Use of Military Power Within Zionism." *Modern Judaism* 7 (February 1987).
Manor, Reudor. "The Conception of Borders in Allon's Strategic Thinking." *Shorashim* (Hebrew) 3 (1982).
Markus, Gregory B., and Converse, Philip E. "A Dynamic Simultaneous Equation Model of Electoral Choice." *American Political Science Review* 73 (December 1979).
Medding, Peter. *Mapai in Israel.* Cambridge: Harvard University Press, 1972.
Mendilow, Jonathan. "Israel's Labor Alignment in the 1984 Elections: Catch-All Tactics in a Divided Society." *Comparative Politics* 20 (July 1988).
Miller, David Aaron. "The Arab–Israeli Conflict, 1967–1987: A Retrospective." *Middle East Journal* 41 (Summer 1987).
Morgan, Patrick M. *Deterrence.* Beverley Hills, Calif.: Sage Publications, 1977.
Morgenthau, Hans. *Politics Among Nations.* 4th ed. New York: Knopf, 1967.
Nakdimon, Shlomo. *Tammuz in Flames* (Hebrew). Jerusalem: Edanim, 1986.

Naor, Arye. *The Writing on the Wall* (Hebrew). Tel Aviv: Edanim, 1988.
Neumann, Sigmund. *Modern Political Parties*. Chicago: University of Chicago Press, 1956.
Niemi, Richard G., and Weisberg, Herbert F., eds., *Controversies in Voting Behavior*. 2nd ed. Washington, D.C.: Congressional Quarterly Inc., 1984.
Page, Benjamin I., and Jones, Calvin C. "Reciprocal Effects of Policy Preferences, Party Loyalties and the Vote." *American Political Science Review* 73 (December 1979).
Peres, Shimon. "Strategy for a Transition Period." *International Security* 2 (Winter 1978).
Peres, Shimon. *Tomorrow Is Now* (Hebrew). Jerusalem: Mabat, 1978.
Peres, Shimon. "Futurology and Foresight." In Alouph Hareven, ed., *Towards the 21st Century: Targets for Israel* (Hebrew). Jerusalem: Jerusalem Van Leer Foundation, 1984.
Perlmutter, Amos. *Israel: The Partitioned State*. New York: Scribner's, 1985.
Porat, Yehoshua. *The Emergence of the Palestinian–Arab National Movement, 1918-1929*. London: Frank Cass, 1974.
Porat, Yehoshua. *The Emergence of the Palestinian–Arab National Movement, 1929-1939*. London: Frank Cass, 1977.
Quandt, William B., Jabber, Fouad, and Lesch, Ann Moseley. *The Politics of Palestinian Nationalism*. Berkeley: University of California Press, 1973.
Rabin, Yitzhak. *Memoirs* (Hebrew). Tel Aviv: Maariv Library, 1978.
Rabin, Yitzhak. "Political Illusions and Their Price." In *The Lebanon War: Between Protest and Compliance* (Hebrew). Tel Aviv: Hakibbutz Hameuchad, 1983.
Rabin, Yitzhak. *The War in Lebanon* (Hebrew). Tel Aviv, 1983.
Rabin, Yitzhak. "In the Aftermath of the War in Lebanon: Israel's Objectives." In Joseph Alper, ed., *Israel's Lebanon Policy: Where To?* Jaffee Center for Strategic Studies Memorandum, No. 12. August 1984.
Rabin, Yitzhak. "The Israeli–Egyptian Relationship: Whereto?—An Israeli Perspective." *Dapei Elazar* 9 (1986).
Roper, John. "The Labor Party and British Foreign Policy." In Werner J. Feld, ed., *Foreign Policies of West European Socialist Parties*. New York: Praeger, 1978.
Sahliyeh, Emile. "Jordan and the Palestinians." In William B. Quandt, ed., *The Middle East: Ten Years After Camp David*. Washington: Brookings Institution, 1988.
Sandler, Shmuel. "The Protracted Arab–Israeli Conflict: A Temporal-Spatial Analysis." *Jerusalem Journal of International Relations* 10 (December 1988).
Sandler, Shmuel, and Frisch, Hillel. *Israel, the West Bank and the Palestinians*. Lexington, Mass.: Lexington Books, 1984.
Sartori, Giovanni. *Parties and Party Systems*. Cambridge: Cambridge University Press, 1961.
Schelling, Thomas C. *Arms and Influence*. New Haven: Yale University Press, 1966.
Schiff, Zeev. "Green Light, Lebanon." *Foreign Policy* 50 (Spring 1983).
Schiff, Zeev, and Yaari, Ehud. *Intifada* (Hebrew). Tel Aviv: Shocken, 1990.
Seliger, Martin. "Fundamental and Operative Ideology: The Two Principal Dimensions of Political Argumentation." *Policy Studies* 1 (Fall 1970).
Sella, Amnon. "Custodians and Redeemers: Israeli Leaders' Perceptions of Peace, 1967–1979." *Middle Eastern Studies* 22 (April 1986).
Sella, Amnon, and Yishai, Yael. *Israel the Peaceful Belligerent, 1967–1979*. London: Macmillan, 1986.

Shalev, Arye. *The West Bank: Line of Defense.* New York: Praeger, 1984.
Shalev, Arye. *The Intifada: Causes and Effects.* Tel Aviv: Papyrus, 1990.
Shamir, Michal. "Realignment in the Israeli Party System." In Asher Arian and Michal Shamir, eds., *The Elections in Israel—1984.* Tel Aviv: Ramot, 1986.
Shapira, Anita. *Visions in Conflict* (Hebrew). Tel Aviv: Am Oved, 1988.
Shapira, Yonatan. "The End of a Dominant Party System." In Asher Arian, ed., *The Elections in Israel—1977.* Jerusalem: Jerusalem Academic Press, 1980.
Shavit, Yaakov. *The Mythologies of the Zionist Right Wing* (Hebrew). Beit Berl: Beit Berl and the Moshe Sharett Institute, 1987.
Sheffer, Gabriel. "Resolution vs. Management of the Middle East Conflict." Jerusalem Papers on Peace Problems, No. 32. Jerusalem: Magnes Press, The Hebrew University, 1980.
Shlaim, Avi, and Yaniv, Avner. "Domestic Politics and Foreign Policy in Israel." *International Affairs* 56 (April 1980).
Shueftan, Dan. *The Jordanian Option* (Hebrew). Tel Aviv: Hakibbutz Hameuchad, 1986.
Sorokin, Pitrim. A. *Man and Society in Calamity.* Westport, Conn.: Greenwood Press, 1973.
Thompson, Neville. *The Anti Appeasers.* Oxford: Oxford University Press, 1971.
Touval, Saadia. *The Peace Brokers.* Princeton: Princeton University Press, 1982.
Wagner, Yigal. "Politics and Ideology in the Controversy on Greater Israel." In Adam Doron, ed., *State of Israel and Land of Israel* (Hebrew). Beit Berl: Beit Berl College, 1988.
Yaniv, Avner. *Deterrence Without the Bomb: The Politics of Israeli Strategy.* Lexington, Mass.: Lexington Books, 1987.
Yaniv, Avner. *Dilemmas of Security: Politics, Strategy and the Israeli Experience in Lebanon.* Oxford: Oxford University Press, 1987.
Yishai, Yael. "Party Factionalism and Foreign Policy: Demands and Responses." *Jerusalem Journal of International Relations* 3 (Fall 1977).
Yishai, Yael. "The Israeli Labor Party and the Lebanon War." *Armed Forces and Society* 11 (Spring 1985).
Yishai, Yael. *Land or Peace: Whither Israel?* Stanford: Hoover Institution Press, 1987.

NEWSPAPERS AND PERIODICALS

Al Hamishmar
Davar
Haaretz
Hadashot
Jerusalem Post
Kol Ha'ir
Maarachot
Maariv
Mibifnim
New Outlook
Newsweek
Skira Hodshit
Sunday Times
Yediot Aharonot

ISRAELI LABOR PARTY PUBLICATIONS

Baavoda
Bama
Emda Medinit
Israeli Labor Party
Migvan
Minutes of the Fourth Party Congress, 1986
Mivzak
Party Platform
Sidra Medinit
Spectrum

KNESSET MINUTES

LIST OF MAIN INTERVIEWEES

MK Nava Arad (July 19, 1990)
MK Uzi Baram (July 16, 1990)
MK Yossi Beilin (February 25, 1988)
MK Binyamin Ben-Eliezer (May 1, 1990)
MK Eli Ben-Menachem (May 3, 1990)
MK Avraham Burg (July 16, 1990)
Dr. Amos Carmel (November 25, 1987; December 5, 1988)
MK Eli Dayan (July 22, 1990)
MK Raanan Cohen (January 13, 1988)
MK Lova Eliav (July 17, 1990)
MK Gedalia Gal (July 10, 1989)
MK Mordechai Gur (December 28, 1987; August 2, 1990)
MK Shlomo Hillel (March 4, 1990)
MK Massalha Nawaf (May 3, 1990)
MK Shimon Peres (June 18, 1979; July 24, 1990)
MK Amir Peretz (July 2, 1990)
MK Chaim Ramon (January 31, 1988; June 16, 1990)
MK Nachman Raz (December 12, 1987)
MK Yossi Sarid (January 19, 1987; May 23, 1990)
MK Shimon Shitrit (May 21, 1990)
MK Edna Solodar (December 12, 1987; August 5, 1990)
MK Shevach Weiss (July 13, 1990)
MK Immanuel Zisman (December 30, 1987)

Index

Achdut Haavoda, 17, 18–19, 20, 88
al-Assad, Hafez, 57
Allon, Yigal, 2, 18, 27(table), 44, 87, 91
Allon Plan, 2, 4, 7, 45, 87–88, 96, 105, 154; defensible borders in, 90–91; development of, 19, 45; support of, 92, 95, 113, 150, 151
Aloni, Shulamit, 153
Amir, Jacques, 27(table), 94
Arabs, 47, 95, 149; agreements with, 14, 36–37, 40, 57; military strength of, 43, 50; nationalism, 58, 62; political views of, 29(n5), 33, 48–49; relations with, 39–40, 44–45, 103; territorial compromise with, 12–13, 110; as threat, 33–34
Arad, Nava, 26, 27(table), 78
Arbeli-Almozlino, Shoshana, 17, 19, 25; political views of, 26, 69, 91, 94, 128, 136
Arafat, Yasser, 59, 60, 76
Arens, Moshe, 23
Arms deals, 43–44
A'Shawa, Rashad, 64
Autonomy: territorial, 2, 69, 107–110, 115(n12)

Baker, James, 155
Baram, Uzi, 18, 23, 25, 26, 28, 49, 142; on Palestinian relations, 69, 77
Bar-Lev, Chaim, 17, 19, 22, 25, 26, 48, 50, 60, 122; on Allon Plan, 91, 95; on Lebanon War, 128–129; on military force, 123, 134, 136, 137, 139, 140; on Palestinian issues, 65, 76
Bar-Zohar, Michael, 25, 26, 27(table)
Begin, Menachem, 67, 68, 107, 122, 151, 154
Beilin, Yossi, 16, 21, 26, 27(table), 36, 80, 110; on Palestinian issues, 63, 68, 69, 71, 72, 77, 102

Beirut, 22
Ben-Aharon, Yitzhak, 110
Ben-Gal, Avigdor (Yanosh), 102
Ben-Gurion, David, 19, 20, 153
Ben-Meir, Dov, 27(table), 128
Ben-Menachem, Eli, 21, 27(table)
Ben-Natan, Asher, 20, 30(n17)
Ben-Porat, Mordechai, 153
Benvenisti, Meron, 87
Borders, 87; adjustment of, 86, 87, 95; defensible, 90–91, 161–162, 163; security of, 98–99
Burg, Avraham, 16, 21, 26, 27(table), 40, 80, 139, 142; on Palestinian issues, 71, 77, 78, 102
Bush administration, 75, 76

Camp David Accords, 30(n9), 44, 59, 68, 91, 151, 155; impact of, 5–6, 34, 65; Palestinian issues, 63, 67, 107; shared rule in, 2–3
Central Council, 22, 24, 69, 155
Central Stream, 19–20, 76, 102–103
Chemical weapons, 34; Arab use of, 132–133; training for, 131–132
Christian Phalangists, 126
Citizens Rights Movement, 69, 103, 153
Cohen, Raanan, 20, 26, 27(table), 72, 76

Dayan, Moshe, 2, 3, 19, 26, 27(table), 80, 153; on Palestinian issues, 78, 90
Defense, 2, 132, 167; Rabin's views, 130–131. *See also* Security
Democratization, 39
Demography: changes in, 41, 53(n43); of territories, 103–104, 154
Dinitz, Simcha, 19, 27(table), 69, 112, 123, 134; on security issues, 47, 105
Dor Hemshech, 20, 76
Dormant war, 121

179

Eban, Abba, 7, 17, 21, 22, 35, 69, 105, 123, 126; on military force, 134, 136; on Palestinian issues, 63, 68, 69, 70–71, 73, 77, 101, 102; on territorial issues, 91, 97
Economy: intifada and, 49–50
Edri, Rafi, 17–18, 26, 27(table), 69, 72
Egypt, 49, 64, 67, 87, 91, 99; peace treaty with, 4, 5, 13, 34, 65, 66, 86, 106, 124, 149, 155, 165–166; relations with, 35–36, 43, 47, 48, 135, 136
Ein Vered circle, 152–153
Elections, 6, 25, 29; 1988, 12, 21, 98, 111, 112; 1989, 12, 78–79; in territories, 40, 70, 71–72, 76
Eliav, Lova, 26, 27(table), 28, 42, 80, 101, 153; on Palestinian issues, 64, 69, 77, 97, 107
Eshel, Tamar, 27(table), 91, 94, 99, 128
Executive Bureau, 22, 24, 126–127

Forum for the Promotion of Peace, 21
Freij, Elias, 76

Gal, Gedalia, 26, 27(table)
Galili, Israel, 94, 128
Galili Document, 90
Gaza Strip, 1, 2, 13, 49, 57, 62, 63, 67, 71, 97, 99, 108, 121, 137, 155, 163, 164; annexation of, 88, 95; control of, 109, 164, 165; Jordan and, 95–96, 149; Palestinian issues in, 64–65, 100; as security zone, 24, 92, 94, 113; unilateral withdrawal from, 110–111, 112
Generals' Plan, 98
Gil, Yaakov, 21, 27(table)
Golan Heights, 1–2, 59, 95; annexation of, 19, 92, 93, 94, 113; control of, 90, 105; as security zone, 91, 94; Syrian negotiations over, 57, 87
Goldman, Micha, 20, 26, 27(table), 94, 112
Great Britain, 43
Green Line, 90, 98
Gulf Emirates, 49
Gulf War. See Iran-Iraq War
Gur, Mordechai, 16, 17, 20, 22, 27(table), 47–48, 50, 105, 122; on military force, 129, 131, 133, 134, 139; on Palestinian issues, 60, 73, 76, 87, 102, 107
Gush Etzion, 88, 93

Hadar, Amos, 27(table), 67, 69, 91, 99
Hadash Party, 126

Hakibbutz Hameuchad, 18–19, 20
Harel, Aharon, 20, 21, 27(table)
Harish, Micha, 18, 20, 22, 79, 139–140
Hashemites, 58, 61, 62, 68
Havereinu, 22
Hebron, 88
Herzog, Chaim, 27(table), 123, 128, 133
Hillel, Shlomo, 19, 22, 26, 72, 91, 108, 128, 139; on Palestinian issues, 69, 76; on territorial issues, 94, 95, 99
Hurvitz, Yigal, 153
Hussein, King, 13, 34, 65, 69, 136; negotiations with, 38, 58–59, 60, 61–62, 68, 149
Hussein, Saddam, 80, 154

IAF. See Israeli Air Force
IDF. See Israel Defense Forces
Immigration, 41, 53(n43), 154
Independent Liberals, 26
Intellectuals, 153–154
International Center for Peace in the Middle East, 21
Intifada, 6, 65, 102; controlling, 124, 138–139; economy and, 49–50; impacts of, 42, 99, 104, 140–141
Iran, 49
Iran-Iraq War, 4, 34, 44, 49
Iraq, 49; attack on, 6, 127, 133–135; as threat, 34, 46–47
Islam, 49
Israel Defense Forces (IDF), 46, 79, 104, 108, 163; and chemical weapons, 131–132; intifada control by, 138–139; in Lebanon War, 125, 126, 135; power of, 43, 111, 123–124; preparedness of, 131, 167; territorial occupation, 42, 96, 162; use of, 105, 121, 122, 125, 150, 167–169; on West Bank, 93, 98
Israeli Air Force (IAF): strike on Iraq, 133, 134–135

Jericho, 88, 107
Jerusalem, 1, 162; annexation of, 85–86, 88; Greater, 94–95; as security zone, 91, 92
Jihad, Abu, 137
Jordan, 2, 34, 43, 49, 51(n1), 64, 86, 91, 102, 136, 161; joint rule with, 107–108; negotiation with, 13, 38, 58–59, 60–61, 62, 65, 66–67, 69, 74, 76, 95, 135, 159, 163–165; Palestinian issues, 14, 90, 101

Jordan River, 58, 61, 88, 98, 101
Jordan Valley Rift, 93; annexation of, 94, 95, 98; as security zone, 91, 92
Judea, 1, 2, 13, 49, 57, 62, 63, 67, 71, 87, 88, 109, 149, 163; control of, 90, 164, 165; Jewish settlements in, 41, 96, 97; military in, 137, 155; Palestinian issues in, 64, 66, 100, 121

Katz-Oz, Avraham, 17, 27(table), 92, 94
Kfar Hayarok, 21, 28
Kiryat Arba, 88
Kissinger, Henry, 67
Kuwait, 49

Labor Forum for the Promotion of Peace, 77
Labor Party, 4–5, 14, 18, 25–26, 153–154; factions in, 11–12, 15–21; platform, 161–169; policies of, 6–7; power struggle, 27–29
Latrun area, 88
Latrun-Cfar Saba line, 95
Leadership: Labor Party, 4, 11–12, 15–21, 26, 28–29, 151, 154; Palestinian, 61
Lebanon, 48, 57, 79, 99, 121; invasion of, 87, 126; security zone in, 136–137, 166–167. *See also* Lebanon War
Lebanon War, 6, 57, 65, 135, 140; impacts of, 125–133; outbreak of, 22, 87
Leshiluv, 20, 69
Libai, David, 21, 25, 27(table)
Likud Party, 1, 5, 6, 18, 28, 29(n5), 48, 75, 80, 151; autonomy, 3, 108; in National Unity government, 12, 23; political views of, 46, 152–153
Lin, Amnon, 20, 27(table), 76, 136
Lishkah. *See* Executive Bureau
Litani Operation, 127
London Agreement, 38, 59
Lubelski, Masha, 25–26

Maale Adumim, 88, 94, 95
Mapai Party, 18, 19, 21, 88
Mapam Party, 26, 27(table), 69, 103, 126
Mashov, 21
Massalha, 26
Meir, Golda, 3, 61, 90, 123
Merkaz. *See* Central Council
Merom, Hagai, 21, 27(table)
Military, 22, 43, 48, 50; air strike by, 133–135; defense role of, 167–169; in Lebanon, 126–127; morale of, 140–141; in riot control, 42, 137–138; in security

zones, 88, 136–137; in territories, 104, 155; use of, 121, 123–124, 129–131, 135–136, 150
Missiles, 34, 105, 132
Movement for a Greater Israel, 152

Naamat Organization, 26
Naim, Raanan, 27(table), 94, 128
Namir, Ora, 21, 25, 26, 28, 40, 42, 142; on military force, 135, 136, 139, 140; on Palestinian issues, 36, 69, 74, 77, 102
National Unity government, 6, 12, 16, 18, 57, 72, 80, 97, 108, 136, 139, 151, 153; peace initiatives of, 38, 43, 46, 75, 138; PLO negotiations by, 73, 74, 78; security issues of, 22–23; on territories, 98–99
Navon, Yitzhak, 17, 20, 26, 27(table), 64, 101–102, 123, 142; on military force, 131, 136, 137, 139
Nehamkin, Aryeh, 17, 19, 25, 27(table), 46, 128
Nuclear weapons, 45, 106, 132, 133
Nuclear Weapons Free Zone, 45, 132

Obeid, 137
October War, 87, 90, 121
Ofer, Avraham, 88
Osirak nuclear reactor, 6, 127, 133–134

Palestine, 41, 85, 97, 103–104, 114(n7)
Palestine Liberation Organization (PLO), 6, 13, 14, 46, 51(n1), 59, 61, 62, 65, 70, 100, 110, 128, 149, 164; attack on, 133, 135; changing role of, 67–68; negotiations with, 15, 48, 58, 62–64, 73–80; policy changes of, 72–73; recognition of, 66–67, 155; representation by, 71–72; terrorism by, 135–136; as threat, 34, 36; United States and, 4, 60, 102, 112
Palestinian National Council, 59–60, 72–73
Palestinian National Covenant, 36, 61, 62, 67, 68, 74, 77
Palestinians, 4, 7, 36, 63, 68, 121, 138, 149, 150, 164; autonomy of, 69, 101, 107–110; in Gaza, 110–111; intifada of, 6, 45–46, 65; and Jordan, 14, 61; leadership of, 71–72; nationalism, 103, 155; negotiations with, 64–65, 68; political participation by, 75–76;

political recognition of, 69–71; representation by, 66–67. *See also* Palestinian state; Palestine Liberation Organization
Palestinian state, 60, 66, 74, 100, 107; acceptance of, 101–102; Central Stream and, 102–103; negotiation for, 68, 79
Partitioning, 58
Peace, 85, 100, 114–115(n10); and National Unity government, 46, 75; initiatives for, 37–38, 42, 45, 47, 72, 138; plan for, 159–160; process of, 65–66, 80, 99; U.S. initiatives, 38–39
Peace for Galilee Operation, 126
Peace Now movement, 26, 39
Peres, Shimon, 3, 19, 20, 26, 28, 50, 59, 60, 100, 142, 122–123, 125, 154, 156, 161, 163; on Arab relations, 39–40; autonomy plan of, 108–109; decisionmaking by, 24–25; on intifada, 42, 141; leadership of, 4, 11–12, 16–17; on Lebanon War, 22, 126, 128, 130; on military force, 123, 131, 134, 136, 137, 138; on Palestinian issues, 69–70, 102, 166; peace efforts by, 37–39, 47, 72; and PLO, 63, 74–75, 76, 77, 78; on security, 23, 105; on territories, 90, 93, 98, 106, 107, 112
Peretz, Amir, 20, 26, 27(table), 77, 80, 110, 131
Plan for Peace and Security, 93, 97, 108, 109, 159–160
PLO. *See* Palestine Liberation Organization
Political Center, 21
Politicide, 33, 35, 46–47, 51(n1)
Prevention of Terrorism Act, 79

Rabat Arab Summit, 67
Rabin, Yitzhak, 4, 22, 23, 26, 42, 46, 50, 60, 97, 109, 112, 121, 122, 129, 156, 162, 166; on Arab relations, 44–45; on chemical weapons, 132–133; decisionmaking by, 24–25; on defense strategy, 130–131, 132; on joint rule, 107–108; leadership by, 11–12, 17, 20, 28; on military force, 123–124, 134, 135–136, 137, 138, 139, 140–141; on Palestinian issues, 67, 69, 70, 71; on peace process, 65–66; PLO and, 63–64, 68, 74–75, 76, 77, 78; on refugees, 99–100; on security zones, 94–95; on strategic situation, 43–44; on territories, 72, 88, 90–91

Rafi, 18, 19, 88
Rafiah, 91, 92
Ramallah, 88
Ramon, Chaim, 20, 21, 25, 26, 27(table), 28, 92, 110, 129, 139, 142, 150; and Arab negotiations, 37, 40; on Palestinian issues, 63, 68, 69, 77, 102; on peace treaty, 98–99
Ratz. *See* Citizens Rights Movement
Raz, Nachman, 20, 27(table), 128, 140, 141
Reagan administration, 73
Reagan Plan, 155
Refugees: Palestinian, 61, 99–100, 126
Riots: control of, 137–138. *See also* Intifada
Rosolio, Dani, 22, 27(table), 69, 91, 94, 128

Sabra (refugee camp), 126
Sadat, Anwar, 5, 43
Samaria, 1, 2, 49, 57, 62, 63, 71, 87, 108, 109, 121, 163; control of, 90, 164, 165; Jewish settlement in, 41, 96, 97; military in, 137, 155; negotiation over, 13, 69, 149; Palestinian issues in, 65, 66, 100
Sareinu, 23–24
Sarid, Yossi: political views of, 11, 22, 27(table), 40, 51(n11), 69, 101, 128, 152
Saudi Arabia, 34, 43, 49, 64
Security, 1, 2, 7, 11, 54(n71), 86, 105, 108, 130; of borders, 98–99; force and, 121, 124–125, 129; Labor Party stance on, 3, 12, 13, 33; National Unity government stance on, 22–23; plan for, 159–160; politics of, 7–8; in territories, 86, 92, 96, 105; threats to, 33–34, 44. *See also* Security zones
Security zones, 24, 88, 91, 92, 96, 103, 113, 154; annexation of, 94–95; in Lebanon, 166–167; military force in, 136–137; sovereignty of, 16, 93
Settlements, 41, 151; Jewish, 85, 96–97; refugee, 99–100
77 Circle, 92, 153
Shahal, Moshe, 16, 17, 20, 50, 110, 112, 137; on Arab relations, 48–49; on Palestinian issues, 69, 77, 102
Shamir, Yitzhak, 23, 28, 46, 80, 164
Shared rule, 2–3
Sharm-el-Sheikh, 91

INDEX 183

Sharon, Ariel, 61, 129
Shatilla (refugee camp), 126
Shemtov, Victor, 68
Shitrit, Shimon, 26, 27(table)
Shochat, Avraham, 21, 25, 27(table), 100
Shultz, George, 38, 59, 73, 164
Sinai: withdrawal from, 48, 87, 90, 106, 151
Sinai II agreement, 106, 155
Six Day War, 1, 35, 58, 121
SLA. *See* South Lebanese Army
Socialist International, 153
Solodar, Edna, 20, 26, 27(table)
South Lebanese Army (SLA), 137
Sovereignty, 2, 16, 24, 93
Soviet Union, 43, 44
Syria, 2, 34, 59, 86, 91, 93, 127, 133, 136, 167; Golan and, 57, 87; negotiation with, 48, 78; Soviet Union and, 43, 44

Taba enclave, 135
Tabenkin, Yitzhak, 19
Telem, 153
Territories, 1, 2, 3, 46, 58, 65, 85; annexation of, 94–95; changes in, 92–93; compromise over, 12–13, 19, 86–91; control of, 62, 107–110; demographic problem in, 103–104, 154; elections in, 40, 70, 71–72, 76, 138; military force in, 139, 155, 162; Palestinians in, 63, 70; security of, 92, 105; significance of, 105–106; withdrawal from, 106–107, 110–113. *See also* Gaza Strip; Golan Heights; Judea; Samaria; West Bank
Terrorism: combatting, 79, 124, 164; PLO and, 68, 72, 77, 135–136
Treaties, 132; with Egypt, 4, 13, 34, 44, 99, 149, 155, 165–166; interim, 106–110
Tunisia, 135, 136
Tzadok, Chaim, 21, 27(table), 28, 71, 77, 88, 101, 110, 139
Tzur, Yaakov, 17, 20, 27(table), 140; on Arab negotiations, 40, 60; on Lebanon War, 128–129; on Palestinian issues, 65, 72; on territories, 94, 111–112

United Kibbutz Movement, 94
United Nations, 110; Security Council resolutions, 72–73, 77, 88, 164
United Nations Conference on Chemical Warfare, 132
United States, 4, 9(n14), 44, 49, 107, 124–125, 127, 155; influence of, 14, 90; relations with PLO by, 40, 60, 73, 78, 79–80, 102, 112; peace efforts, 38–39, 164
Uprising. *See* Intifada

Violence, 121; controlling, 137–138; impacts of, 124–125

Weiss, Shevach, 21, 26, 27(table), 136
Weizman, Ezer, 17–18, 26, 27(table), 28, 49, 95, 122, 132, 142; on Arab relations, 36–37, 40, 60; on Egyptian relations, 35–36; on military force, 134, 136, 137; on Palestinian issues, 64, 72, 73, 74, 77
West Bank, 2, 13, 42, 58, 68, 90, 95, 101, 113; IDF on, 93, 98; Jewish settlements in, 96–97; Palestinian influence in, 59–60; withdrawal from, 106–107

Yaakobi, Gad, 17, 20, 40, 49–50, 95, 111, 139, 141; on Palestinian issues, 77, 101
Yariv, Aharon, 68, 101
Yariv-Shemtov formula, 68
Yatir region, 92
Young Guard group, 20

Zakai, Yehezkel, 27(table), 30(n9), 91
Zionism, 2, 61, 97, 122, 158, 161
Zisman, Immanuel, 19, 26, 27(table), 28, 94; on Palestinian issues, 72, 76
Zvili, Nissim, 21

About the Book and the Author

Disagreements over national security issues, primarily between Likud and Labor (the two major political forces in Israel), have gradually become the central topic of dispute in Israeli politics. Likewise, the distinction between the political left and right increasingly concerns questions of national security, rather than other cleavages in Israeli society.

Efraim Inbar investigates the Labor Party's positions on national security in the 1980s and into the summer of 1990, thus shedding light on the broader issues of Israel's politics. Beginning with a discussion of the hawk vs. dove schism within the party, Inbar goes on to discuss party leaders' perceptions of threat with regard to the Arab-Israeli conflict—perceptions that have constituted, to a large extent, the basis for positions on national security matters. Succeeding chapters focus on the party debate over the appropriate partner in peace negotiations and the increased willingness to accept the Palestinians in this role; the likely shape of the party's proposals for interim and permanent peace agreements; and the attitudes of Laborites toward the use of force. In a final chapter, Inbar attempts to explain the leftward move of the Labor Party, especially intriguing in the context of the apparent shift of the electorate toward greater hawkishness.

EFRAIM INBAR is a senior lecturer in political studies at Bar-Ilan University and is also research fellow at the Leonard Davis Institute for International Relations, the Hebrew University of Jerusalem.

LIBRARY OF DAVIDSON COLLEGE

Books on regular loan may be checked out for four weeks. Books must be presented at the Circulation Desk in order to be renewed.

A fine is charged after date due.

Special books are subject to special regulations at the discretion of the library staff.